E. Franklin Frazier

ON RACE RELATIONS

THE HERITAGE OF SOCIOLOGY

A Series Edited by Morris Janowitz

E. Franklin Frazier
ON RACE RELATIONS

Selected Writings

Edited and with an Introduction by

G. FRANKLIN EDWARDS

THE UNIVERSITY OF CHICAGO PRESS

CHICAGO AND LONDON

Library of Congress Catalog Card Number: 68–8586

THE UNIVERSITY OF CHICAGO PRESS, CHICAGO 60637
The University of Chicago Press, Ltd., London W.C. 1

© *1968 by The University of Chicago. All rights reserved*
Published 1968

Printed in the United States of America

Contents

IV. THE NEGRO FAMILY

V. THE NEGRO MIDDLE CLASS

VI. THE NEGRO AND DESEGREGATION

Introduction

THE SOCIOLOGICAL writings of E. Franklin Frazier (1894–1962) cover a variety of subjects, but underlying the publications of his more mature years two major themes may be found to characterize his work. The first is his preoccupation with the historical development, structure, and functions of the Negro family. The second is his concern with an analysis of the problems and processes of race relations, not alone in the United States but in Brazil, the Caribbean, Africa, and other parts of the world as well. These basic themes, in fact, are interrelated, for, as Frazier himself pointed out in evaluating his work, his interest in the family was not alone in the Negro family as a pivotal institution, but as well in the manner by which the larger social environment determined family organization and functions in different parts of the world. While he maintained an interest in "studying such purely sociological problems as the development of masculine authority and discipline in the family and the influence of family traditions on the stability of the family and the behavior of its members,"[1] the linkage between his interests in the studies of the family and of race relations is supplied by him in the following statement:

I feel that my work in sociology falls into two major fields of interest: *Race and Culture Contacts* and *The Family*. This has been owing partly

[1] Howard W. Odum, *American Sociology: The Story of Sociology in the United States through 1950* (New York: Longmans, Green and Co., 1951), p. 238.

vii

to the fact that I have felt that the most fruitful approach to the study of *Race and Culture Contacts*, especially those aspects as regards acculturation and assimilation, was through the study of the family.[2]

It is possible, of course, to classify Frazier's writings under several headings, as suggested by the categories into which they appear to fall logically. To some extent this has been followed in the present work. The recurrent appearance of such concepts as urbanization and middle class in the titles of his papers provides a warrant for organizing his work around headings which incorporate these titles. But the reader of Frazier's works would do well to remember that central to his concern with urbanization was the manner in which this process produced changes in Negro life— primarily in the family and in forms of social and economic status, and secondarily in individual behavior. It was the influence of the larger community forces upon the institutions of Negro life, and, conversely, the impact made by the presence of the Negro upon the larger society of which he was a part, that were the central focuses of Frazier's research interests. He was not engaged primarily in the development of stratification theory, ecological theory, or personality theory, or of a general theory of urbanization. To the extent, however, that his research findings documented or modified existing theories in these areas, it may be stated that he made a contribution to them.

Intellectual Development and Sociological Views

Like many sociologists of his generation, Frazier did not begin the study of sociology until after he had completed his undergraduate education. At Howard University, from which he was graduated *cum laude* in 1916, sociology was not an established part of the curriculum. He once stated that he was told (by fellow students) that the few courses which were offered in this field were not presented in a serious fashion. At Howard he did receive a broad education in the arts and sciences, including mathematics,

[2]   *Ibid.*

physical science, literature, Latin, Greek, French, German, and social sciences. These were taught by well-prepared teachers, for many of whom Frazier developed a high respect.[3]

The training he received during his undergraduate years provided the fundamental background knowledge which Frazier believed all sociologists should possess. He maintained, for example, a lively interest in languages, later adding Portuguese to those he had studied at Howard. Although he was not a skilled linguist, he made effective use of his knowledge of French, German, and Portuguese in the work in which he later became engaged.

The training at Howard also provided the credentials and qualifications for a succession of teaching positions in high schools, beginning in 1916 at Tuskegee Institute, Tuskegee, Alabama, where he taught mathematics. This was followed by a year at Saint Paul's Normal and Industrial School, Lawrenceville, Virginia, where he conducted classes in English and history. In 1918 he taught mathematics and French in a high school in Baltimore, the city in which he was born, in 1894, and in which he spent his pre-college years.

The three years spent in secondary-school teaching furnished Frazier an opportunity for the development of insights into Negro educational institutions at that level. He was mindful of these early experiences when late in life, after having taught at some of the best institutions in the country, he was wont to state that he knew something of American educational institutions in general and of Negro educational institutions in particular. The years at Tuskegee, Lawrenceville, and Baltimore also furnished Frazier with a more intimate knowledge of the racial mores of southern and border American communities. His early interest in race problems, doubtless the result of a close association with an intensely race-conscious father, was stimulated by these experiences. It was at this period that he developed the ambition to take graduate work in sociology because it appealed to him as "the social science

[3]   See Odum, *American Sociology*, pp. 233–34 and A. Davis, "E. Franklin Frazier: A Profile," *Journal of Negro Education* 31, Fall, 1963, p. 430.

which most nearly provided an explanation of race and class conflicts."[4]

Frazier's early interest in race problems was combined with an interest in socialism.[5] At Howard he had been a member of the Intercollegiate Socialist Society. He opposed the World War I draft on the theory that it was a war between imperialistic powers and was not related in any meaningful way to the American claims that it was being fought to preserve democracy. So intense was his feeling on the subject that he wrote a tract entitled "God and War," which he had privately printed and distributed. In a later assessment of his concerns with social and economic problems during this period, against the background of his desires for advanced study in sociology, Frazier stated: "As I look back now, it appears to me that during this period I was developing an objective outlook on racial and other social problems which was divorced in a sense from my reactions to these problems as a person and as a member of society."[6]

Frazier's first serious encounter with the formal study of sociology came during the academic year 1919–20, which he spent in graduate study at Clark University, from which institution he received the Master of Arts degree in sociology in 1920. The subject of his Master's thesis, "New Currents of Thought Among the Colored People of America," reflects his continued interest in the race problem. His mentor at Clark was Professor Frank Hankins, whose theory courses Frazier credits with having introduced him to the possibilities offered by sociology for the analysis of social problems on a high intellectual level. Frazier frequently mentioned that it was during his year at Clark that his career as a sociologist began and that the year of study with Hankins had a profound ef-

---

4   Odum, *American Sociology*, p. 234.
5   In an introduction to the paperback edition of *Negro Youth at the Crossways* (New York: Shocken, SB 161, 1967), p. ix, Saint Clair Drake refers to Frazier as a neo-Marxist and dates his interest in socialism to his return from foreign study in Denmark in 1922. It is clear, however, that this interest was developed at an earlier period.
6   Odum, *American Sociology*, p. 234.

fect upon his intellectual development. He was always quick to add to this assessment, however, that he did not always agree with Hankins' position on race and other social problems.

In 1920–21 Frazier was a research fellow at the New York School of Social Work and he conducted, during that period, a study of the longshoremen of New York City. The following year, 1921–22, he studied in Denmark as a fellow of the American-Scandinavian Foundation. While in Denmark he studied the folk high school of that nation. Upon returning to the United States he accepted a position which combined instruction in sociology at Morehouse College (Atlanta, Georgia) with the direction of the Atlanta School of Social Work.

It was during his years in Atlanta that Frazier began his writings on the Negro family and the processes of differentiation and stratification in the Negro community. Two articles listed in the Bibliography for this volume, "Durham: Capital of the Black Middle Class" and "The Pathology of Race Prejudice," were written during that period. The latter article provoked such a strong emotional reaction in some members of the white community that Frazier's life was threatened, and he was forced to leave Atlanta almost immediately after the article appeared. This reaction resulted from the article's comparison of the mechanisms which operate in prejudiced behavior with those which characterize mental illness. Both race prejudice and the behavior of mentally-disturbed persons are characterized by irrationality, and in both the prejudiced person and the mentally-disturbed person the psychological mechanisms of dissociation and projection are operative. The most sensitive portion of this essay, and doubtless the cause of greatest disturbance, was the reference to the operation of projective mechanisms in white women who accuse Negro males of attempted rape. It was not safe for a Negro person to express such views in 1927, and only a person with Frazier's "mental toughness," who dared to state the truth as he conceived it, would have undertaken to have such an essay published.

Frazier's experience at Atlanta was followed by two years of graduate study at the University of Chicago, from which he received the doctoral degree in sociology in 1931. It was at Chicago that Frazier became thoroughly socialized into what later came to be called the "Chicago School of Sociology." As a graduate student he came under the influence of distinguished teachers and promising student colleagues, included among whom were Robert E. Park, Ellsworth Faris, Ernest W. Burgess, William F. Ogburn, George H. Mead, Louis Wirth, and Herbert Blumer. His doctoral dissertation, later published in 1932 by the University of Chicago Press under the title *The Negro Family in Chicago*, was clearly in the Chicago tradition of an empirical study of one aspect of community life to illuminate larger aspects of social reality.[7] Frazier's study of the Chicago Negro community was distinctive inasmuch as it was the first investigation of community life to combine two methodological tools, the method of human ecology and the use of personal documents, which were being emphasized by University of Chicago sociologists at the time.[8]

Formal study at Chicago did more than acquaint Frazier with the techniques of sociological investigation developed at that institution. It also imbued him with a fundamental conception of sociology which he stated in numerous articles and which served to guide his researches. A clear expression of this conception is given in his article on "Theoretical Structure of Sociology and Social Research," in which Frazier states that the various systems of social relationships that come into existence as a result of association are the proper subject matter of sociology. A social system may be an institution, such as the family; an association, such as a labor union; or a larger unit, such as a nation. "The character of the social system depends upon such factors as the spatial distribution of people, the division of labor, institutions, social

[7] For a discussion of the Chicago School, see Morris Janowitz's Introduction to *W. I. Thomas on Social Organization and Social Personality*, Heritage of Sociology Series (Chicago: University of Chicago Press, 1967), pp. vii–ix. See also Robert E. L. Faris, *Chicago Sociology, 1920–1932* (San Francisco: Chandler Publications, 1966).

[8] Personal communication to the author form Professor Ernest W. Burgess which was read at the Memorial Services for Professor Frazier at Howard University, October 19, 1962.

stratification, and the nature of contacts and communication among its members."[9]

Moreover, economics and politics have their place in sociological study and research. "According to our point of view," Frazier states, "sociological analysis must include economic and political factors relevant to the particular system of social relations which is being studied. This is quite different from claiming that sociology is a general social science discipline confronted with the impossible task of synthesizing the data of all the social sciences."[10]

While for Frazier the major objective of sociological study was the structural and associational aspects of social life, he recognized that there was a subjective element which could not be ignored, as behavior involves meanings which become the basis of understanding or consensus and social control by which collective life is made possible. Sociological study, however, should not be limited to, or even mainly centered upon, the study of interactional factors or the study of attitudes. Such a limitation neglects the contribution of contextual or organizational factors to the behavior under study and thus misses important meanings.

Frazier's position on attitude studies was a reaction in part to the increased use of this mode of investigation during the 1940's and 1950's. The possibility such studies offered for quantification of data gave them an aura of scientific respectability, but the validity of the results was often suspect. This was revealed when their findings were put to predictive tests, as they were increasingly in connection with efforts to predict community reactions to desegregation of public education and to desegregation in areas of public accommodations. Such studies often missed the "social reality," to use a favorite Frazier expression.

The "social reality" to be grasped in the understanding of attitudes and other aspects of individual behavior was the objective social situation to which the individual reacted. Frazier made frequent use of W. I. Thomas' "definition of the situation" in at-

[9]   "Theoretical Structure of Sociology and Social Research," *British Journal of Sociology* 4, December, 1953, p. 294.
[10]   *Ibid.*

tempting to explain the behavioral responses of the individual. In his construction of typical personality profiles of Negro youth in the border cities of Washington, D. C., and Louisville, Kentucky, in *Negro Youth at the Crossways: Their Personality Development in the Middle States* (1940), Frazier's analysis took account of the socialization influences provided by the family, church, school, and neighborhood contacts. He also had his subjects react to a number of themes which were known to be relevant to Negro life. This approach to meaningful situations, involving the understanding of the roles of social and community factors and the interpretations of the youth themselves, served to document Frazier's subscription to the view of Ellsworth Faris that personality was the subjective aspect of culture and to Thomas' and Znaniecki's postulation that attitudes were to be viewed as responses to social values.

It was not only the application of attitude measurement to the study of personality which reinforced Frazier's conviction that such an approach was not the most meaningful one for the study of individual behavior. He was equally opposed to studies of conflicts between nations which employed such concepts as psychological tensions and attitudes. It was partly in reaction to such studies during his period of service as Chief of the Division of Applied Social Sciences of UNESCO, 1951–53, that he wrote the article on "The Theoretical Structure of Sociology and Social Research."

The reader of this volume should note that in those articles reproduced in this volume which deal with desegregation, Frazier's analysis of the process gives foremost consideration to the institutional aspects of the problem. Only in a subordinate sense does he consider individual interests and attitudes; these are derived or imputed from the relationship of the individual to his community identifications.

The basically non-quantitative approach espoused by Frazier at a time when sociology, along with the other social sciences, was becoming increasingly preoccupied with methodological problems, in which major consideration was given to techniques of quantification, brought his works under careful scrutiny. Critical evaluations of them were inevitable. This is illustrated, for example, in the evaluation of his use of personal documents.[11] To such criticisms Frazier was sensitive and was prone to overreact. He took advantage of every opportunity to spell out and emphasize the sociological approach he employed. A good example of this is gained from his Presidential Address to the American Sociological Society in 1948 on "Race Contacts and the Social Structure."

In concluding this part of the Introduction, it should be pointed out that Frazier's views on sociology as a body of knowledge and as an area of research, and his close intellectual kinship with the Chicago school, are well illustrated in his volume on *Race and Culture Contacts in the Modern World*. There his analysis of race relations takes account of demographic, ecological, economic, and political factors in explaining race relations problems which are found in various parts of the world. "It is not difficult," he wrote, "to show that the character of race and culture contacts is determined, partly, by the spatial distribution of people, their method of gaining a livelihood, and the distribution of economic power. Moreover, the traditions and culture of people with different racial backgrounds shape their attitudes toward each other. Finally, the existing political structures, the distribution of political power, and the laws regulating the relations of people with divergent racial and cultural backgrounds are all determinants of the kinds of group contacts and interpersonal relations which exist at any moment in history. . . ."[12]

Students familiar with Robert E. Park's writings on the subject of race and culture will recognize that the approach is essentially that advanced by him for study in this area. It remained, however, for Everett C. Hughes, another of Park's students, to point out that "Park himself never wrote a book in which he put his scheme for study of race and culture contacts together. It is

[11]   See, for example, Robert Angell's "A Critical Review of the Development of the Personal Document Method in Sociology, 1920–1940," in *The Use of Personal Documents in History, Anthropology and Sociology* [New York: Social Science Research Council (Bulletin 53), 1945], pp. 189–92; 197–99.

[12]   E. Franklin Frazier, *Race and Culture Contacts in the Modern World* (New York: A. A. Knopf, Inc., 1957), pp. 31–32.

greatly to Frazier's credit that, late in his career, he took the time
and trouble to give us a book which does it; it is Frazier's book,
however, not Park's; the mature work of a disciple who valued,
but bettered, the Master's instruction—a disciple who had himself
become Master."[13] Hughes went on to state that, in his judgment,
Frazier was Park's most complete student.

Substantive Considerations

The Family

Doubtless Frazier's most important work is *The Negro
Family in the United States* (1939), which built upon the author's previous works on the family. The volume won the Anis-
field Award as the most significant work on race relations in the
year of its publication. Ernest Burgess, in an Editor's Preface to
the work, stated that it was the most important contribution to the
literature of the family since the publication, twenty years earlier,
of *The Polish Peasant*. This comprehensive analysis provides a
natural history of the Negro family in the United States as it re-
sponded to forces encountered in that environment—the breakdown of the African heritage, slavery, emancipation, urbanization,
and, cutting across all of these, race prejudice and discrimination.[14]

Deviations in Negro family life from many normative patterns
of American family behavior, such as the high incidence of divorce, desertion, illegitimacy, female-headed families, were explained in sociological terms. This viewpoint offered an important
corrective to prevailing explanations of the first third of the century which attributed deviations in Negro family life to biological
factors. The Negro had been regarded as a defective, dependent
and delinquent, who was incapable of full participation in American civilization.

[13]   From "Remarks of Everett C. Hughes" on the occasion of the
Memorial Services for Frazier, Howard University, October 19, 1962.
[14]   The view that the Negro family was a peculiar expression of response to the American environment involved Frazier in a lively controversy with Melville Herskovits, an anthropologist, who claimed that the
Negro family continued to be influenced by African survivals.

The volume is significant also for its contribution to our knowledge of the disorganizing effects of urban life upon the Negro family, and, to a great extent, it exercised an influence on social work theory and practice in dealing with problems of the Negro.

As pointed out in the first section of this Introduction, the interrelated themes of the Family and Race Relations led Frazier to an analysis of the effects of the increasing urbanization upon the Negro family. The migration to the cities of the North during World War I produced increasing occupational differentials in the Negro population. The volume built upon the discovery of gradients in the Negro community, first pointed out in *The Negro in Chicago*, and delineated two major classes—The Brown Middle Class and The Black Proletariat. The point which Frazier made, whether in discussing the effects of urbanization upon Negro life or in tracing the evolution of the Negro family, was that there were stable as well as disorganized family units in the Negro community.

Using his own research experience, Frazier has pointed to differences in the family life of Negroes in the United States and Brazil resulting from the manner in which the Negro was introduced into the two countries, differences in the plantation systems of the two nations, and variations in the racial attitudes of the Portuguese and English. (See "A Comparison of Negro-White Relations in Brazil and in the United States.")

One finds in his analysis of the Negro in the United States, Brazil, and Africa certain common preoccupations with the reorganization of family life as a result of urbanization.

The Middle Class

Frazier's concern with the traditions of the Negro family and with the urbanization of the Negro population led to considerable attention on his part to the Negro middle class. His first article on this subject was "Durham: Capital of the Black Middle Class" in 1925. In that essay he attempted to describe the evolution of a business class in a southern city and some of the forces which contributed to it. The spirit of business enterprise which characterized American businessmen in general was found among the black entrepreneurs of Durham. At the same time that Frazier extolled the virtues of the group about which he wrote, he pointed to the difficulties which beset Negro businessmen in general as a result of their isolation from the white business world.

One finds in the Durham article Frazier's characterization of the Negro as "a strange mixture of the peasant and the gentleman" in his outlook on life. "Two hundred years of enforced labor," he wrote, "with no incentive in its just reward, more than any inherent traits, explain why the Negro has for so long been concerned with consumption rather than production. Peasant virtues are middle class faults. And so are the gentleman's; and the Negro has come by these in curious but inevitable ways."[15]

This theme is picked up in *Black Bourgeoisie* (1957), in which Frazier writes of the passing of the peasant and the gentleman that resulted from the mass migration to cities. The old middle-class virtues were lost and a new middle class, concerned with conspicuous display, came into being. This stratum of the population was, indeed, highly mobile, and, in most instances, demonstrated the breakdown which had occurred in Negro family life. Its style of life was entirely at variance with older middle-class virtues.

Some persons were wont to regard *Black Bourgeoisie* as a polemic, and others viewed it as an exaggerated profile of the behavior of the class described. These arguments are not entirely without merit. But the book, regardless of its methodological faults, makes a contribution to our knowledge of behavior under conditions of rapid mobility. The larger significance of the work, in line with so much of Frazier's writing, is that it offered a case study of the impact of American environment upon a particular stratum of the Negro population. The exaggerated behavior of the Negro middle class was to be viewed as a departure from middle class norms occasioned by the isolation under which Negroes lived.

Overall Evaluation

Frazier's major contribution lies in his demonstration that the isolation under which the Negro lived in the United States produced serious attenuations in his community and institutional life

[15]   Durham: Capital of the Black Middle Class," p. 339.

and, as a result, had a profound impact upon his self-conception. His family life was characterized by serious disorganization and deviations from the normative American family patterns. His relatively small middle class was the result of lack of economic opportunities and departed significantly from American middle-class values in general. Moreover, the Negro lacked a true upper class. Negro business, at best, was small business, and in many respects the hope of racial uplift through business enterprise was mythical in character. The Negro press reflects the extent to which Negro self-conceptions were out of line with social realities. Its exaggerations of Negro accomplishments showed, according to Frazier, that Negroes lived in a world of make-believe. The Negro church was the single strongest institution of the Negro community and profited from the segregation under which Negroes lived. This isolation is physically symbolized by the ghetto, which itself is a pathological phenomenon.

Frazier made no claim to having made any substantial contribution to the methodology of sociology. In a rejoinder to William T. Fontaine's critical evaluation of the race relations views of Negro scholars from the standpoint of the sociology of knowledge, Frazier wrote:

It is not difficult to explain the scientific outlook of the Negro scholar and the conceptual tools he utilizes. If . . . the Negro scholar has arrived, he has become only a competent thinker and craftsman. The techniques and conceptual tools which he utilizes have been acquired during the course of his education. Doubtless, he has made some worthwhile contributions in the various fields, but so far he has not broadened our own intellectual vistas or forged new conceptual tools . . ."[16]

Except for comments on Frazier's education and some of his professional experiences, very little has been mentioned of the personality of the man himself. Something of his intellectual vigor is gained from a reading of the articles produced in this volume. He sought constantly to broaden his knowledge and took advantage of numerous professional experiences which were offered him.

[16]   " 'Social Determination' in the Writings of Negro Scholars," *American Journal of Sociology* 49 (1943/44) : 314.

These opportunities permitted him to view the problems of Negro-white relations in a broad perspective. His foreign travel and work experiences provided a comparative perspective for the study of race and culture contacts and the family.

Frazier knew the meaning of racial discrimination, for on occasion he had been its victim. He always reacted vigorously to such experiences. But he was deeply concerned with understanding behavior, including discrimination, and sought to analyze it objectively. He conceived his role as that of an intellectual, not of a policy maker. This is why he refused offers in which he would be expected to play the role of race relations expert or race relations adviser. He thought that the only hope for the Negro American was full integration into American society. To achieve such equality the Negro must be able to compete, even if this involved struggle against the handicaps he suffered. For this reason he would be opposed to the separatist objective of contemporary "Black Power" advocates. He would have subscribed, however, to programs, short of complete separation, designed to produce in the Negro a sense of racial identity and self-respect.

The numerous articles included in the Bibliography were the result of a busy academic life spent largely at Fisk University, Nashville, Tennessee (1929–34) and at Howard University, Washington, D.C. (1934–62). They add to our knowledge of the subjects discussed and provide a base upon which contemporary scholars may build. As a student of social change, Frazier realized that his works would become dated, and sought always to keep informed of the contributions that others made to the areas in which he was interested.

G. Franklin Edwards

I. Theoretical Perspectives

THEORETICAL STRUCTURE OF SOCIOLOGY AND SOCIOLOGICAL RESEARCH

1953

THE PURPOSE of this article is to discuss the basic concepts of sociology in relation to some concrete problems with which sociological research has been concerned and to call attention to the necessity of relating empirical research to the theoretical structure of sociology. Such a discussion seems to me to be especially important to-day both because vast sums of money are being devoted to sociological studies and because sociology is becoming diffused with the spread of Western civilization. The first part of this article will be devoted, then, to a brief presentation of the conceptual standpoint of sociology in regard to social reality. This will be followed by an analysis of the problems of race and culture contacts within a sociological frame of reference. One phase of this analysis will be carried out in greater detail in the discussion of the role of the family in social assimilation.

I

Sociology in the broadest sense may be regarded as the science of human nature—not the human nature which has been regarded as a biological datum but the human nature which is a

This article is a condensation of a series of three lectures given by the author as Special University Lectures in Sociology at the University of London, 4th, 7th and 8th May, 1953. Reprinted from the *British Journal of Sociology* 4 (December, 1953) : 292–311.

product of human association. Human association involves inter-action between human beings which is made possible through different forms of communication. Since for human beings social behaviour involves meanings, there is a subjective element which cannot be ignored since it provides the basis of understanding or consensus and social control which enable men to carry on a collective existence. As the result of collective living, institutions and other structured forms of behaviour come into existence and in turn determine the behaviour of individuals. This is essentially an organic conception of social life, since, according to this view, individual acts become meaningful or socially significant as the result of the organization of the behaviour of individuals. This view is opposed to the atomistic conception which regards society as an aggregate of individuals whose behaviour is to be explained in terms of the similarity of individual responses and attitudes. For certain purposes, of course, men in society may be studied as an aggregation of discrete units and not in their social relations with each other. This is true in regard to demographic studies and in the case of human geography or human ecology where account is taken of the fact that man modifies his environment. In the study of human ecology, the sociological element is absent in as much as one is concerned with human interactions on a symbiotic level and not with human interaction involving social definitions and communication.

The various systems of social relationships which come into existence as the result of association are, according to our view, the proper subject matter of sociology. A social system may consist of a family group, a labour union, or a nation. The character of the social system depends upon such factors as the spatial distribution of people, the division of labour, institutions, social stratification, and the nature of contacts and communication among its members. For example, the polarity which is involved in the distinction between *Gemeinschaft* and *Gesellschaft* or between sacred and secular societies represents two ideal types of social systems. It is hardly necessary to add that the nature and boundaries of a particular social system should be established on the basis of empirical data. A community may be studied as a social system having a location in space, which may be defined by the means of transportation and communication.

Here it is necessary to consider the relevance of economic and political factors to sociological study and research. Some sociologists, especially the majority of American sociologists, have regarded economic and political factors as irrelevant to sociological inquiry. They have generally confined their studies to the investigation of social interaction or the measurement and analysis of attitudes, or they have utilized some vague concept as mores and folkways which they regard as *sui generis* sociological phenomena. According to our point of view, sociological analysis must include economic and political factors relevant to the analysis of a particular system of social relations which is being studied. This is quite different from claiming that sociology is a general social science discipline confronted with the impossible task of synthesizing the data of all the social sciences.

In order to make clear the viewpoint expressed here, I shall undertake to show how the conception of sociology presented here may be utilized in the study of the system of race relations which has emerged especially in the southern part of the United States. The most general explanation is that racial antagonism and racial prejudice, which resulted in the creation of a legalized system of racial separation and racial taboos and resembles a caste system, were the result of attitudes having their roots in slavery. A closely related explanation is that the system of race relations that emerged in the South was based upon the mores which grew up spontaneously as the result of the association of the two races. However, from the standpoint of the historical development of race relations in the South, it should be noted that the inauguration of the system of the legal separation of the races and the disfranchisement of the Negro did not occur until twenty-five years after the Civil War. Moreover, another fact deserves emphasis: namely, for fifteen years after white supremacy was established in the South, no attempt was made to establish a legal system of racial separation and disfranchisement.

According to the point of view presented here, the sociological explanation of the system of racial separation and the disfranchisement of the Negro is to be found in the unresolved class conflict and the resulting political struggles among the whites in the South. Let us begin with the restoration of white supremacy in the South. What did this mean in regard to class relations in the white South? The Civil War, as the Beards have called it, was a second American Revolution. The defeat of the planter class did not result simply in the emancipation of the slaves. It also provided an opportunity for the landless poor whites to resist the domination of the white planter class. In this connection it should not be overlooked that some of the so-called Radical Republicans were in favour of ex-propriating the white planter class and creating a white and black peasantry. But the more conservative Republicans stated frankly that such a policy would set an example for white indus-trial workers in the North who might seek to expropriate the owners of factories. The restoration of white supremacy resulted in the political domination of the commercial and industrial classes who were known as Southern Bourbons. But it did not result in the complete disfranchisement of the Negro or in a system of racial separation. In fact, many leaders of the planter class utilized their former relationship with the Negroes to win the support of black voters against the poor whites who continued to struggle for land and a higher standard of living.

Out of the unresolved class conflict in the white South devel-oped the Populist Movement in the 1890's which was a struggle on the part of the landless poor whites against the planters and the new commercial and industrial interests. One of the problems faced by the leaders of the Populist Movement was the Negro. Despite the efforts of the planters and new capitalist classes to di-vide poor whites and Negroes, the leaders of the Movement suc-ceeded to a large extent in bringing about co-operation between whites and Negroes. In the end the Populist Revolt was defeated, not, however, simply because of race prejudice but mainly because of the superior economic power of the planter and capitalist. Never-theless the collapse of the Populist Movement as an organized political movement did not end the unrest on the part of the dis-inherited whites. It was then that the Southern demagogues seized the opportunity to gain political power.

In order to gain political power, they sought the support of the wealthy as well as the poor whites. First, they offered no threat to the economic interests and political power of the planters and industrial capitalists. Secondly, they convinced the poor whites that their condition was due to the presence of the Negro. Therefore, they proposed and carried through legislation which accomplished the following: (1) the disfranchisement of the Negro; (2) the public school funds which were appropriated on a per capita basis of children of school age were diverted from Negro to white schools (until then white and Negro children received the same per capita appropriation and white and Negro teachers the same salaries); and (3) the establishment of a legalized system of racial segregation designed to maintain the social and economic subordination of the Negro. In order to justify this programme before the nation, the demagogues with the support of planters and capitalists carried on a propaganda campaign for a quarter of a century against the Negro. This propaganda aimed to prove that the Negro was subhuman, morally degenerate and incapable of intellectual development. Therefore, an adequate sociological analysis of racial attitudes in the South cannot ignore the role of propaganda and the deliberate inculcation of racial prejudices.

The analysis which I have given of the development of race relations in the Southern States is an illustration of the necessity to study social attitudes within the context of a system of social relations. But it is necessary to add a few remarks concerning the study of attitudes as the central problem of sociological analysis. For the social psychologist who is interested in the development of personality, attitudes may be the focus of research, though even the social psychologist must take into account the social context in which attitudes are formed. Although this fact is generally recognized, there is still the tendency to treat attitudes without reference to their organic relation to the social situation. This is due largely to the attempt to introduce quantitative techniques and measurements and to take over uncritically the concepts of physical science. For example, let us begin with the assertion that attitudes are either positive or negative in regard to persons and objects. This uncritical application of the concept of physical science to socio-psychological phenomena is an over-simplification of the problem. The same may be said of the attempt to classify attitudes according as they indicate approach or withdrawal. An attitude of hostility, for example, may involve either approach to or withdrawal from a hated person. Or to characterize the attitude of whites towards Chinese, Negroes and Indians as negative tells us nothing concerning the behaviour of whites. If I understand the meaning of negative, I am sure Negroes in the United States would often prefer a negative attitude to a positive attitude on the part of whites. The general attitude on the part of whites in the United States which may be characterized as a tendency not to take the Negro seriously explains more about their behaviour towards Negroes than so-called measurements of positive and negative attitudes or degrees of approach and withdrawal in regard to Negroes. Moreover, the results obtained from the techniques used to measure social distance cannot be taken as indications of how people will behave in social situations. Fortunately, there is a growing recognition that attitudes and social distances are multi-dimensional. What is still needed is the study of the attitudes of individuals as members of specific collectivities.

There are indications in some recent studies that sociologists are beginning to study attitudes and behaviour in relation to the social structures within which they develop. I may refer to a recent study of racial segregation in Washington, the capital of the United States. The usual procedure in such studies is to make a study of the attitudes of white people or to give a description of the pattern of race relations. The study to which I refer was unique in that it undertook to study the groups or systems of social relationships that were responsible for the pattern of segregation and discrimination and caused it to function. It was recognized that no study of the racial attitudes of individual whites could explain the social reality which was represented by the system of racial segregation. The so-called public opinion of the Washington community which was supposed to be interpreted if not reflected in the newspapers turned out to be the public opinion of certain groups. Likewise, the so-called mores of race relations which were invoked as a reason for not attempting to change the racial pattern turned out to be non-existent. This was not strange since, as any sociologist knows, the behaviour of individuals in the mass societies which have come into existence as the result of urbanization is no longer governed by the mores of the community. Individual behaviour is determined by the various collectivities or systems of social relations of which the individual is a member. The collectivities—labour unions, property associations, etc.—define the objectives of the individuals and determine the role they play in different situations. As a result there is not only a contradiction between what is regarded as the individual's racial attitude and his behaviour in a specific situation but a contradiction in his behaviour towards members of the same racial group in different situations.

The discussion so far has been concerned with the analysis of race relations in the United States. In the following section the general sociological frame of reference within which this analysis was made will be made more explicit as a frame of reference for studying race and culture contacts in the modern world.

II

In conformity with our conception of sociology, the general characteristics of the systems of social relationships which emerge during the course of race and culture contacts will be analysed. The scheme presented here represents a logical rather than a chronological scheme for the study of the problem though it provides an evolutionary frame of reference for studying the changing character of race relations.

The first stage or, perhaps better, phase of race and culture contacts is characterized by contacts which are not truly social in the sense that people with different racial and cultural backgrounds who are brought together are not members of a single moral order. They may look at each other with a certain fascination, but they hardly regard each other as completely human. The initial contacts between peoples with different racial and cultural backgrounds involve barter and trade which have often assumed a form known as the silent trade, a transaction involving an exchange of goods between people who do not even see each other. Trade and barter between European and native peoples has often resulted in conflict. These conflicts may result from cheating or robbery on the part of Europeans or misunderstandings arising especially from the fact that native peoples do not understand a system of exchange based upon economic values. These misunderstandings have been frequent in regard to the ownership of land since native peoples generally do not regard land as an object of commerce.

For our purposes, the important fact that should be noted in regard to the conflicts which arise during the first stage of race and culture contacts is that they are carried on on a biological plane. Since the two parties in conflict are not members of a single moral order, there are no codes to regulate these conflicts, nor is there a basis for human sympathy to prevent these conflicts from assuming a savage character. The entire history of conflicts between peoples with different racial backgrounds has been characterized by unrestrained savagery on the part of Europeans as well as the non-European peoples. Often race riots in the United States have assumed the character of a struggle on a biological plane while the lynching of Negroes has only emphasized the fact that they were not regarded by whites as really human. It should be pointed out, also, that at this stage the ecological organization of race relations is taking form and that it is influenced by such factors as climate, geographic and demographic factors, but more especially by the type of economic exploitation.

Out of the system of barter or exchange of goods during the initial stage of contacts of Europeans and indigenous people there grew up organized systems of economic exploitation. The transition from the first stage to the second stage has been aptly characterized as a transition "from barter to slavery." In fact, the plantation system and slavery or some form of forced labour have been characteristic of this phase of race and culture contacts. In modern societies the factor of compulsion has often been disguised. The system of indentured labour in Africa and parts of Asia and peonage in the southern part of the United States are essentially forms of forced labour. The essential fact concerning this phase of race and culture contacts is that economic relations assume an organized or institutional character. Thus slavery may be regarded from this standpoint as an industrial institution. Where slavery has assumed the character of a purely industrial institution, the members of the subjugated or subordinate races are treated, in the words of Aristotle, as animate tools. For example, on the sugar plantations of Louisiana and on the larger cotton plantations, the Negro slaves were regarded as mere instruments of production and in the same category as work animals. The same situation has existed in South-East Asia and in Africa where slavery and other forms of forced labour including indentured labour have existed.

The industrial organization which develops as a result of the contact of different races and culture groups represents a racial division of labour. In its initial stages the racial division of labour is simple where Europeans confront primitive peoples. But as the new society emerges, the racial division of labour becomes more complex and involves the question of social organization which will be discussed later. In this connection, one might cite, as examples, the racial situation in South Africa and in the southern part of the United States. On the other hand, when Europeans have confronted the older civilizations of Asia, economic relations and control have been established through capital investment and different forms of financial control. Then, too, a native bourgeoisie has generally emerged which has played a subsidiary role in relation to foreign capitalists and industrialists.

The economic phase of race and culture contacts cannot be separated from the political phase. The plantation system, which also involves the exercise of arbitrary power and social control with certain sanctions, is a type of political institution. Even where the recruitment of labour on a voluntary basis is undertaken there is need for some kind of political control in dealing with native peoples. Moreover, there is need to maintain order generally when new systems of economic exploitation are introduced among so-called primitive peoples. The British system of "indirect rule" may be taken as representative of this type of political control. But in a certain sense a system of "indirect rule" is characteristic of all systems of political control where people with different racial and cultural backgrounds are involved.

In the southern part of the United States where the Negroes were disfranchised, it was necessary to set up an informal and extra-legal system of social control which was essentially political in character and had much in common with a system of "indirect rule." In the Southern States, Booker T. Washington was the accepted spokesman for the Negro and practically dictated the appointment of Negro educators and other leaders to positions of responsibility within the Negro communities. Even on the national scene his authority represented a type of indirect rule in that he dictated the few political appointments which Negroes received at the time. Likewise, the activities of the philanthropic foundations which devoted themselves to the welfare of the Negroes may be placed in the same category. In distributing funds for education and welfare, the various foundations selected certain Negroes for leadership and these leaders played a predominant role in maintaining control within Negro communities.

It might be added that the various forms of political control established by the Europeans over the older civilization of Asia involved various degrees of "indirect rule." This was as true of India where political control was established through the conquest of practically the entire country, as of China and other areas in Asia where domination was limited by agreements as to extra-territoriality and treaty ports.

It would be difficult to conceive of an institution as a purely industrial organization, however dehumanized it might be. Thus the plantation, though primarily an industrial institution, may develop traditions and means of social control which transform it into a type of social institution. This is most likely to happen where slavery becomes an established way of life involving the close association of masters and slaves. Social control is not maintained simply by physical force and fear of punishment. Traditions, custom, and habits become more important elements in social control. A social ritual develops and a sentiment of submission on the part of slaves may correspond to a sentiment of loyalty and paternalism on the part of the masters. Where this occurs one may discover the germs of a social organization which, as it matures, involves the problems of culture and personality.

It will not be necessary to define the meaning of culture though it will be useful to clarify the significance in this discussion of the terms: amalgamation, acculturation and assimilation. Amalgamation will be used to designate the result of the mating of members of different racial stocks. Amalgamation, which may occur within or without marriage, is preferable to the term miscegenation, since the latter has certain invidious connotations. The term acculturation, which is a social process, refers to the process by which a person takes over the culture of the group or one group takes over the culture of another group. During the process of acculturation there is generally an exchange of cultural elements. Although the process of assimilation is closely related to acculturation, it should be differentiated from the latter because it includes something more fundamental than the latter. It involves complete identification with a group. Thus, American Negroes have been amalgamated to a large degree with whites and they are acculturated in respect to European culture. But they are not assimilated in American society, since they are regarded as American *Negroes*, seldom even as Negro *Americans*, and they think of themselves as Negroes first and only secondarily as Americans.

In the final phase of the development of race and culture contacts one is concerned primarily with the problem of social organization. Where race and culture contacts have developed beyond the stage of slavery, the classical form of social organization has been a system of castes or the hierarchical division of society along racial lines. This type of social organization represents a form of accommodation in which conflicting interests are resolved, if not permanently, at least to the extent that a collective life is possible. The accommodation which is established is based upon a racial division of labour while the system of power relations which enables the upper ranks of the caste system to maintain their dominant position is supported by traditions and sentiments rather than a show of force.

There is another form of social organization which may emerge where race relations have developed beyond slavery, namely, the biracial organization of society. In a biracial organization of a society each racial group has its own institutions and associations which enable it to carry on a separate social life and, theoretically at least, no difference in social status exists between the two racial groups. Social distance is maintained between the two races on a horizontal rather than a vertical plane. Some students of race relations have regarded the biracial organization of society as a stage of race relations growing out of the system of castes. But it appears more likely that the two systems of social organization develop out of different economic and social situations. In fact, the system of castes and the biracial organization may be closely associated in a more inclusive system of race relations. For example, in the southern part of the United States following the Civil War and Emancipation, both patterns of racial accommodation developed. During recent years the breaking down of the system of castes has also undermined the biracial organization.

There has been much controversy over the question whether the racial situation in the Southern States constitutes a caste system or is simply the result of race prejudice. Anyone who studies the situation without attempting to prove certain preconceived notions about race relations will find that there are many elements in the racial situation which resemble a caste system and there are other features which differentiate it from a caste form of social organization. The idea of caste is opposed to American democratic ideals and Christian teachings and consequently the Negroes are constantly in revolt against the attempt to impose upon them an inferior status. Moreover, one may even go further and say that in an urbanized, industrial society it does not seem possible to maintain a biracial organization.

At this point it would be well to devote some attention to the phenomenon of race prejudice since it is generally regarded as the major obstacle to the creation of a single moral order involving people with different social and cultural backgrounds. Since so many studies have been made to establish the fact that racial prejudice is not inborn and since knowledge of this fact has been so widely diffused, it is unnecessary for me to dwell upon it here.

Children, who are not acquainted with racial concepts, do not define experiences with people of a different colour as racial. In other words, they have not learned to categorize people racially on the basis of colour and other features. The essence of race prejudice is, according to our viewpoint, that it is an emotionalized attitude toward a person who is treated as a member of a racial category and not as an individual or, better, that when he is categorized from the standpoint of race, this fact affects any other manner in which he may be perceived. Race prejudice not only blinds one to the actual physical traits and behaviour of the individual of a different race but it endows the individual with traits that constitute the categoric picture of the race. That is why all Negroes look alike to prejudiced white peoples and all Chinese look alike to prejudiced Negroes. Recent experiments have revealed that prejudiced whites cannot tell one Negro from another while unprejudiced whites are able to see Negroes as individuals.

Since race prejudice is a social attitude it is communicated to individuals through the means of communication which create other social attitudes and conceptions. The origin of racial prejudice is to be discovered in the system of economic and social relations which are established between different racial groups. When a system of accommodation has been established between two races, the harsher expressions of race prejudice may disappear and the categoric picture of the subordinate race may include some desirable human traits. But where the traditional pattern of race relations is being broken down and individuals of different races become competitors, new social attitudes emerge and the categoric picture of the subordinate race includes only undesirable traits. While the Negro was a slave, race prejudice as such tended to disappear towards the Negro slave and the categoric picture included many admirable human traits. On the other hand, there was considerable projudice against the free Negro before the Civil War and after the Civil War. The categoric picture of the free Negro which was created and propagated lacked human characteristics. Consequently race prejudice may be regarded as a conservative force utilized to preserve the traditional order. It is interesting to compare the categoric picture of the Negro which is presented over the radio to-day with that which was presented twenty-five or thirty years ago, not to mention what was printed in Southern newspapers forty years ago. Likewise, attitudes towards the Chinese on the West Coast of the United States have changed and the categoric picture of the Chinese has changed in recent years to meet the exigences of the international political situation. This all seems to emphasize the necessity of studying racial attitudes in the context of the social organization in which they exist. The measurement of the racial attitudes of individuals and the social distances between members of different races as if they lived in a social vacuum will not provide an understanding of race and culture contacts.

One might say that the central sociological problem to be studied in the final stage of race and culture contacts is the manner in which the racial divsion of labour is broken down and racial competition in the economic sphere gives way to competition on an individual basis and political power is identified with class rather than race. But even when members of different races may compete as individuals and exercise political rights, there is still a final barrier to be broken down before they are completely assimilated into the social organization. This barrier is the family which plays a unique role in transmitting the social heritage and in giving the child a conception of himself as a member of the group. It is in this intimate phase of race and culture contacts that one comes to grips with the problem of culture and personality. It is in this area of the problem that social psychology and other disciplines dealing with personality and the subjective aspects of culture are needed.

In this stage or phase of race and culture contacts, the marginal man and his role in the social organization become important. The marginal man is a cultural hybrid since he is the product of two cultural worlds and is not at home in either. Here one can differentiate between the processes of acculturation and assimilation. The marginal man may be thoroughly acculturated from the standpoint of the dominant racial or cultural group but he cannot identify himself with the dominant racial or cultural group. This is because there are still barriers to intimate association with members of the dominant group especially in regard to inter-marriage. The marginal man may become an intellectual and he may develop an objective attitude toward both the minority and the dominant racial group. Very often it is these marginal men who become leaders of nationalistic movements.

Nationalistic movements should be studied in this phase of race and culture contacts because they involve the problem of social organization. Although nationalistic movements may have an economic and political basis, they also have a cultural aspect which is of great significance since nationalistic movements bring about a transvaluation of values so far as the minority is concerned. The values of the minority group supersede the cultural values of the dominant group. In the nationalistic movements the marginal men resolve their personal conflicts and identify intellectually and emotionally with a group which has acquired a new status. While nationalistic movements appear in this last phase of race and culture contacts and should be studied as a part of the final phase, they are not the inevitable outcome of race and culture contacts. They represent the failure on the part of people with different racial and cultural backgrounds to achieve a social organization. Where the barriers to intermarriage are broken down and complete assimilation is achieved, the different cultural traditions are mingled in the family traditions and people with different racial backgrounds become identfied as members of a single moral order.

The utility of the sociological frame of reference, presented here, in the study of race and culture contacts, becomes apparent when one undertakes, for example, a comparison of race relations in Brazil and in the United States. The usual approach to this problem is to make a study of racial attitudes in the two countries. In the case of Brazil the absence of a serious race problem has been explained by the fact that the Portuguese had already become accustomed to the presence of the Negro in the Iberian peninsula. Undoubtedly, the attitude of the Portuguese toward darker races played a role in the development of race relations in Brazil. But the history of race relations in Brazil clearly shows that there were periods of racial discrimination and that there was a struggle for equality on the part of the mulattoes as well as on the part of the blacks. Therefore, the course which race relations followed in Brazil differed from that in the United States for more fundamental reasons than a mere difference in racial attitudes.

The first important fact to be taken into account in comparing race relations in Brazil and the United States is that from the beginning the symbiotic relations established between the European and the Negro were different for the two countries. In Brazil, the Negro found a geographic environment very much the same as that from which he came. Consequently, on the biological plane he enjoyed an advantage in the racial competition that developed. Secondly, even as regards technical competence the Negro often enjoyed some advantages over the Portuguese. Finally, the African social organization was never completely destroyed in Brazil. In the United States, on the other hand, the Negro did not enjoy any of these advantages. He was introduced into a geographic environment that was more favourable for the European; whatever techniques he acquired he had to learn from Europeans; and his traditional family system was completely destroyed.

There were many similarities between the plantations in Brazil and in North America both as regards the personal relations between masters and slaves and the systems of social control. But in Brazil the plantation system with slave labour had not produced a large class of landless poor whites who were thrown into competition with the emancipated Negro slaves as was the case in the United States. After the abolition of slavery the transformation of Southern society in the United States was carried through largely by the rise of the poor whites or descendants of the non-slaveholding whites. On the other hand, in the evolution of Brazilian society during the nineteenth century, the mulatto played a predominant role since he represented the most mobile element in the society. Because of the position of the mulatto in the social structure, it was impossible to establish a system of discrimination based upon racial descent as in the United States. The integration of the Negro and mulatto into the social organization of Brazil was inevitable under the circumstances. A dark colour might constitute a temporary barrier to complete assimilation but because of intermarriage the fact of racial descent could not play the role which it did in North America.

III

Because of the importance of the family in acculturation and assimilation, a more detailed analysis of its role becomes necessary. The important role of the family in acculturation and assimilation is due to the nature of contacts within the family as compared with other types of human association. In stable agricultural societies, educational institutions, including those which transmitted a formal type of instruction, only tended to supplement the role of the family in transmitting the culture of the society. But as modern societies have become mobile and more differentiated as the result of urbanization and industrialization, educational as well as other institutions and associations have played an increasingly important role in acculturation. Through the contacts provided in these different types of associations and new means of mass communication, certain formal aspects of the culture of a society are transmitted to individuals. This results in a large degree of uniformity in overt behaviour while the basic values and personalities of individuals with different cultural backgrounds are unchanged. But it is almost exclusively through the intimate contacts of family living that the sentiments and ideals characteristic of a society are transmitted and become a part of the personalities of the members of society.

In studying the role of the family in acculturation, it is necessary to distinguish the "natural" family group from the institutional type of family. The "natural" family group is based upon maternal affection and the sympathetic ties which bind together members of the same household. It does not originate as the result of marriage nor are the obligations of its members defined by law. The mother, or if there are two generations, the grandmother, occupies the dominant role in such family groups while the role of the father is adventitious, depending upon feelings of sympathy and the growth of common interests. This type of family may also come into existence as the consequence of desertion on the part of the father or where unmarried motherhood is due to the fact that intermarriage is prohibited by law and custom. In these "natural" family groups, the mother becomes the chief agent by which the culture of the society is transmitted to the child. The institutional family, on the other hand, is based upon marriage and possesses stability and continuity which are due sometimes to its material possessions but more generally to its social heritage. This social heritage consists of the family traditions which shape the character and personality of the family members and give direction to their lives. While this type of family is rooted in the mores, it is generally integrated into the institutional life of the community. Therefore, the institutional type of family tends to influence the status of the individual in the community.

The "natural" family groups which came into existence as the result of the mating of white males and Negro or coloured females in the United States provide excellent material for studying the role of "natural" family groups in acculturation and assimilation. During the period of slavery when a large number of these families existed, the character of the relationship of the white male to his coloured concubine and coloured children varied considerably. At one extreme, the white father took no interest whatever in his nameless coloured offspring and they were left to be reared by their mothers. Where the coloured offspring were abandoned, they became slaves if their mothers were slaves and shared in the common fate of the slaves. If their mothers were free and they were abandoned by their white fathers their future development varied according to the social development of their mothers. At the other extreme, the white father, if unmarried, would live with his coloured family and if married would live with his coloured mistress and white wife in a polygamous relationship. Under such conditions he would not only provide for the economic needs of his coloured offspring but would see that they were carefully reared.

The relation of the white father to his coloured family had a decisive influence upon the extent to which the coloured offspring acquired European culture. On the basis of abundant documentary material, including published biographies and autobiographies, it is possible to trace the process by which the coloured offspring acquired European culture. They were generally subjected to a strict family discipline under the supervision of the white father. This discipline included literary and religious instruction and the inculcation of moral ideals. These white fathers often sent their coloured offspring to the free States of the North to complete their education. Moreover, they saw to the economic welfare of their coloured children either during their lifetime or made provision for it in their wills.

In the majority of cases these coloured offspring did not identify themselves with their white fathers but rather with their coloured mothers. This was due not entirely to the relationship which was established between the white father and his offspring but also to the manner in which the coloured offspring was defined racially by the society. In some countries, as for example in Latin America, the coloured offspring have tended to identify themselves with their white fathers because the society defined them as white or European. But in the United States where there was a principle of colour or racial caste, if the coloured offspring did not identify themselves with their mother's race, they became marginal men. In many areas of the South these mulattoes constituted an intermediate caste between the white slaveholders and the black population both slave and free.

Even under the most favourable conditions there are certain limitations placed upon the "natural" family as an instrument of assimilation. The first limitation is the absence of a male to serve as a model for the children, especially the male offspring. Studies have indicated that while affection and feelings of security are necessary for the normal development of children, they are not sufficient for the full development of their personality. In the drama of family life, the child needs models with whom he can identify and towards whom he can develop attitudes or obligations. Since every culture has a well-defined role for the male, the absence of the male model in the family group deprives the male child of the opportunity of identifying himself with this model and assuming the conception of himself which the model would provide. In the absence of the male model the mother may attempt to create an ideal image of the absent father. Sometimes a wise mother has created an ideal model that would help the child to assume the male role expected of him by society. The difficulties of creating an ideal male model are increased when the child's father is of a different race. Even when his father is of the same race there are difficulties which cannot be overcome. For example, in the United States, where a huge proportion of Negro males, especially in the South, have never been permitted to play the male role as defined by American culture, the male model created by the mother has generally been disparaging to the male.

This leads me to say something concerning the "natural" family groups that are not the result of race mixture, or at least are not directly the result of race mixture. In the United States, a large number of these "natural" family groups originate in unmarried motherhood in which Negro fathers are involved. This is, of course, no new phenomenon and has a long history. The mothers who play the major role in socializing the child are the repositories of the folk culture of the Negro. Therefore, they have been unable to contribute much to the acculturation of the child to live in American society. The same observations could be made concerning the numerous "natural" family groups with the Negro mother as the mainstay which result from desertion on the part of the male. The "natural" family groups resulting from unmarried motherhood and desertion on the part of the male constitute the major portion of the large number of "broken" Negro families, as they are known to social workers, in the cities of the United States. Lacking an institutional character and passing on to the children the remnants of a folk culture which has lost its meaning in the urban environment, these families contribute nothing to the assimilation of Negro children in American culture. It is the public school, their experience as workers, and the chance contacts of city life which bring about their acculturation in American life. Those who have acquired these new ways of thinking and behaving may become the fountainhead of a family tradition if they establish a family along institutional lines.

When we consider the role of the institutional family in assimilation we must confront the stubborn fact that the institutional family constitutes a barrier to the assimilation of divergent racial elements. In order to continue its function of conserving the traditions and values of a society, it must maintain a certain exclusiveness. This does not mean that the institutional family cannot play an important role in assimilation. But in order to study its role in assimilation we must study it in the course of its formation and development when race and culture contacts are involved.

Once more I shall draw principally upon my studies of the development of the Negro family in the United States, especially those studies having to do with the manner in which an institutional type of family developed among the free mulattoes in the pre-Civil-War South. These families grew out of the sexual association between white men and Negro women. The mulatto offspring were recognized by their white fathers to the extent that their fathers made provisions for their economic welfare and saw that they were properly reared. Very often their white fathers took care that they learned a skilled trade and these skilled mulatto artisans soon acquired a monopoly of the skilled trades in many areas of the South. Their privileged position in the economic structure of the pre-Civil-War South was such as to discourage European immigrants from going to the South and aroused the envy and hatred of the non-slaveholding whites. As we have seen, the same development occurred in Latin American countries with the important difference that the mulatto offspring enjoyed a certain social recognition and became the backbone of the new societies, whereas in the post-Civil-War South these mulattoes and their descendants were shunted to the Negro communities.

Nevertheless, the free mulattoes who were not subject to the restrictions in regard to education which were imposed upon the slaves in the South acquired property in land and even in slaves and founded families of a patriarchial character similar to that of the slaveholders. They developed educational, religious, and welfare institutions and literary societies. They took over the ideals and values of the aristocratic slaveholding whites and took pride in their relationship to this class. Their philosophy of life and style of living were not a mere pretence since they rested upon a solid foundation of property and civilized behaviour. After emancipation it was the descendants of these same families who constituted an upper class in the Negro communities and became the leaders of the Negroes. A study of the institutional life which developed among Negroes after emancipation reveals that they established schools and churches and businesses and became the leaders in the professions. This accounts for the fact, for which American sociologists have often sought an explanation in biology, that during the first decade of this century the vast majority of the educated leaders and successful men and women among Negroes were mulattoes or mixed-bloods.

In connection with the important role which these free mulattoes and their descendants played in the creation of Negro communities, it is necessary to say something concerning the role of the Northern white missionaries who went South after the Civil War and devoted their lives to helping the freedmen to become educated and responsible American citizens. It is no exaggeration to say that these missionaries were chiefly responsible for the gains which the Negro made in civilization following Emancipation. How did they accomplish so much? They did this by creating a social situation that closely resembled that of the family group. They set up schools in which they were truly *in loco parentis* as regards their students. Later generations have accused them of paternalism towards the Negro. This was true in the finest sense of the word. But, in addition, it was exactly what was needed in the task which they undertook. They lived with the Negro students twenty-four hours a day. They ate with them and prayed with them and subjected them to the same kind of discipline to which they would have been subjected in a well-organized family. Education was a part of daily living. The result was that the students learned to speak and write English; they learned civilized manners; and more than that, they acquired the moral ideals and sentiments of their teachers. Of course, when these missionaries undertook their task they could isolate their charges in a way that would be impossible to-day with the radio and movie and automobile.

Of special interest to our discussion is the fact that the graduates of these schools became heads of families which represented the most stable and civilized elements in the Negro community. Some of the students who attended these schools were the descendants of the free mulattoes among whom family traditions were solidly established. But, on the other hand, the majority of the students were the black children of ex-slaves or mulatto children without a background of coventional family life. The descendants of the free mulattoes intermarried with the successful members of this group who represented the first generation of freedmen. Thus the old upper class, who regarded themselves as aristocrats, constantly received fresh recruits, which enabled it to continue in its role of leadership until the First World War.

As the result of Emancipation, a type of family with a history different from that of the free mulattoes acquired an institutional character and played an important role in the acculturation of the Negro and prepared the way for his ultimate assimilation. The founders of these families had had close contacts with their masters in their homes or they had been taught skilled trades and had occupied a fairly respected position, as far as it was possible for a slave, in the economic life of the pre-Civil-War South. Under favourable conditions and where slavery assumed a paternalistic character, the house servants were integrated into the families of their masters. They received religious and moral instruction, generally attending the same churches as their masters, and were subject to a discipline that initiated them into European culture. Although legal marriage was not permitted, they were encouraged in forming stable unions and were permitted to exercise paternal control over their children. This was especially true in regard to the skilled mechanics who formed with the house servants a sort of upper class in the slave community.

After Emancipation, the slaves who had enjoyed such advantages engaged in trade, became independent mechanics, or began buying land. From the standpoint of family life, the first advantage which the Negro derived from freedom was the dominant position of the male in the household. Under slavery the authority of the Negro father or husband was always subject to the higher authority of the white master. The change in status was given recognition when, for example, contracts for the renting of land were signed by the Negro male and he was held responsible for the conduct of his family. But the development of the father's interest in his family rested upon more material considerations. When the father entered into a contract to purchase land, his interest in his wife and family became identified with his own interests. His sacrifices and labour became a part of the family traditions. Moreover, the ideas which he had acquired during slavery from his white masters concerning family life—masculine authority and responsibility, female faithfulness, obedience on the part of children, a family name, inheritance of property—became real values for him.

It is no wonder that these families represented an important accession to the stable elements in the Negro population and that from these same families came the most ambitious members in the Negro communities. The increase in the size and influence of this class in the Negro population coincides roughly with the increase in land home ownership among Negroes up to the First World War. It was among this same group of families that there developed a certain racial pride and a determination to measure up to the standards of the white community. In a sense these families represented a type of black puritanism. They were eager to maintain the highest standards of behaviour especially in regard to family and sex. They were the main support of the churches and other institutions while the children in these families seldom engaged in delinquent or criminal behaviour.

As the Negro population became urbanized these families withstood the shock of city life better than the loosely organized families without traditions of stable family life. It was from these families that came the most efficient and stable workers who entered industry. As the result of their new contacts in the urban environment and their new relation to the great body of American industrial workers, these families are changing. But the point of interest here is that the new outlook on life and the new values and patterns of behaviour which members of these families have acquired through wider contacts with American life are becoming a part of their family traditions.

The manner in which a new type of family is emerging among the Negro industrial workers in the United States has some value for the study of the family problem in those areas where the impact of Western industrial civilization is uprooting people from their traditional ways of life. As these non-European peoples are drawn into industry and into urban areas, not only is the traditional family being destroyed but there is little opportunity for creating new family groups of an institutional character. This is the case, for example, in many parts of Africa where males are herded into compounds or they are treated as machines or work animals. Much has been written about the laziness, crime, and inefficiency of the urbanized African worker. From the studies which have been made it is apparent that the first step in improving the situation is to make possible a normal and stable family life for the detribalized and urbanized African. Only through the creation of opportunities for a new family life in which children can receive the proper discipline and develop a new orientation towards community living can shiftlessness, crime, and delinquency be reduced. But the family cannot thrive in isolation; it must be integrated into a community.

The main emphasis of this discussion may be summed up in some general remarks concerning the place of methods and techniques in sociological research. The question of methods and techniques in sociological research just as in other fields of scientific enquiry is inseparable from the conceptual organization of the discipline. Many problems concerning human beings may be interesting but they may not be sociological problems, either because the data involved cannot be studied in a sociological frame of reference or because of the manner in which the problems have been defined. In many so-called sociological studies this simple fact is forgotten and virtuosity in the use of methods and techniques becomes an end in itself. Therefore, the first task in sociological study is to define or formulate a problem in terms of the concepts of the discipline. Then the problem of methods and techniques resolves itself into one of utilizing the appropriate methods and tools. That this viewpoint is not shared by some sociologists was indicated during a recent meetings where sociologists were divided over the question of methods and techniques. Neither side justified its espousal of certain methods and techniques on the grounds of their relevance to sociological concepts but on the grounds that its own methods were more "scientific" than those of its opponents.

The emphasis here on the need for sociologists to define their problems in terms of the basic concepts of their discipline should not be confused with the search for new concepts. According to our point of view, there is no pressing need for new concepts. Many of the generalizations of the early sociologists provided fundamental concepts, which could be made more precise by sociological research, and important hypotheses which could be tested by empirical studies. Unfortunately, in the effort to pile up a mass of so-called objective studies which have little or no sociological significance, these important generalizations have been ignored or forgotten. Often when the attempt has been made to introduce new concepts into sociology, it has resulted in a substitution of new verbal symbols for old terms. The conceptual tools of sociological research—whether labelled by old or new verbal symbols—will become more precise as they are utilized to reveal significant relationships between social phenomena.

From the standpoint of this discussion, significant relationship between social phenomena refers especially to the organic relation between the data on human behaviour. Many statistical studies lack sociological significance because they fail to show any organic relationship among the elements which they utilize for analysis. The problem of crime among American Negroes, to which sociologists have given attention, comes to mind. The lack of education has generally been isolated as the most important factor in the high crime rates among Negroes and to support this claim statistics were cited to show that graduates of Negro colleges had never been convicted of crimes. This manner of treating education without reference to its organic relationship to other factors has led to a false sociological analysis of Negro crime. Two facts will make this clear: educated Negroes, including the graduates of the colleges, have been increasingly convicted of crimes in recent years, while on the other hand, small semi-rural Negro communities with a high degree of illiteracy have remained relatively free of crime. The sociological explanation of the fact that formerly the graduates of Negro colleges were not convicted of crime is in all probability due to the fact that the graduates were educated in relatively isolated institutions characterized by a system of social control based upon the intimate association of teacher and students and that these graduates found positions in a stable social world where they enjoyed a high social status and economic security.

This type of sociological analysis will be open to criticism on the grounds that it involves subjective judgments and evaluations. This is inevitable at the present stage of the development of methods and techniques and it is not certain that all aspects of social reality are susceptible to statistical treatment. But this is no justification for the sociologist, in his striving to be "scientific," to abandon the study of significant and fundamental sociological problems because quantitative and precise tools of research have not been developed to deal with such problems. Only during the course of studying significant sociological problems will the necessary scientific tools be forged to enhance the validity of sociological analysis and generalization. Awareness of this responsibility on the part of sociologists is especially important to-day when they are being called upon to study the pressing problems of the modern world. Chief among these problems are those posed by the new societies which are coming into existence in Africa and Asia as the result of the impact of Western civilization. The study of these problems provides a great opportunity for sociology to become a serious and respected social science discipline. But the achievement of this end will depend upon the extent to which sociologists have a clear conception of their distinctive field of enquiry and are willing to deal with significant problems in the area of social relations.

2

SOCIOLOGICAL THEORY AND
RACE RELATIONS

1946

THE FIRST sociological treatise to be published in the
United States were concerned with race relations. In 1854 there
appeared Henry Hughes' *Treatise on Sociology, Theoretical and
Practical*[1] which undertook to demonstrate that the slave system
was "morally and civilly good" and that "its great and well-known
essentials" should "be unchanged and perpetual." During the same
year there appeared George Fitzhugh's *Sociology for the South:
or the Failure of Free Society*,[2] which possessed more significance
because of the political philosophy upon which it was based. As
indicated in the title, this book was not only a justification of
Negro slavery, but was opposed to the democratic theory of social
organization. Fitzhugh declared that the Declaration of Independence was opposed to "all government, all subordination, all
order."[3] In his attack upon laissez-faire and a competitive society,
he stated that a society did not exist in the free countries where
each man acted for himself.[4] Expressing a philosophy closely resembling Fascist doctrines, he declared that liberty, equality and

---

Paper read before the annual meeting of the American Sociological Society, Chicago, Ill., December 27–30, 1946. Reprinted from the *American Sociological Review* 12, no. 3 (June, 1947) :265–71, by permission of the American Sociological Association.

[1]   Philadelphia, 1854.
[2]   Richmond, 1854. See Harvey Wish, *George Wish: Propagandist of the Old South* (Baton Rouge, La., 1943).
[3]   *Sociology for the South*, p. 175.
[4]   *Ibid.*, p. 33.

freedom had brought crime and pauperism to Europe and that socialism and the struggle of women for equality with men were the results of the failure of a free society. Only in a society built upon slavery and Christianity as the South was built, could morality and discipline be maintained.

The sociological theories of Hughes and Fitzhugh undertook to provide a philosophical justification of slavery. Although their sociological theories cannot be ignored in the history of sociological theories of race relations in the United States, they have scarcely any relation to the later development of sociological thought in this field. Therefore, we shall turn to the so-called fathers of sociology—Ward, Sumner, Giddings, Cooley, Small and Ross—who established sociology as an academic discipline.

Although Lester Ward did not make any specific contribution to the theory of race relations in the United States, his sociological theories contain implications concerning the racial problem. Ward accepted the position of Gumplowicz and Ratzenhofer that the state and other phases of social organization such as caste and class had grown out of group conflict, especially the struggle of races.[5] But in accepting the theory of race struggle Ward did not accept the theory of fundamental racial differences. He rejected the theories of Galton concerning superior races and superior classes. In fact, he took the position that the dominant position of the superior races in the world was due to "the longest uninterrupted inheritance and transmission of human achievement."[6] Through what he termed "sociocracy" or the scientific control of the social forces by the collective mind, equal opportunities for all races and classes would remove the differences in achievement in civilization. Finally, he looked forward to the "period in which the races of men shall have all become assimilated, and when there shall be but one race—the human race."[7]

Sumner's sociological theories have had an influence upon the study of race relations that is still reflected in studies of race relations at the present time. I refer especially to his concept of the

[5] Lester F. Ward, *Pure Sociology* (New York, 1921), pp. 203–20.
[6] *Ibid.*, p. 238.
[7] *Ibid.*, p. 220.

mores. First, it should be pointed out that Sumner took the position that "modern scholars have made the mistake of attributing to race much which belongs to the ethos" of a people.[8] Therefore, the most important factor that separated the various races were their mores. In the South, before the Civil War the two races had learned to live together and mores had developed regulating their relations. The Civil War had destroyed the legal basis of race relations and the resulting conflict and confusion had prevented the emergence of new mores. However, new mores were developing along lines different from those advocated by reformers and legislators who could exercise no influence on the character of the developing racial patterns. Myrdal in his *An American Dilemma* has pointed out the fatalism contained in this conception of the problem of race relations and in fact the inapplicability of the concept of mores to a modern urban industrial society.[9]

Giddings did not offer any broad and systematic theory of race relations although he thought his concept of the "consciousness of kind" explained racial exclusiveness. In regard to the racial mixture, he accepted current notions concerning the instability of mixed races.[10] He was of the opinion, however, that the mental plasticity of mixed races was an important contribution to the development of nations. The social disabilities suffered by the Negro and Indian were an indication of the extent to which the social constitution had not become differentiated from the social composition of the nation.[11]

Cooley's position in regard to the native endowment of different races is set forth in a criticism of Galton's theories in an essay which appeared in *The Annals* in 1897. In that essay, he pointed out that even Galton admitted that Negroes and whites could not be compared because they do not mingle and compete in the same

8   William G. Sumner, *Folkways* (New York, 1906), p. 74.
9   Gunnar Myrdal, *An American Dilemma* (New York, 1944), 2: 1031–32.
10   Franklin H. Giddings, *The Principles of Sociology* (New York, 1908), pp. 324–35.
11   *Ibid.*, pp. 316–17.

social order under the same conditions.[12] However, Cooley's socio-logical theory regarding race relations was set forth in his *Social Organization.* He stated: "Two races of different temperament and capacity, distinct to the eye and living side by side in the same community, tended strongly to become castes, no matter how equal the social system may otherwise be."[13] In a chapter devoted to caste, Cooley presented a clear analysis of the caste character of race relations in the South. In his *Social Process* which was pub-lished nine years later in 1919, he continued his analysis of Negro-white relations in a chapter on "Class and Race." In this chapter he pointed out the lack of positive knowledge of racial differences but felt it reasonable to assume that during the process of bio-logical differentiation of races, mental differences had developed.[14] His conclusion was that race should not be dealt with as a separate factor. He recognized that caste and democracy could not be re-conciled and hoped for some form of cooperation and good-will between the races. He concluded, however, that Orientals should be excluded from the United States and whites from Oriental countries in order not to create racial problems.

The remaining two "fathers" of American Sociology, Ward and Ross, did not make any contributions to sociological theory in regard to race relations. Ross was of the opinion that there was a "Celtic temperament" and that there was no doubt that races dif-fered in regard to intellectual ability.[15] Moreover, he felt that the more intelligent white race had an obligation to civilization to pre-vent Negroes from overwhelming it by mere numbers. He did not believe, however, that the superior race should exploit or mal-treat the inferior race.

[12]   Charles H. Cooley, "Genius, Fame and Comparison of Races," *An-nals of the American Academy of Political and Social Science*, 9 (May, 1897) :1–42; reprinted in *Sociological Theory and Social Research* (New York, 1930), pp. 121–59.

[13]   *Social Organization* (New York, 1923), p. 218.

[14]   *Social Process* (New York, 1925), pp. 274 ff.

[15]   Edward A. Ross, *Principles of Sociology* (New York, 1921), pp. 59 ff. In his autobiography *Seventy Years of It* (New York, 1936), pp. 276 ff., Ross repudiated his former notions concerning racial differences.

In discussing the development of sociological theory and race relations, one cannot overlook a book by one of Giddings' students which had considerable influence on thinking in regard to the Negro. In 1910 Odum published his *Social and Mental Traits of the Negro*, which became for many students a source of information on the mental and social condition of the Negro. When one views today the opinions expressed in the book, it is clear that they reflect not only outmoded conceptions concerning primitive people but all the current popular prejudice concerning the Negro.

The point of view of Odum's book was that the Negro was primarily a social problem and would remain a social problem because he could not be assimilated. It is not strange, therefore, that in the treatment of the Negro as a social problem there is an implicit sociological theory concerning race relations. We might take as typical of the first two decades of the present century two books. In his *Sociology and Modern Social Problems*, first published in 1910, Ellwood devoted a chapter to the Negro problem. In this chapter it is assumed that the Negro has a "racial" temperament and that his "shiftlessness and sensuality" are partly due to heredity and that he is inferior in his adaptiveness to a complex civilization. The infiltration of white blood is responsible for ambition and superiority on the one hand and vice and immorality on the other. It is not strange that since "industrial education" was one of the shibboleths at the time, industrial training is regarded as one of the means of solving the problem. The problem of the Negro is recognized to be a moral problem—not in the sense that Myrdal said that it was a moral problem; namely, the moral obligation of whites to live up to the American creed of human equality. According to Ellwood, it is a moral problem in the sense that the socially superior race should have good will and assist the socially inferior race on the other side of the fence.

The second book on social problems, first published in 1920, by Dow, not only regards the Negro as an unassimilable element in the population but proposes his gradual segregation in a single area or state.[16] Dow accepts as true many of the stereotypes con-

[16]   Grove S. Dow, *Society and Its Problems* (New York, 1920), pp. 157 ff.

cerning the racial traits of the Negro but states that he believes selection and environment are stronger. While Ellwood thinks that more white teachers should be employed to help the inferior Negro race, Dow thinks that white teachers should not be employed because of the possible tendency toward social equality. White teachers from the North did more harm than good, and the Fifteenth Amendment to the Constitution was the worst political blunder in the history of the American people. Northern people do not understand Negro nature. Mulattoes are addicted to crime because, as Dow states, they have the degenerate blood of good white families. Industrial education is a partial solution and caste is the solution for the present though ultimate segregation is necessary.

In considering these books, one should not overlook an article by Weatherly which appeared in the *Journal* in 1910 on "Race and Marriage."[17] The author took the position that there was a natural aversion to intermarriage which was designed to preserve race purity as a necessary condition for social development. Another article along similar lines, entitled "The Philosophy of the Color Line" by Mecklin appeared in the *Journal* in 1913.[18] This writer found justification for "white supremacy" in the necessity to preserve purity.

The sociological theory in regard to race relations which was current during the first two decades of the present century was doubtless not unrelated to public opinion and the dominant racial attitudes of the American people. The racial conflict in the South had subsided and the North had accepted the thesis that the South should solve the racial problem. The southern solution had been the disfranchisement of the Negro and the establishment of a quasi-caste system in which the Negro was segregated and received only a pittance of public funds for education and social services. The famous formula of Booker T. Washington, involving the social separation of the races and industrial education, had become

[17]   Ulysses G. Weatherly, "Race and Marriage," *American Journal of Sociology* 15 (1910) :433–53.
[18]   John M. Mecklin, "The Philosophy of the Color Line," *American Journal of Sociology* 19 (1913) :343–57.

the accepted guide to future race relations. The sociological theories which were implicit in the writings on the Negro problem were merely rationalizations of the existing racial situation.

During this period there began to emerge a sociological theory of race relations that was formulated independent of existing public opinion and current attitudes. As early as 1904, W. I. Thomas presented in an article entitled "The Psychology of Race Prejudice," in the *Journal*, a systematic theory of race relations.[19] Thomas undertook first to determine the biological basis for the phenomenon of race prejudice. He thought that he discovered this in certain reflex and instinctive reactions of the lower animals to strange elements in their environment. But in the case of human beings, he held that the development of sympathetic relations was the important factor. Sympathetic relations were most highly developed within the family group and only gradually included larger social groupings. Although race prejudice had an organic basis and could not be reasoned with, it could be dissipated through human association. Thus Thomas assumed that race prejudice could be destroyed and he did not assume that people of divergent racial stocks must inevitably remain apart or could only live together in the community where a caste system existed. The relation between caste and race prejudice is summed up by him in the following statement:

Psychologically speaking, race-prejudice and caste-feeling are at bottom the same thing, both being phases of the instinct of hate, but a status of caste is reached as the result of competitive activities. The lower caste has either been conquered and captured, or gradually outstripped on account of the mental and economic inferiority. Under these conditions, it is psychologically important to the higher caste to maintain the feeling and show of superiority, on account of the suggestive effect of this on both the inferior caste and on itself; and signs of superiority and inferiority, being thus aids to the manipulation of one class by another, acquire a new significance and become ineradicable. Of the relation of black and white in this country it is perhaps true that the antipathy of the southerner for the negro is rather caste-feeling than race-prejudice, while the feeling of the northerner is race-prejudice proper. In the North, where there has been no contact with the negro and no activity connections, there is no caste-feeling, but there exists a sort of *skin*-prejudice—a horror of the external aspect of the negro—and many northerners report that they have a feeling against eating from a dish handled by a negro. The association of master and slave in the South was, however, close, even if not intimate, and much of the feeling of physical repulsion for a black skin disappeared.[20]

Thus as early as 1904 Thomas had shown the caste character of race relations in the South and had shown how race relations there differed from race relations in the North. Moreover, Thomas in another article had undertaken to show how social and mental isolation had been responsible for the failure of the Negro to make outstanding achievements in civilization.[21]

The sociological theories of Park in regard to race relations were developed originally in close association with Thomas. Park, who was observing race relations in the South, was in constant communication with Thomas. Park's theories, which represent the most comprehensive and systematic sociological theories of race relations developed by American sociologists and have had the greatest influence on American sociology, began to appear at a time when the Negro problem was assuming a new character in American life. The migration of Negroes to the metropolitan areas of the North had destroyed the accommodation that had been achieved to some extent following the racial conflict during and following Reconstruction. The publication of *Introduction to the Science of Sociology* by Park and Burgess coincided with the study of the race riot in Chicago in 1919. The new impact of the Negro problem on American life undoubtedly helped Park as much as his experience in the South in the formulation of a sociological theory.

For Park the phenomenon of race relations is to be studied within his general sociological frame of reference—competition, conflict, accommodation, and assimilation. "Nowhere do social

[20]   *Ibid.*, pp. 609–10.
[21]   "Race Psychology: Standpoint and Questionnaire," *The American Journal of Sociology*, 17:745, ff.

contacts so readily provoke conflicts as in the relations between the races, particularly when racial differences are re-enforced; not merely by differences of culture, but of color."[22] Concerning the nature of race prejudice he wrote:

Race prejudice, as we call the sentiments that support the racial taboos, is not, in America at least, an obscure phenomenon. But no one has yet succeeded in making it wholly intelligible. It is evident that there is in race prejudice, as distinguished from class and caste prejudice, an instinctive factor based on the fear of the unfamiliar and the uncomprehended. Color, or any other racial mark that emphasizes physical differences, becomes the symbol of moral divergences which perhaps do not exist. We at once fear and are fascinated by the stranger, and an individual of a different race always seems more of a stranger to us than one of our own. This naïve prejudice, unless it is re-enforced by other factors, is easily modified, as the intimate relations of the Negro and white man in slavery show.[23]

Although Park held that there was an instinctive element in race prejudice, he nevertheless stated that the conflict of culture was a more positive factor in race prejudice. The central fact in the conflict of culture was, he wrote, "the unwillingness of one race to enter into personal competition with a race of a different or inferior culture." In a later article he made the factor of status the most important element in race prejudices.[24] In making status the most important factor in race prejudice, Park took the position that race prejudice was based upon essentially the same attitudes as those at the basis of class and caste. A prejudiced reaction to members of another race is the normal tendency of the mind to react to individuals as members of categories. The categories into which people are placed generally involved status. Since the Negro is constantly rising in America, he arouses prejudices and animosities. Race prejudice is "merely an elementary expression of conservatism."[25]

[22]   Robert E. Park, *Introduction to the Science of Sociology* (Chicago, 1924), p. 578.
[23]   *Ibid.*, p. 578.
[24]   Robert E. Park, "The Basis of Race Prejudice: The American Negro," *The Annals*, 140 (1928) :11–20.
[25]   Park, *ibid.*, p. 13.

Up to about 1930, Park's sociological theory in regard to race relations in the United States did not go beyond the theory of a biracial organization in which vertical social distance between the two races would become a matter of horizontal social distance. A biracial organization would preserve race distinctions but it would change its content in that there would be a change in attitudes. The races would no longer look up and down but across.[26] The development of the biracial organization marked a fundamental change in status, since the Negro was acquiring the status of a racial or cultural minority. In an article published in 1939, Park presented the case of the American Negro in the general frame of reference which he had developed for the study of race relations in the modern world.[27] In that article he showed how the migration of the Negro to northern cities had changed the character of race relations and he pointed out that caste was being undermined and that the social distance between the races at the different class levels was being undermined. Moreover, he regarded race relations in the United States as part of a world process in which culture and occupation was coming to play a more important role than inheritance and race. Thus for Park, the "racial frontiers" that were developing in various parts of the world were the seed-beds of new cultures.

In Park's development of a sociological theory in regard to race relations, there are several important features which are significant for the future of sociological theory in this field. The original emphasis of his theory was upon the social psychological aspects of race contacts. It was concerned primarily with providing an explanation of behavior in terms of attitudes. This was not only peculiar to Park's theory but it was characteristic of the theories of other scholars. In this connection one might cite Faris' penetrating analysis of race prejudice in an essay entitled, "Race Attitudes and Sentiments."[28] In the social psychological approach there was a tendency to ignore or pay little attention to the struc-

---

[26]   *Ibid.*, p. 20.
[27]   "The Nature of Race Relations," in Edgar T. Thompson (ed.), *Race Relations and the Race Problem* (Durham, N.C., 1939).
[28]   Ellsworth Faris, *The Nature of Human Nature* (New York, 1937), pp. 317–28.

tural and organizational aspects of race relations on the one hand and the dynamic aspects of the problem on the other. The so-called "caste and class" school of students of race relations who have challenged the position of the sociologist has focused attention upon this phase of the problem. However, it should be pointed out that while the "caste and class" school has focused attention upon the structural aspects of race relations, they have only documented the concept of caste. They have not provided any new insights concerning the attitudes and behavior of whites and Negroes. Since the concept of caste has been an essentially static concept, it has failed to provide an orientation for the dynamic aspects of race relations. This brings us to another phase of the sociological theories of Park in regard to race relations.

Park's sociological theory was originally a static theory of race relations. His theory not only contained the fatalism inherent in Sumner's concept of the mores. His theory was originally based upon the assumption that the races could not mix or mingle freely. This is apparent even in his concept of the biracial organization. But as Park saw the changes which were occurring in the United States and other parts of the world, he modified his theory to take into account these changes. His latest theory of race relations in the modern world took into account the dynamic elements in the situation. It remains for his students and other scholars to make a more precise formulation of these theories through research and reflection.

This last statement seems appropriate since Park's last formulation of his theory of race relations indicates a trend in research, only a brief reference to which can be made here. Current sociological research has not only discarded the older assumptions about racial characteristics but it is approaching the problem of "race relations" from a different standpoint. For the sociologist the problem of "race relations" has become a problem of inter-group relations. This change in viewpoint, it might be pointed out, is evident even in the programs of so-called "inter-cultural education" which are gradually becoming programs of "inter-group" relations. Sociological theory has had some influence on this new orientation.

In summary, the development of sociological theory in regard to race relations may be stated as follows:

(1) The sociological theories of the founders of American sociology as an academic discipline were only implicitly related to the concrete problems of race relations. Their theories concerning race relations were derived from European scholars who were concerned with the universal phenomenon of race contact. Cooley was an exception in that he offered an analysis of race relations in the South based upon his theories of the origin and nature of caste and its relation to class.

(2) Sociological theories relating to the concrete problems of race relations in the United States were implicit in the sociological analysis of the Negro problem as a social problem. The analysis of the Negro problem was based upon several fairly clear assumptions: that the Negro is an inferior race because of either biological or social heredity or both; that the Negro because of his physical character cannot be assimilated; and that physical amalgamation is bad and undesirable.

(3) The sociological theories implicit in the studies of the Negro problem were developed during the period when the nation held that the attempt to make the Negro a citizen was a mistake and a new accommodation of the races was being achieved in the South under a system of segregation. Therefore, these theories were rationalizations of American public opinion and the dominant attitudes of the American people.

(4) Sociological theory in regard to race relations began to assume a more systematic formulation following the first World War. Park was the chief figure in the formulation of this sociological theory which provided the orientation for empirical studies of race relations. These studies were based upon the theory that race was a sociological concept and utilized such social psychological tools as attitudes and social distance and Sumner's concept of the mores. As the relation of the Negro to American life changed and the problems of race relations throughout the world became more insistent, Park developed a more dynamic theory of race relations.

(5) A so-called new school of thought, utilizing the concept

of caste and class, has undertaken new studies of race relations. Whereas this new school has focused attention upon the neglected phase of race relations—the structural aspects—it has documented the concept of caste rather than provided new insights.

(6) What is needed is the further development of a dynamic sociological theory of race relations, which will discard all the rationalizations of race prejudice and provide orientation for the study of the constantly changing patterns of race relations in American life.

3

RACE CONTACTS AND
THE SOCIAL STRUCTURE

1949

IN THE PRESENT meeting of The American Sociological
Society, we have returned to the central theme of the annual meeting of 1928, Race and Culture Contacts. That the Society has
turned its attention once more to this subject is not due to any
lack of other important problems deserving attention in the field
of sociological inquiry. During the twenty years that have elasped
since the 1928 meeting an economic depression of almost global
dimensions and a second world war have caused the problem of
the relations of peoples with different racial and cultural backgrounds to become one of the most important problems of human
relations in the modern world. Although the phenomenon of race
and culture contacts involves economic and political factors, it is
of primary concern to the sociologist since he is interested in the
manner in which men are able to achieve a basis of understanding
or consensus in order to carry on collective life.

In regarding consensus as the basis of social life, I am not un-
mindful of the recurrent problem in sociology concerning the
nature of society or the frame of reference in which sociological
research should be undertaken. This problem, which involves the
nature of the relation of the individual to the collectivity which we
call society, is not unrelated to the phenomenon of race contacts.
According to one school of sociologists, the nominalist, society is

The Presidential Address read before the annual meeting of the American
Sociological Society held in Chicago, Illinois, December 27-30, 1948. Reprinted from the *American Sociological Review* 14, no. 1 (February, 1949) :
1–11, by permission of the American Sociological Association.

an aggregate of individuals, and the key to an understanding of society is to be found in the study of the behavior of individuals as discrete units. The other school, known as the realist or organic school, has focussed its attention upon the social processes and the organized aspects of the collective life arising out of communication and interaction. Although the thinking of many American sociologists has been dominated by the latter point of view, their researches have reflected the former conception of society. This has been especially true in the study of race contacts where the members of the different racial groups have been treated as a mere aggregate of individuals. As a consequence, studies of race relations have often been based upon individual reactions, without reference to the behavior of men as members of a social group.

It is my purpose to indicate how the study of race contacts in the context of social relations or an organic conception of society will yield significant results for sociology. For this purpose I shall discuss Negro-white contacts from the standpoint of the social structure of the Negro world.

Since the Negro has been chosen as the basis of this discussion it may be well to review briefly the general orientation of studies of the Negro by American sociologists. These sociologists fall into three groups, whose works coincide roughly with historical periods in the development of American sociology. The first group consisting of the so-called fathers of American sociology—Ward, Sumner, Giddings, Cooley, Small and Ross, who established sociology as an academic discipline—did not deal specifically with the problem of race relations. Their theories concerning race relations were derived largely from European scholars who were concerned with the universal phenomenon of race contact. Ward, who accepted the theories of Gumplowicz and Ratzenhofer concerning the role of the struggle of races in the social development of mankind, did not accept the theory of race differences. He took the position that the superior status of the dominant races was the result of their having had "the longest uninterrupted inheritance and transmission of human achievements." Sumner regarded race differences as primarily a reflection of the ethos of different peoples. Consequently, the most important factor in race relations was the mores which gradually changed to meet new life conditions but could not be influenced by legislators and reformers. Although Giddings did not deal specifically with Negro-white relations, he thought that his concept of the "consciousness of kind" explained racial exclusiveness. He accepted the current notion of the instability of mixed races and regarded the "mental plasticity of mixed bloods" as a contribution to the development of nations. Although Small was influenced by Ratzenhofer, he did not make any contribution to theory in this field. Ross offered only some generalizations concerning racial temperament and felt that the more intelligent white race had an obligation to civilization to prevent Negroes from overwhelming it by their numbers. Cooley was an exception in that he offered an analysis of race relations in the South based upon his theory of the origin and nature of caste and its relation to class. Cooley's point of view not only anticipated a current approach to race relations, but placed the subject in a sociological frame of reference.

When the sociologist began to direct his attention to the Negro, it was to study him as a "social problem" in American life. The general point of view of the books and articles published by this group of sociologists was that the Negro was an inferior race because of either biological or social heredity or both; that the Negro because of his physical characteristics could not be assimilated; and that physical amalgamation was bad and therefore undesirable. These conclusions were generally supported by the marshalling of a vast amount of statistical data on the pathological aspects of Negro life.

The third group of American sociologists who have dealt with race relations was represented by W. I. Thomas and Robert E. Park, who did not study the Negro as a "social problem" but as a subject of sociological research. As early as 1904, Thomas presented an analysis of race prejudice and caste-feeling that has not been superseded by later analyses. Park studied race relations within the frame of reference of his general sociological theory. He became the chief figure in a more systematic formulation of a theory of race relations following World War I when the mass migration of Negroes to northern cities changed the entire character of Negro-white contacts in the United States. His theory of the emergence of the Negro as a racial minority provided a frame of reference in which to study the changing character of race relations. In this connection the appearance of the so-called new school of thought, utilizing the concept of "caste and class," should be mentioned since it appeared at the time when sociologists were turning their attention to "the original interest of sociologists in the actual problems of man in society."[1]

The emergence of the so-called "caste and class" school of students of race relations offered a challenge to the sociologist from two angles. First, they opposed the conception of race relations since, they argued, the Negro was not a race in the biological sense; and, secondly, the pattern which Negro-white relations assumed in the United States was essentionally a caste system. The sociologist has been able to defend his definition of Negro-white relations as race relations because Negroes are regarded as a race and are treated as if they were a race. Contrary to the prediction of Vacher de Lapouge in 1880 that in the twentieth century "millions will cut each other's throats because of one or two degrees more or less of cephalic index," racial conflict has never been based upon the refined racial indices of anthropologists. On the other hand, many features of Negro-white relations have resembled a caste system. But when one realizes that the pattern of Negro-white relations has not only lacked both religious sanctions and a political ideology, but has been resisted by Negroes, it is clear that such a conception may introduce confusion. The studies of the "caste and class" school have rendered a service by focusing attention upon the structural aspects of race relations. But the caste concept of race relations has been utilized in studies as a static concept. Consequently, while failing to provide any new insights into the attitudes and behavior of whites and Negroes, these studies have ignored the dynamic aspects of race relations, especially under the changing conditions of urban living.

Some day the growing interest of American sociologists in the sociology of knowledge will probably reveal the reason for the

[1]   Louis Wirth, "American Sociology, 1915–47" in *The American Journal of Sociology, Index to Volumes I–LII, 1895–1947*, p. 274.

changes in the conception of the problem of Negro-white relations and the status of research in this field. Here are offered only some tentative hypotheses which may be tested by those who are interested in this branch of sociology. The emphasis upon the study of the Negro as a "social problem" rather than a problem for sociological analysis is understandable in the light of its prominence among American social problems. But what needs further analysis from the standpoint of the sociology of knowledge is why the Negro was defined sociologically as essentially a racial problem involving an unassimilable group. The hypothesis that is offered here is that the sociological definition of the problem represented a rationalization of the social attitudes of the class in the white community from which sociologists were recruited. With the earlier sociologists, the founding fathers of the discipline, the Negro was remote, the majority being concentrated in the South. Moreover, the earlier sociologists based their generalizations upon knowledge acquired from books rather than empirical studies. Later, when the impact of the Negro upon the main stream of American life following World War I required a re-definition, the concepts of sociology and the techniques which sociologists were employing in empirical studies had achieved some maturity.

There remains another reflection on the status of studies of the Negro which is relevant at this point. There has been a rather widespread feeling or belief that studies of the Negroes did not have the same academic status or did not require the same intellectual maturity or discipline as the study of other sociological problems. It appears that there was a feeling, perhaps unconscious and therefore all the more significant, that since the Negro occupied a low status and did not play an important role in American society, studies of the Negro were of less significance from the standpoint of social science. As a consequence of this attitude, the study of vitally important sociological problems, for which the Negro provided incomparably valuable materials, was left to anyone who might occupy himself with such lowly sociological materials. It is only recently that the sociological study of the Negro has acquired the academic status of studies of other groups and has attracted the serious attention of sociologists.

Of course, the relegation of the sociological study of the Negro to a lower academic status has been involved with the essentially political aspects of the problem. By political aspects of the problem, reference is made to the question of social control. Sociologists have practically ignored the system of social control which the white community has utilized to maintain a certain equilibrium between the Negro community and the more inclusive community. Here I do not refer to legal controls but to the invisible forms of social control which have been utilized by agencies outside of the governmental structure. Although this phase of Negro-white relations has been ignored, many studies of the Negro have been a reflection of a certain philosophy of race relations rather than an analysis of the social processes involved in race relations. Consequently, it is not surprising that what were essentially political programs for amicable race relations or diplomatic commentaries on race relations by so-called inter-racial statesmen have passed for scientific sociological analysis.

The interest in recent years in the study of race relations as a problem of intergroup relations is an indication of the growing consciousness of the need to study such relations within a sociological frame of reference. Workers in the field of race relations who are concerned with programs of social action are becoming aware of the Negro community and its institutions or the social world of the Negro and its various relations to the social world of the more inclusive white community. But students who are engaged in formal or academic studies of race contacts are still inclined to employ tools of research which are designed to discover how individuals may act towards individuals of another racial group without reference to the social context in which this behavior occurs. An excellent example of this type of approach to racial contacts may be found in the numerous studies of racial attitudes. Attitude studies attempt to probe the behavior and mental processes of sociologically isolated individuals. Even when the attitudes of individuals are related to their occupational or educational status, they do not become sociologically significant. The sociologist is interested in discovering how people are likely to behave by virtue of the fact that they are members of a certain group or are placed in a type of social situation.

In order to illustrate the frame of reference to which I am suggesting that race contacts should be studied, we might take the question of intermarriage. I should begin by saying that the definition of marriages between Negroes and whites contains a bias since it is assumed that the attitudes of recent immigrants and their descendants are the same as the attitudes of the older American stocks. But this is not the phase of the problem in which we are primarily interested. Intermarriage is a sociological problem which has been more or less tabooed or when it has been subjected to study, the so-called sociological analysis has been little more than a rationalization of current prejudices. There have been attempts to make objective analysis of available statistics on marriage between white and Negroes. In the statistical studies an attempt has been made to determine the volume and trend of intermarriage and an analysis has been made of the occupational status of whites and Negroes and the national origin of the whites who entered into marriage.

While all of these factors have had some relevance to the sociological problem, they have been related only inferentially to the social and economic structure of the white community and they have almost completely ignored the social reality which we have called the Negro community and its institutions. Not only have both whites and Negroes been treated as atomized individuals without family relations and social status, but such sociologically relevant factors as the effects of urbanization and mobility upon the character of racial contacts and social status have been left out of account. What I wish to emphasize is that if studies of intermarriage are to have sociological significance, they must analyze intermarriage within the frame of reference of two social worlds or the social organization of the white and Negro communities. Outside of this frame of reference, the extent and trend of intermarriage as measured by statistics becomes a meaningless abstraction and no extrapolation of statistical trends on intermarriage will provide any key to the future course of this relationship. If intermarriage were studied within the frame of reference of the changing nature of the contacts which are occurring between the social world of the whites and the social world of the Negroes, both the extent and trend of intermarriage would acquire meaning and provide a basis for prediction. Although this prediction could not be presented in the form of graphs, it would nevertheless be based upon an analysis of intermarriage within the social context in which it occurs.

The study of racial contacts in relation to the social reality which we have designated as the social world of the Negro will make such concepts as communication and interaction more meaningful as tools for sociological research. As sociologists we have been interested in the means by which individuals and groups take over the culture and become identified inwardly as well as outwardly with other groups. We have devised techniques and tools such as the social distance scale in order to state in a quasi-quantitative form the degree of intimacy and identification existing between different racial, cultural and national groups. These techniques and tools have yielded much information on the attitudes and presumptive behavior of persons who have been treated as discrete individuals. But these questions may be asked, for example: What does the position of a person on a social distance scale indicate in regard to his behavior as a member of a labor union or a member of a baseball team? In view of the increasing integration of the Negro into various phases of American life, what do the various attitude studies tell us about this process? Have these scales not been employed without reference to the fact that sociologists are primarily interested in the behavior of people as members of society?

Since my aim is to show how the study of race contacts in the context of social relationships will increase our understanding of this aspect of human relations, it is necessary to give some attention to the social world of the Negro. Attention is directed almost entirely to the social world of the Negro because it is still a vague or unknown quantity in sociological studies.

I shall begin by considering the effects of the spatial segregation of the Negro community on race contacts. The studies in the field of human ecology have revealed that the location of people and institutions in the modern urban environment is not a haphazard or adventitious phenomenon. As the result of the competition for land or space, there is a process of selection and segregation of persons on the basis of education, occupation, wealth, and racial or cultural background and of institutions on the basis of function. Where there are no legal barriers or resistance on the part of organized white groups to the expansion of the Negro population, the location of the Negro community and persons and institutions within the community can be explained on the basis of the findings in human ecology. Of course, these studies are concerned with the modern urban community where competition for space determines the location of people and institutions. If one studies the location of Negro communities in the older cities of the South, one finds that their original pattern has not been determined so much by impersonal economic factors involved in competition as by historical factors. The Negro population in these cities is widely scattered because the whites settled their slaves close to their residence and later generations of Negro tenants and owners have occupied the homes or the same land. Consequently, one finds that from the standpoint of spatial relations the Negro communities which have emerged in northern cities since the migrations beginning with World War I are more segregated than the Negro communities in older southern cities. In the border cities, it appears that the location of Negro communities has not been influenced decidedly either by impersonal economic and social forces as in the North or by historic factors as in the older southern cities. Moreover, it is important to note that in the newer cities of the South, and as the older southern cities acquire a more industrial and commercial character, the Negro community is becoming more segregated.

I shall refer to only the more important effects of the spatial segregation of Negro communities on racial contacts. In the South the spatial proximity of the races has not led to the integration of the Negro into the more inclusive community. Yet the relations between whites and Negroes living in the same neighborhoods have not been symbiotic relationships except in the case of the white owners of grocery stores who cater to the Negro community. This can even be said of the relationship of the two races where Negroes live close to whites for whom they work. Their relationships have been similar to some extent to the traditional patterns of Negro-white relationships evolving out of the slave status. Where this relationship has been broken or there is no traditional basis for race relations—where, for example, white neighbors are descendants of the non-slave-holding class—then race relations will depend upon various types of personal relationships which may develop between individuals. In any case the life of the Negro outside his economic relationships with whites revolves chiefly about the organized social life of the Negro community. On the other hand, in northern cities where there is greater concentration of Negroes, the members of the two races have more frequent contacts of an impersonal nature. For example, there are more contacts in the field of employment, and because of the greater mobility of the population there are many more opportunities for casual contacts between individual members of the two races. Another difference which needs to be emphasized is that although the Negro population may be more segregated from the standpoint of residence, there is greater opportunity for Negroes and whites to be members of the same functional groups which characterize modern civilization. At the same time, the existence of two social worlds results in the tendency for each group to see the other through the press and other media of mass communication in the city. The Negro press provides a mirror in which the Negro sees himself in a different role from that presented in the white press and gives a picture of the white world quite different from that which the white press reports. Only in the mixed areas on the fringe of the Negro and white communities where some approach to neighborly relations may develop, do members of the two races see each other more or less as individual human beings. It is noteworthy that such areas in southern as well as northern cities have been free from violence when race riots have raged in other parts of the city.

In a number of studies of race relations in cities, there has been an uncritical use of such concepts as mores and caste. For example, it was claimed by a social scientist that Negroes could not be employed on the buses and streetcars in the District of Columbia because their employment in this capacity was opposed to the mores of the community. It should be clear to any sociologist that the term mores as used by Sumner has only a limited application to behavior in the modern urban community. The opposition to the employment of Negroes in the District of Columbia was due to the opposition of an organized group of workers who desired to defend their interests in this field of employment. Likewise, the segregation of the Negro population in our cities is not a reflection of the mores of the community, nor is it always the result of the operation of impersonal social and economic forces which are responsible for the ecological pattern of our cities. In the recent study of segregation in the nation's capital it was clearly shown that the restriction of the Negro population to certain areas of the city has been accomplished by the activities of the organized real estate, commercial, and financial interests. Unless one includes in a study of race relations the influence of this aspect of the social organization of the white world, studies of racial contacts in the urban community will have little validity.

In considering the relation of the social organization of the Negro community to racial contacts, one must begin of course with the family. The changes in race relations following Emancipation affected the internal organization and function of this most scared and exclusive form of human association. The transfer of authority in the Negro family from the white master to the Negro father or mother was one of the primary factors in the estrangement of the two races. Where formerly the intrusion of the white master was accepted, the interference of the white employer or landlord was resented. The claim of family loyalty superseded loyalty to the white employer. As the family has acquired an institutional character, it has increasingly become a barrier to close contacts between the two races. At the same time the culture of the Negro family has had a decided influence on the manner in which contacts with the white world have affected individual Negroes.

For example, the influence of the culture of the family is evident in the case of the children of southern migrants in the public schools of northern cities. The standard American education to which these children are exposed represents a world of ideas and beliefs which are markedly different from the beliefs and ideas which are received through family training. The response of the children to new ideas and beliefs is dependent upon the manner in which they are defined in the family. The apathetic attitudes of the children of southern migrants toward education may be understood when one is acquainted with their family training and experience. In fact, the same could be said today of the large body of Negro students who are entering the colleges at the present time. These students are being drawn from a stratum in the Negro population with a folk and plantation background that has been transmitted through the family. Consequently, the response of these students to a liberal education is quite different from that of the small body of Negro students who attended college in the past. The latter students were drawn largely from the descendants of Negroes who were free before the Civil War and the descendants of those house-servants and artisans among whom a tradition of literate culture had become established.

The family also plays a role in racial contacts that is more patently related to this discussion, in that it defines the attitudes and reactions of Negroes toward whites. This was revealed in the studies of the effect of minority status upon the development of the personality of Negro youth sponsored by the American Council on Education. The character of the influence exercised by the family on the response of Negro youth to racial contacts was related to the class position of the family. Lower-class families tended on the whole to accept the white man's conception of the Negro, and parents in lower-class families taught their children techniques —often involving lying and clowning and other forms of deception—for getting along with whites. On the other hand, middle-class families rejected the white man's conception of the Negro but accepted his culture as the means of enhancing their own personal dignity. The children in upper-class families with traditions representing a blend of upper-class and middle-class American pattern of behavior revealed an ambivalent attitude toward the Negro world. While they sought to escape from the Negro masses, they were inclined to resist the breaking down of racial barriers in those areas of contacts which offered a threat to their privileged position behind the walls of segregation.

The relation of cultural institutions in the Negro community to racial contacts has generally been ignored. I shall consider only one of these institutions, the church, not only because of its long history and importance in Negro life but more especially because it will show most clearly the crucial role of the social structure in racial contacts. The Negro church arose as an institution among free Negroes in the North as a protest against segregation and a subordinate status in the white church organizations. After Emancipation the Negro church organizations absorbed what Woodson has aptly called "the invisible church" which had grown up among the slaves. Consequently, the Negro church came to embody more than any other institution the traditional culture of the Negro with its roots in these two sources of racial experience. In fact, before the migrations of Negroes to the metropolitan areas of the North, which resulted in an upsurge of race consciousness, for the masses of southern rural Negroes identification with the large church denominations represented their widest group identification. In other words, to be a Baptist or Methodist had more meaning for them than the fact that they were Americans or even Negroes. Although the importance of the Negro church in the social organization and culture of the Negro community has declined, it remains the chief repository of the cultural traditions of the Negro masses and embodies some of their most deeply rooted vested interests. The Negro church has provided a field for the development of leadership and self-expression, and in those sections of the country where Negroes have been excluded from political participation it has been the area of social life in which their talents for politics could be developed. Then it is important to add that the church has provided patterns of behavior which have left their imprint on other phases of the social life of the Negro community.

These facts are important not only when one undertakes to study the phenomenon of race contacts but also if one is engaged in a program for the integration of the Negro into the larger American commuity. There are widespead efforts on the part of Protestants and Catholics to break down the racial barrier in the field of religion. The church, it is claimed, should set the example for other associations and institutions in the American community. While this may be a praiseworthy goal from the standpoint of Christian ethics and democratic ideals and if carried out would undoubtedly have some influence on racial attitudes and public opinion, this type of thinking involves a misunderstanding of the nature of social institutions and their role in the culture of a group, and their relation to the changing pattern of race contacts. There is the failure to differentiate between a church organization and a theater or some other place of public entertainment and recreation. If evidence were lacking, it should be clear to sociologists why it is easier to integrate the Negro or any other outgroup into a secular institution characterized by casual and impersonal contacts than into a sacred institution based upon families and the peculiar cultural traditions of the group. Therefore, the admission of Negroes to theaters and restaurants will not depend upon their integration into white churches. Moreover, and this is the fact which I want to emphasize, even if white churches should welcome Negro communicants, the vast majority of Negroes will continue to maintain their own church organizations since these institutions embody the cultural traditions of the Negro as well as other vested interests. On the other hand, organizations in the Negro community which represent the more secular interests which Negroes have in common with whites will dissolve more quickly into the functional organizations of the more inclusive community.

I shall turn now to the social norms and values in the Negro community which have an influence on racial contacts and contribute to the isolation of the Negro world. Many years ago W. I. Thomas undertook to show the effects of isolation on the intellectual development of Negroes, peasants, women and savages. Thomas' attention was directed to the manner in which the absence of contacts restricted the communication of ideas to Negroes. At the same time he pointed out that, unlike the Negro, the oppressed Jew in Russia and Roumania had been able to overcome the effects of isolation because he possessed resources, traditions, and techniques upon which he could draw. My purpose here is to direct attention to the manner in which the isolation of the Negro results from such social factors as the traditional patterns of behavior and values which are associated with the institutional life of the community and its class structure. The social organization of Negro life and its dominant values act as a social prism through which ideas, patterns of behavior, and values current in the larger American community are refracted or distorted. I would even suggest the hypothesis, which might be tested by empirical studies of racial contacts, that the degree of refraction or distortion is in inverse ratio to the extent that Negroes participate in the larger American society. Or stated otherwise, the degree of refraction or distortion is proportional to the extent that Negroes are integrated into the institutions and culture of the Negro community.

What I am referring to here is, of course, what Thomas called the definition of the situation provided by the culture or other persons. A few examples will enable us to understand how certain patterns of behavior and prestige values which are found among different classes in the Negro community affect racial contacts or tend to isolate the Negro. The most mobile elements in the Negro population are likely, because of their incomes and education, to have upper-class status within the Negro world. This means that they are drawn into a social world with certain values and style of life. These upper-class values generally involve conspicuous consumption and forms of leisure and recreation which are characteristic of upper-class white Americans. Therefore, a Negro with the same income and occupational and educational status as a middle-class white person is likely to have a different conception of his status and to live according to a different style of life. This creates a barrier between the two races that is not broken down even when whites and Negroes are employed in the same institutions in the community. For the Negro is still bound by the traditions and expectations of the class in the Negro community with which he and his family and friends are identified. There may even be a resistance to the style of life of his white associates when the latter attempt to establish friendly and intimate relations with him. Moreover, it is likely that the impact of ideas and other influences originating in the more inclusive community will have a different meaning for him.

The vested interests of the members of a class in the Negro community influence their attitudes toward race contacts. As the result of segregation, the professional Negro has enjoyed a monopoly in regard to some services in the Negro community. Because of these vested interests the professional Negro is often not inclined to welcome the lowering of racial barriers in the interest of abstract democratic ideals when it will result in the loss of his monopoly. It should be noted, however, that the interests of this class are opposed to those of the great mass of Negro workers who gain by the breakdown of segregation because they are thus able to compete in the American labor market. Therefore, in the study of race contacts it is necessary to understand how the conflicting interests of these two classes affect their attitude toward race contacts.

The influence of certain prestige values may be seen in the contrast between the tradition of the book or learning in the Jewish community and the absence of such a tradition in the Negro community. Because of the dominating position of the church and its influence on the general orientation of the Negro toward the world, there is no deeply rooted intellectual tradition in the Negro community. Some observers have noted a certain anti-intellectual bias as one of the features of Negro culture. Although this has not been established by empirical study, there can be no question concerning the absence of a distinct class in the Negro community which has become the bearer of an intellectual tradition. Increasingly, individual Negroes are acquiring the best intellectual culture that America offers in the institutions of the country. But when such persons return to the Negro community, they generally become identified with a class in the community that has no appreciation of intellectual values. Even when they become identified with educational institutions, intellectual achievements may not count for much except as symbols of status which is associated with power relations within the Negro community. This is not a phenomenon peculiar to the Negro community, but it becomes important because of the difference in the definition of intellectual attainments and the almost complete absence of a class to give support to intellectual values. For example, when a Negro professional man was recently appointed to a white institution, the Negro newspapers did not mention a single fact concerning his profession, but identified him by noting his various activities in social and fraternal organizations in the Negro community.

I have referred briefly to the extra-legal control exercised by agencies in the white community over the Negro community. I wish to refer more specifically to the manner in which this type of control has influenced the thinking of Negroes, especially those who have occupied strategic positions in educational institutions. It is common knowledge that the selection of the leadership and personnel of the separate educational institutions in the South has been based upon the philosophy of race relations of the ruling group in the white community. But the influence of the white community has not been so obvious in the case of private institutions. Because of the poverty of Negroes and the failure of the southern states to provide for their higher education, the support of the private institutions has depended upon philanthropic individuals and foundations and church organizations in the North. At one time a few of the Negro institutions were supported by philanthropic whites who represented the abolitionist tradition. But with the gradual disappearance of this group, the support of the private institutions passed into the hands of foundations and church organizations with a conservative philosophy of race relations. The extent to which these organizations have deliberately selected a certain type of educational leader has varied. Whatever the policy the foundations have followed in the selection of Negro leaders, the leaders themselves have not been unaware of the philosophy of race relations of their supporters.

Since the social structure of both the Negro community and white community has been undergoing rapid changes, the analysis of race contacts should be related to a changing structure of social relationships. The most important factor which has been responsible for the change in race contacts has been the urbanization of the Negro population. To some extent the urbanization of the Negro population has limited the role of the family in defining race contacts. On the other hand, urbanization has created a substantial group of middle-class families whose position in the class structure of the Negro community has erected barriers to intimate contacts between the races. From the standpoint of secondary contacts the development of middle-class standards of behavior has decreased the social visibility of the Negro in the general community. Urbanization has changed the structure and function of every institution and association in the Negro community and their role in race relations. For example, as the Negro church has acquired a more intelligent leadership and has become concerned with secular matters, it has increasingly played a role in mass movements for civil rights and wider opportunities for employment.

As the bi-racial organization has been breaking down in the metropolitan community, even more important changes have occurred in the nature of race contacts. The growth in the size and importance of the Negro professional class has brought members of this class into closer association with white members of this class in the wider community. The integration of Negroes into industry and labor organizations has reduced the social distance between the races even to the extent of breaking down the barriers to intimate association between individuals of the two races. Moreover, as the result of urbanization, the control formerly exercised by various philanthropic and other organizations over the leadership of the Negro is disappearing. The educated Negro is no longer dependent for employment exclusively upon segregated schools and social welfare organizations which derive their support from agencies representing a conservative philosophy of race relations. They are finding employment either in organizations supported by Negroes or in institutions and organizations in the more inclusive American community.

In this discussion my purpose has been to call the attention of sociologists, who are concerned with the nature and changing character of race contacts, to the necessity of studying this phenomenon within the context of the social relationships wherein race contacts occur. Whether the sociologist employs case studies as a tool for analysis or utilizes statistics or attitude and social distance scales, the significance of his results for sociology will depend upon the extent to which they throw light upon the behavior of men in society. There are indications that sociologists are becoming increasingly aware of the necessity to redefine their problems of research in terms of the study of men in their social relationships. In this connection I might refer only to a recent article by Blumer on the polling of public opinion. Negro-white relations were chosen as the basis of the present discussion not only because it is the field in which I have worked but more especially because it is an area in which sociologists have labored long, and there are no signs of their diminishing interest in the subject. If our concern with race contacts over a long period has not yielded the results for sociological theory which should have been expected from so much labor, it is because we have failed to study race contacts as a phase of men's behavior as members of groups. With this orientation toward race contacts, we can sharpen our research tools and become better prepared to study race contacts not only in this country but in other parts of the world where the problem of race contacts is assuming increasing importance.

II. Race Relations

4

THE PRESENT STATE OF SOCIOLOGICAL KNOWLEDGE CONCERNING RACE RELATIONS

1959

THE SOCIOLOGICAL study of race relations has progressed as sociology and has developed as an independent social science discipline. At the same time, however, the problems with which sociologists have been concerned in this field as well as their conceptual approach and methods of study have been influenced largely by the changes in race relations during the present century. Originally, sociological interest in race relations was dominated by the biological concept and viewpoint concerning race and reflected the political interests of Europeans in regard to non-European peoples.[1] With the development of anthropology, racial differences were increasingly redefined in terms of cultural differences and race relations in terms of cultural contacts.[2] As the result of two world wars which undermined and destoyed on the whole the colonial system and changed the relations of Europeans and non-Europeans the sociological viewpoint in the study of race relations

Reprinted from *Changes in Education, Transactions of the Fourth World Congress of Sociology*, vol. 5 (Amsterdam, 1959), pp. 73–80.

[1]   Richard Hofstadter, *Social Darwinism in American Thought* (Philadelphia: University of Pennsylvania Press, 1944).

[2]   Edward B. Reuter, "Fifty Years of Racial Theory," *The American Journal of Sociology*, 50:452–61. E. Franklin Frazier, "Sociological Theory and Race Relations," *American Sociological Review*, 12:265–71.

has gained ascendency. In this summary analysis of sociological studies of race relations which provides a sort of introduction to the papers in this section, the purpose is to indicate the nature and significance of the sociological contributions to the study of race relations and to point out some of the problems which call for further study.

One may note the shift from the biological to the sociological study of race and race relations in the statement by Fouillée at the First Universal Races Congress in London in 1911.[3] At that meeting he insisted that a factor of supreme importance which had been neglected in discussions of race had been the idea which a race had of itself, which included race-consciousness in relation to other peoples. Moreover, while Fouillée recognized the role of skin colour in identifying different races, he nevertheless called attention to the role of language and customs, and especially religion, in creating racial unity and solidarity. However, the clearest expression of the sociological approach to race relations was probably formulated by Park. Although he states that his formulation is in terms of the definition of the race relations in the United States, it provided a clear sociological approach as distinguished from other approaches to race relations. According to Park, "Race relations . . . are relations existing between peoples distinguished by marks of racial descent, particularly when these racial differences enter into the consciousness of the individuals and groups so distinguished, and by so doing determine in each case the individual's conception of himself as well as his status in the community."[4] This conception of the sociological approach in the study of race relations may be criticized on the grounds that it fails to take into account the ecological, economic, and political aspects of race relations. Moreover, since Park conceived race relations to be relations "which are not now consccious and personal" but "are fixed in and enforced by custom, convention and the routine

[3]   Alfred Fouillée, "Race from the Sociological Standpoint," in *Papers on Inter-Racial Problems*, G. Spiller (ed.) (London: P. S. King and Son, 1911), pp. 24–29.
[4]   Robert E. Park, *Race and Culture* (Glencoe, Ill.: The Free Press, 1950), p. 81.

of an expected social order,"[5] his definition is essentially a static conception which omits the dynamic aspects of race relations.

Without undertaking a formal definition of race relations which would expand Park's definition, I shall proceed to an examination of sociological studies which are representative of a more inclusive sociological approach to race relations.[6]

Although most of the earlier sociological studies of race relations dealt with problems of race prejudice, assimilation and other social aspects of the problem, a systematic review of studies in this field would logically begin with ecological studies of race relations. In fact, while ecological studies of race relations deal with a presocial stage or extra social aspect of race relations, they are important for a number of reasons. First, they are concerned with the demographic aspects of race relations, with racial competition and survival, and with the distribution of races with reference to geographic factors and natural resources. In this sense, ecological studies provide an understanding of the background in which the economic relations of races are rooted and out of which political institutions emerge in order too maintain certain patterns of race relations. Then, too, ecological studies of race relations reveal the impersonal aspects of race relations or those relations which are characterized as symbiotic relations.

Although the migrations of races have generally been studied by geographers, it appears that increasingly sociologists have been working in this field. In this connection there come to mind the studies which are being made of the migration of West Indians to Great Britain. There are important studies dealing with the succession of races, outstanding among which are the studies of Lind in Hawaii.[7] Perhaps some of the most noteworthy studies dealing with the ecological aspects of race relations are concerned with

5   *Ibid.*, p. 83.
6   E. Franklin Frazier, *Race and Culture Contacts in the Modern World* (New York: Alfred A. Knopf, 1957), pp. 31–36.
7   See Andrew W. Lind, *An Island Community: Ecological Succession in Hawaii* (Chicago: University of Chicago Press, 1938). See also Otis Dudley Duncan and Beverly Duncan, *The Negro Population of Chicago* (Chicago: University of Chicago Press, 1957).

segregation.[8] In fact, the study of racial segregation in the cities of the United States has engaged the energies of many American sociologists who have attempted to develop precise quantitative methods in order to measure degrees of segregation.[9] There are indications that sociologists in other parts of the world are beginning to study the ecological aspects of race relations in cities. The study of the racial ecology of the city of Durban in South Africa is an indication of this trend.[10]

Since the ecological aspect of race relations is concerned with the competition of races, studies of the racial division of labour provide a transition from the ecological to the economic aspects of race relations. The racial division of labour, as understood here, refers to a racial division of labour based upon an impersonal process of competition free from legal and other restraints. There have been a number of studies in this field from various parts of the world but not as many as the importance of the subject warrants. Some studies have been made of the situation in the United States but there the racial division of labour is complicated by legal, political, and customary restrictions upon the employment of Negroes on the part of both capital and labour. More valuable studies have been made of the racial division of labour in Canada by Hughes, in Hawaii by Lind, and in the West Indies by Broom.[11] From the standpoint of economic institutions one may refer to

[8]   See, for example, Ernest W. Burgess, "Residential Segregation in American Cities," *Annals of the American Academy of Political and Social Science*, vol. 140; E. Franklin Frazier, "Negro Harlem: An Ecological Study," *The American Journal of Sociology*, 43:72–88.

[9]   See Duncan and Duncan, *The Negro Population of Chicago*, passim.

[10]   Leo Kuper, Hillstan Watts, and Ronald Davies, *Durban: A Study in Racial Ecology* (London: Jonathan Cape, Ltd., 1958).

[11]   Leonard Broom, "The Social Differentiation of Jamaica," *American Sociological Review*, 19:115–24; Clarence E. Glick, "The Position of Racial Groups in Occupational Structures," *Social Forces*, 26:206–11; Everett C. Hughes and Margaret L. McDonald, "French and English in the Economic Structure of Montreal," *Canadian Journal of Economics and Political Science*, 7:493–505; Andrew W. Lind, "Occupation and Race on Certain Frontiers," in Andrew W. Lind (ed.), *Race Relations in World Perspective* (Honolulu: University of Hawaii Press, 1955), chap. 3.

the work of Thompson on the plantation and Hughes' studies of race relations in modern industry.[12] Since the problem of the integration of Negro workers is so important in the new policy of the integration of Negroes into American society, sociologists have begun to give more attention to this phase of race relations. Moreover sociologists, especially in the United States, are beginning to appreciate the necessity of taking into account the political elements in the analysis of race relations. For this reason, a recent study, *Race, Jobs and Politics*, of the Fair Employment Practices Committee assumes special importance.[13]

On the whole, however, the political aspects of race relations have been neglected, especially in the United States. By political aspects I am referring to political institutions and the power structure which are so important in shaping the relations of persons with different racial backgrounds. Lohman's study of racial segregation in the capital of the United States represented a radical departure from the usual approach to the problem.[14] Instead of studying the attitudes of whites, Lohman studied the social structure of the dominant white community which maintained racial segregation and moulded the attitudes of citizens. Increasingly, the political elements in race relations are forcing themselves upon the attention of all sociologists as the result of the break-up of colonialism and the emergence of new nation-states. Different types of racial frontiers are being recognized and defined as areas for research. Attention is begin focused especially upon the areas in the world where multi-racial communities exist or where multi-racial societies are beset with problems of social organization.

In the United States where major emphasis was generally placed upon the social psychological aspects of race relations, little

[12]   See Everett C. Hughes, "Race Relations in Industry," in William F. Whyte (ed.), *Industry and Society* (New York: McGraw-Hill, 1946), chap. 6, and Edgar T. Thompson, "The Plantation as a Race-Making Situation," unpublished statement before the conference on Race Relations in World Perspective (Honolulu: University of Hawaii, 1954).

[13]   Louis Ruchames, *Race, Jobs and Politics: A Story of the F.E.P.C.* (New York: Columbia University Press, 1953).

[14]   J. D. Lohman, *Segregation in the Nation's Capital* (Chicago: National Committee on Segregation in the Nation's Capital, 1949).

attention was directed to the study of the problem from the stand-point of social structure and institutions. What came to be known as Warner's "caste-class" school of race relations tended to direct attention to the structural or essentially sociological aspects of race relations.[15] However, a number of scholars challenged the relevance and utility of the caste concept in studying race relations in industrial-urban societies not only in the United States but also in South Africa.[16] Nevertheless, there is still the need to investigate race relations from the standpoint of social organization in the United States. For example, no one can provide an adequate understanding of the resistance to desegration of public schools in the Deep South without studying its against the background of the economic structure of the Deep South and its political power which is aligned with northern industrialists and capitalists. Unfortunately, most of the literature on racial desegregation in the United States is devoted to the legal and social psychological aspects of the problem.[17] Simpson and Yinger have shown the relevance and utility of structural-functional theory in the study of race relations especially in relation to racial desegregation.[18] Perhaps the most important study so far of the relationship of social

[15]   Here it should be noted that as early as 1904, William I. Thomas, in "The Psychology of Race Prejudice," *The American Journal of Psychology*, 9:609–10, had stated that the antipathy of whites for Negroes in the South "is rather caste-feeling than race prejudice, while the feeling by the northerner is race-prejudice proper."

[16]   See Brewton Berry, *Race Relations* (New York: Houghton Mifflin Co., 1951), pp. 317–19; George Simpson and F. Milton Yinger, *Racial and Cultural Minorities* (New York: Harper and Brothers, 1953), pp. 327–30; I. D. MacCrone, "Race Attitudes: An Analysis and Interpretation," in Ellen Hellmann (ed.), *Handbook on Race Relations in South Africa* (New York: Oxford University Press, 1949), p. 685; and Oliver C. Cox, *Caste, Class and Race* (New York: Doubleday and Co., 1948).

[17]   See, for example, studies listed in George E. Simpson and J. Milton Yinger, "The Sociology of Race and Ethnic Relations," in *Sociology Today* (New York: Basic Books, 1959), p. 392. n. 23. Concerning the Negro in the United States see St. Clair Drake, "Recent Trends in Research on the Negro in the United States," *International Social Science Bulletin*, 9: 475–92.

[18]   *Ibid.*, pp. 384–94.

organization to race relations is the study of segregation in the nation's capital referred to above.

Race relations in Brazil have generally been studied in the context of the economic and political organization of the country. This was true of Freyre's studies in which he described and analysed the role of the Negro and mulatto in the structure of Brazilian society.[19] Moreover, in Freyre's studies the process of racial mixture is placed in its true social perspective and the important role of the mulatto in the evolution of an urbanized middle-class society in Brazil during the nineteenth century.[20] The writer undertook some years ago a comparative study of race relations in Brazil and in the United States in terms of ecological, economic, and political differences which provided the background of race relations in the two countries.[21] The work of Pierson, which deals intensively with the situation principally in Bahia, throws light on the racial division of labour and other aspects of racial relations within Brazil.[22] More recently Wagley and Bastide have carried out studies in Brazil which have helped to clarify the racial situation there in relation to the class structure of the country and the changes which are occurring in its social organization.[23]

Africa offers a wide field for the study of race relations. There race relations may be studied in its larger economic and political aspects where Negro independent states are coming into existence and in the multi-racial communities faced with the problem of integrating different races into a social organization. Much work has been done in South Africa but sociologists are being attracted

19   Gilberto Freyre, *The Masters and the Slaves* (New York: Alfred A. Knopf, 1946).

20   Gilberto Freyre, *Sobrados e Mucambas* (Sao Paulo: Companhia Editora Nacional, 1936), chap. 7.

21   E. Franklin Frazier, "A Comparison of Negro-White Relations in Brazil and in the United States," *Transactions of the New York Academy of Sciences*, ser. 2, 6:251–69.

22   Donald Pierson, *Negroes in Brazil* (Chicago: University of Chicago Press, 1942); and "Race Relations in Portuguese America," in Andrew W. Lind (ed.), *Race Relations in World Perspective* (Honolulu: University of Hawaii Press, 1955), chap. 19.

23   Charles Wagley, *Race and Class in Rural Brazil* (UNESCO, 1952).

to other areas.[24] Some of the most important studies of race relations in Africa have been carried on by Balandier in West and Central Africa.[25] In his various studies Balandier has studied the demographic and economic aspects of race relations, including the racial division of labour and has illuminated the role of messianic movements in the nationalistic awakening in Africa. Sociologists are beginning to pay special attention to the emergence of a middle class in Africa.

The racial situation in tropical Africa resembles in some respects the changes which have occurred and are taking place in another tropical area, the West Indies. Although this has been an area which has long been recognized as a laboratory for the study of race relations, only recently have any significant sociological studies been undertaken there.[26] Among recent studies reference should be made to the studies by Williams, Henriques, Clarke and Broom.[27]

The study of the West Indies as a racial frontier naturally leads us to England where the migration of West Indian Negroes has created an important area for the study of race relations in Europe. Little has made an important study of Negroes in Britain and

[24]   Ellen Hellman (ed.), *Handbook on Race Relations in South Africa* (New York: Oxford University Press, 1947); Eugene P. Dvorin, *Racial Separation in South Africa* (Chicago: University of Chicago Press, 1952); Hilda Kuper, *The Uniform of Colour: A Study of White-Black Relationships in Swaziland* (Johannesburg: Witwatersrand University Press, 1947); and Sheila Patterson, *Colour and Culture in South Africa* (London: Rutledge and Kegan Paul, Ltd., 1953).

[25]   See Georges Balandier, "Race Relations in West and Central Africa," in Lind (ed.), *Race Relations in World Perspective*, chap. 7, which contains references to his various studies.

[26]   Ulysses G. Weatherley, "The West Indies as a Sociological Laboratory," *The American Journal of Sociology*, 29:290–304.

[27]   Eric Williams, *The Negro in the Caribbean* (Washington, D.C.: Associate in Negro Folk Education, 1942); Fernando Henriques, *Family and Colour in Jamaica* (London: Eyre and Spottiswoode, 1953); Edith Clarke, *My Mother Who Fathered Me* (London: George Allen and Unwin Ltd., 1958); Leonard Broom, "The Social Differentiation of Jamaica," *American Sociological Review* 19:115–24; and Vera Rubin (ed.), *Caribbean Studies: A Symbosium* (Jamaica: University College of the West Indies, 1957).

under his direction other studies have been made of race relations by Collins and Richmond.[28] This brief reference to the studies of race relations in England might conclude our survey since it brings to a full circle the cycle of race relations which began with the expansion of the European or white race which created the racial frontiers in the modern world. The descendants of those who manned the slave ships to the West Indies are rubbing shoulders today with the descendants of the slaves on the streets, in the marketplaces, and in the factories of England.

However, I cannot conclude this rather sketchy account of the present status of sociological research in regard to race relations without saying something concerning sociological theories of race relations. Some attempts were made to outline a natural history of race relations. This gave rise to what was known as cycles of race relations.[29] Although these cycles of race relations provide a good descriptive account of successive phases of social contacts under certain conditions, they can hardly be regarded as generalized theories of race relations. More recently Blumer has undertaken to outline a general theory of race relations. After a critical analysis of the theoretical approaches to race relations and of the nature of race relations, he comes to the conclusion that students of race relations can only contribute a "policy theory" rather than a scientific theory of race relations because of the changing character of the phenomena which are being studied.[30] Freedman in his critique of recent studies of race relations reveals

---

[28]   K. L. Little, *Negroes in Britain* (London: Kegan Paul, Trench, Truber and Co., Ltd., 1947); Sidney Collins, *Coloured Minorities in Britain* (London: Lutterworth Press, 1957); Anthony Richmond, *Colour Prejudice in Britain* (London: Routledge and Kegan Paul, 1954); and A. T. Carey, *Colonial Students* (London: Secker and Warburg, 1956).

[29]   See Robert E. Park, "Our Racial Frontier on the Pacific," *Survey Graphic*, vol. 9 (May, 1926); Emery S. Bogardus, "A Race Relations Cycle," *The American Journal of Sociology*, 35:612–17; and W. O. Brown, "Culture Contact and Race Conflict," in E. B. Reuter (ed.), *Race and Culture Contacts* (New York: McGraw-Hill Book Co., 1934), chap. 3.

[30]   Herbert G. Blumer, "Reflections on Theory of Race Relations," in Andrew W. Lind (ed.), *Race Relations in World Perspective* (Honolulu: University of Hawaii Press, 1955), pp. 3–21.

the lack of any genuine theoretical basis of sociological studies of racial relations.[31] Then I would add that, in the sociological approach to the study of race relations, there is still a need to determine whether one can include the contacts, for example, of Chinese and Malayans within the category of race relations. I would go so far as to say that some recent attempts to include racial and religious groups in the single category of minorities only introduces confusion in the study of race relations.

However, when one studies the vast work which has been done in the sociological study of race relations, it is possible to make some generalizations about the definition of problems in the field and the utility and validity of certain approaches. First, it is clear that the social psychological approach is too narrow and that while it may reveal many interesting and important facts, especially concerning interpersonal relations, it does not reveal the important economic, political and other cultural and institutional factors which are determinants of race relations. In the modern world, at least, the economic factor is of primary importance in race relations, and as Voegelin has indicated, the idea of race is a political idea which sets up symbols and welds the diffuse mass of individuals into a group unit.[32] It is especially important for sociologists to take account of this aspect of race relations in view of the emergence of nationalistic movements among the peoples of Africa and Asia. It is probably because of the political implications of the race idea that in the United States, where there is an announced policy of racial integration, it is difficult to secure financial support for the scientific study of race relations. Fortunately, to compensate for this tendency there is a growing interest on the part of sociologists in the study of race relations in Africa, the West Indies, and South America and even in Asia.

[31]   Maurice Freedman, "Some Recent Work on Race Relations: A Critique," *The British Journal of Sociology*, 5:342–54.
[32]   Eric Voegelin, "The Growth of the Idea of Race," *The Review of Politics*, 2:283–86, reprinted in *Race: Individual and Collective*, Edgar T. Thompson and Everett C. Hughes (eds.) (Glencoe, Ill.: The Free Press, 1958), pp. 250–52.

5

AREAS OF RESEARCH IN
RACE RELATIONS

1958

THE FIELD of race relations has long been one of the major interests of American sociologists. Their interest in race relations has been changing, however, during the past two decades partly because of the developments which have occurred in race relations in the United States and partly because of changes in the world at large. As a result of economic, political, and social changes in the modern world, American sociologists have been acquiring a new perspective on race relations generally. In view of their changing interest in race relations and their new perspective, it may be of value to suggest some sociological problems that need further study and to point out the areas of the world in which these problems are found. These problems may be conveniently considered under three headings: (1) the problem of race sentiment and race consciousness, (2) the influence of institutions on race relations and racial attitudes, and (3) the role of racial sentiment and race consciousness in personality formation.

(1) *Race sentiment and race consciousness.* No one can deny the existence of race sentiment and race consciousness in the world today. There is considerable disagreement, however, concerning the nature of race feeling or race sentiment and the conditions under which it comes into existence. Can one say, for example, that race feeling exists in the relations of the Chinese and the peoples of Southeast Asia? Race consciousness which refers to the extent to which race feeling or race sentiment is present in con-

Reprinted from *Sociology and Social Research*, 42 (July–August, 1958): 424–29.

sciousness fluctuates considerably. It has often been stated that whereas race sentiment was present in the Old South during slavery, race consciousness was reduced to a minimum in the social accommodation represented by the slave regime. This clearly indicates that despite the great physical differences between the two races, it was possible for the maximum physical intimacy to exist between whites and blacks along with the maximum social distance. This has considerable significance for the sociologist who is concerned with research on race relations, especially during a period of social change.

What then are some of the questions which need to be answered? There is first the question concerning the nature of race sentiment and race consciousness. More than a half-century ago W. I. Thomas differentiated what he called the caste feeling on the part of Southerners from what he regarded as essentially the race feeling of the northern whites.[1] No sociologist or social psychologist has undertaken to test this hypothesis. In this connection one might undertake to find out if, in view of the traditional racial situation in the South, it is easier for southern whites and Negroes to associate on terms of equality when caste feeling disappears than it is for northern whites and Negroes. This is important because there is much loose talk about race relations resulting from desegregation and many unsupported generalizations concerning race relations in the North as compared with the South.

A somewhat related sociological problem is the relation of race prejudice and color prejudice. That the two types of prejudice should be differentiated first occurred to the writer during his studies in Brazil nearly two decades ago. In the United States race prejudice is a matter of ancestry and descent, but in Brazil, in Spanish America, and in some parts of the West Indies there is undoubtedly prejudice against black or darker people. This prejudice is not based upon racial descent. The prejudice which, in the opinion of the writer, is mistakenly called race prejudice and confused with race prejudice in the United States is very much like the color prejudice which one finds among Negroes in the United

[1]   See William I. Thomas, "The Psychology of Race Prejudice," *The American Journal of Sociology*, 9:593–611.

States. There is, however, a kind of prejudice which is found among the nonwhites in the United States which approximates *race* prejudice. It is the type of prejudice which one finds in the so-called "racial islands" or those mixed groups—generally white, Indian, and Negro—toward Negroes, even toward "Negroes" of the same biological ancestry. The people who comprise these "racial islands" consider themselves a different *kind* of people.

Race sentiment and race consciousness as a field of sociological study have become of special importance with the emergence of new nation states following the collapse of colonialism. This is true not only in regard to the new nation states which have come into existence in Asia. It is of special significance in respect to the nationalistic movements in Africa and in the areas where Africans are struggling for a larger share in self-government in black Africa, as the area of Africa south of the Sahara is known. Although the Mau Mau movement in Kenya was an extreme expression of anti-white feeling, the racial element is present wherever there is a revolt against colonialism. Colonialism has become identified in the mind of the African with white domination. Some African politicians have admitted that the racial factor has been deliberately utilized temporarily to mobilize resistance to white rule. This does not alter the fact that racial sentiment and race consciousness play a role in the revolt against colonialism. The problem for the sociologist is to discover not only the role of the racial factor in the struggle against white domination but what role race is playing in the development of new nation states. This is extremely important when one considers the importance of the racial factor even in those areas where the French have had a policy of assimilation.

(2) *Institutions and race relations.* The next area of research in the field of race relations concerns the relation between institutions and race relations and racial attitudes. Usually the sociological problem in this field has been framed in terms of a debate concerning the relative influence of institutions or the priority of institutions or attitudes in determining the character of race relations. Not only does this appear to the writer to be a falsely defined sociological problem, but it is only one phase of the sociological problem with which we are concerned. First, it is important in

dealing with the problem of segregation to have a clear conception of the nature of the social reality with which we are dealing. But this cannot be determined *a priori* by debating the issue. When one is dealing with interpersonal relations, racial attitudes are important. But we know that racial attitudes do not function as independent variables but always as a function of a social situation. Therefore, it is always necessary to know the social context in which persons with certain racial attitudes function or behave.

This was evident in the study which was made of segregation in the District of Columbia before desegregation was undertaken. It has been stated half seriously by some of us who undertook this study that we did not study the attitudes of white people concerning desegregation because we knew what they were. The problem which we set for ourselves was to determine what social groups were interested in maintaining segregation, what groups and agencies exercised power in maintaining segregation, and what agencies of communication created and perpetuated certain racial attitudes. The program of desegregation was based upon the answers to these questions. Unfortunately, similar studies have not been carried out in other parts of the country. They would have provided empirical data which could have formed the basis of a theoretical body of knowledge in this area. Even one of the foundations, when approached by a group of distinguished scholars and laymen, refused to support a purely scientific study of the process of desegregation.

An important phase of the relations between institutions and racial attitudes becomes apparent whenever one considers the fact that personal relations tend to undermine the institutional and moral order where race relations are involved. For example, in the southern states the "mixing" of the races seemingly never has referred to a purely biological phenomenon, but to a social phenomenon on the institutional or moral plane. Here is an unexplored area of research for the sociologist. Then there is a related phenomenon in the area of race relations that requires study. In some areas of the world the dogma against the "mixing of the races" did not come into existence until white women appeared on the scene. Have we any sociological explanations for this phenomenon?

When one considers the broad problem of race and culture contacts in the modern world, there is a neglected phase of race relations which deserves serious study. This is the racial division of labor which appears in different parts of the world where races meet. Some attention has been given to the racial division of labor in some localities as, for example, in the West Indies. This is becoming an important area of research as the peoples of the world become increasingly mobile and multi-racial communities are growing up all over the world. The sociological problem is chiefly concerned with areas where the racial division of labor is not due to political factors or any other form of social compulsion.

The problem of the racial division of labor is related to the problem of the relation between racial prejudice and color prejudice. It is also related to the class structure of a society. What is the relation between middle-class status and race relations and racial attitudes? This is a field for investigation not only in the United States but in other parts of the world. For example, one often refers to Brazil as a country in which racial and color prejudices have not been important or at least have not become the basis of social stratification. Nevertheless, there is evidence that as the old feudal aristocracy has disappeared in Brazil and the middle class has become dominant, color snobbishness has become important if race prejudice as we know it has not made its appearance. In the new forms of social and recreational life, a black face seldom appears. Is the middle-class way of life associated with similar snobbishness in regard to the pure-blooded Negro and the pure-blooded Indian (American) in other parts of America?

There are a number of problems of sociological interest in the economic relations of different races. One problem involves competition and is related to the racial division of labor to which we have referred. Likewise, there are sociological problems which need study in the area of politics. These problems are important where multiracial communities exist—in the southern states, in South Africa, in the Central African Federation, and in East Africa. These problems are concerned with power and prestige. Despite the denials by some of its leaders, it appears that the new regional bloc known as the Afro-Asian bloc represents to some extent race consciousness on the part of the colored peoples of the world.

(3) *Race and personality*. We come finally to the problem of race and personality which is the special field of the social psychologist. As is well known, many of the leaders of the nationalistic movements in the areas of the world where peoples have secured their independence or are struggling for independence are so-called "marginal men," or cultural hybrids. The study of the western educated man and his role among native or indigenous races or peoples is attracting an increasing amount of attention on the part of social psychologists. Although increasing attention is being given to the study of political leaders, much more needs to be done. Not only is it necessary to study the leaders in order to discover how race feeling has shaped their personalities and determined their roles in the struggles of people for political independence. But studies are also needed at the present time to determine the role of race sentiment and race consciousness in the formation of the new societies in Africa and in the West Indies, as well as in the areas of Central and South America where new societies are struggling to be born.

Some studies have been made of the personality of mixed bloods who are very often "marginal men." But here we are not so much interested in mixed bloods as marginal people but as the forerunners of the "new" races. Above we referred to the "racial islands" or communities of mixed bloods who think of themselves as being a different "kind" of people—different from both Negroes and whites or Indians. Here it seems that we come to grips with the problem of race sentiment and the role of race in the formation of personality. To what extent do people not only as individuals but as collectivities need some form of racial identification? It is especially important today, since on the racial frontiers of the modern world "new" peoples are coming into existence. What role is race sentiment playing in the formation of these "new" peoples?

In this brief article an attempt has been made simply to indicate what appear to be some fundamental sociological problems that are worthy of study in the field of race relations. These problems have emerged both as the result of the change in race relations in the United States and as the result of the sociologist's new outlook on the race problems which are emerging in the modern world. These problems not only offer a challenge to the sociologist, but they provide an opportunity for the continued development of sociology as a scientific discipline.

6

A COMPARISON OF NEGRO-WHITE RELATIONS IN BRAZIL AND IN THE UNITED STATES

1944

SOON AFTER the turn of the present century, Viscount Bryce expressed the opinion that the close and widespread contact of the advanced and backward races was the completion of a world-process which marked a crisis in the history of the world.[1] The process of which Viscount Bryce spoke had its origin in the economic expansion of western Europe during the fifteenth and sixteenth centuries, which resulted, not only in the spread of European culture, but in the expansion of the white race. Until the fifteenth century, the white race had been confined to western Europe and, only toward the close of the century, was the Moor expelled from the Iberian peninsula. In eastern Europe, the Asiatic still threatened the frontier. But in the fifteenth and sixteenth centuries, the maritime nations of Europe, in their quest for spices and gold, circumnavigated the globe and charted the course of their future colonies. Yet, it was to require two centuries before

---

The materials upon which this paper is based were collected during a study of the Negro family in Brazil, made possible through a fellowship grant from The John Simon Guggenheim Foundation for the year 1940–41. Reprinted from the *Transactions of the New York Academy of Sciences*, 6 (May, 1944) : 251–69.

[1]   James Bryce, *The Relations of the Advanced and the Backward Races of Mankind* (Oxford, 1902), pp. 6–7.

the colonizing white nations would secure settlements of importance in the newly discovered lands. The discovery and settlement of Brazil by the Portuguese in the sixteenth century, the settlement of North America by the Spanish and French in the sixteenth century, and by the English in the seventeenth century, were phases of the expansion of European peoples.

Although the initial impulse behind the economic expansion of Europe was the search for precious metals, the colonial powers soon began to exploit the productive powers of their colonies. In the tropical regions, the plantation system of agriculture became the characteristic form of industrial organization. In regions of "open resources," the plantation type of exploitation has required some form of forced labor.[2] In Brazil, as in the southern part of the United States, when the Indian proved inadequate, the African slave trade provided the necessary forced labor. Consequently, in both countries, the question of race relations is concerned primarily with the relations of whites and Negroes.

In order to present an adequate analysis of the differences in race relations in Brazil and the United States, it is necessary to give at least a brief account of the conditions under which the Negroes were introduced into the two countries, their treatment under the plantation system, their emancipation, and their subsequent position in the economy of the two countries. Since Brazil did not offer the ready booty in gold, spices, silks, and precious stones as did the Indies, the Portuguese neglected the country for a quarter of a century. Then, during another quarter of a century, there were explorations along the coast and the country was divided into capitancies, which were held as feudal fiefs of the king of Portugal. During this period, the wifeless Portuguese adventurers began to mix their blood with the Indians and the offspring of such unions provided wives for later settlers. By the middle of the sixteenth century, Thomé de Souza, Captain-General of

[2]   H. J. Nieboer, *Slavery as an Industrial System* (The Hague, 1910), p. 385. "Among the people of the first category (open resources) the means of subsistence are open to all; everyone who is able-bodied and not defective in mind can provide for himself independently of any capitalist or landlord."

the colony, had founded the city of Bahia, or Bay of All Saints, which became the center of the African slave trade. Under Souza's administration, the cultivation and manufacture of sugar was begun in the settlements about Bahia. And it was to meet the demand for laborers that Negro slaves were introduced into the colony.

The southern part of Brazil did not develop as rapidly as the northern part during the early years of settlement. Owing to the failure of the cultivation of sugar, only a few Negro slaves were introduced. The colonists developed a sustenance economy, raising grapes for wine, wheat, and tobacco, and carried on a trade in Indian slaves. These settlers mixed freely with the Indians and there grew up in southern Brazil a population that was largely mixed with Indian. By the close of the seventeenth century, it is estimated there were not more than 100,000 people in Brazil who spoke Portuguese and, in this total, the pure whites were a minority.[3] The Portuguese officials constituted an upper caste, ranking higher than the Portuguese born in the colony. Next in rank came the Indian-white mixtures and, just below them, the mulattoes. After the mulattoes came various crossings of mulatto-Indian and Negro-Indian mixtures. At the bottom of the social pyramid were the slaves, the red slaves ranking above the black slaves.[4]

Beginning in the middle of the sixteenth century, the Jesuits carried on their missionary work for over a hundred years among the Indians. It was in the mission that the Indian submitted to the discipline of regular labor and ceased his resistance to the Portuguese. In 1570, the Jesuits secured a royal decree abolishing Indian slavery in the Bahia area and, in 1640, this decree was extended to all of Brazil. It has been stated that Negro slavery was introduced into Brazil at the suggestion of the Jesuits in order to save the Indian from annihilation. But, as Gilberto Freyre has pointed out, the Indian was not replaced by the Negro because of moral reasons or because of the Indian's pride and courage, as

[3]   Pandiá Calogeras, *Formação Historica do Brasil* 3a (Rio de Janeiro, 1938), pp. 32–33.
[4]   *Ibid.*, p. 33.

Indianphiles have said.[5] The Indian was not only physically inferior to the Negro, but he was a hunter and a nomad and in a more primitive stage of culture than the Negro. The Negroes imported into Brazil came from areas in Africa where agriculture and the arts had reached a high degree of development. Therefore, the Negro, because of his cultural heritage, provided the basis of Brazilian civilization in the north.

The number of Negroes imported into Brazil and their distribution in the country were governed by labor demands and the development of agriculture and industry in various areas. The cultivation and manufacture of sugar in the north drew the largest number of slaves. According to conservative estimates, 350,000 slaves were imported in the seventeenth and 1,000,000 slave in the eighteenth and nineteenth centuries, for the growing of the cane and the manufacture of sugar.[6] Gold was discovered in Minas Geraës toward the close of the seventeenth century and reached its maximum production in the middle of the eighteenth century. For the mining of gold, 600,000 Negro slaves were imported. After coffee production began in 1820, a quarter of a million more slaves were imported. In addition to these importations, a million more slaves were imported for the mining of diamonds, the production of tobacco, cotton, food stuffs, and for domestic and commercial services. Altogether, according to a conservative estimate, three and a third million Negroes were imported into Brazil.

The type of rural civilization which grew up in Brazil on the basis of African slavery has been described by Gilberto Freyre in his celebrated work, *Casa Grande e Senzala*.[7] As indicated in the subtitle of this book, slavery became the basis of a patriarchal economy. Under the patriarchal economy, the Portuguese masters and the Negro slaves lived in a type of close and intimate association that excells the most sentimental and romantic accounts of the social solidarity existing between master and slave in the

[5]   Quoted in Roberto C. Simonsen, *Historia Economica do Brasil, 1500–1820* (Rio de Janeiro, 1937), 1:190–200.
[6]   *Ibid.*, pp. 201–205.
[7]   Rio de Janeiro, 1930. *Casa Grande e Senzala* may be translated as "the 'big house' and the slave quarters."

southern States. The close relationship between the two races in Brazil has been attributed by Gilberto Freyre to the fact that the Portuguese had occupied a marginal position, racially and culturally, between Europe and Africa. Concerning the widespread racial mixture which took place in Brazil, he writes:

One should remember that probably, owing to their intimate contact with the Moors, the Portuguese were from the beginning admirers of dark women. Girls, some of them blonde, were sent to Brazil from Portugal—sometimes by the Queen of Portugal herself—to marry Portuguese gentlemen established there as planters. These girls were sent to Brazil, not so much for the sake of race purity, as to preserve the social rank and the aristocratic status of the planters. But personally many of those gentlemen preferred Indian and even Negro and mulatto girls. . . . Some planters were careful in their importation of slaves from Africa to arrange that pretty girls should come. These sexual preoccupations were unworthy of Christian monogamic gentlemen; they show how much the Portuguese had come under the influence of the polygamous Arabs and the Moors. But one should not forget that those same sexual preoccupations led to the formation of a mixed race, as we have seen. Slaves from African groups far advanced in their culture, like the Mohammedan Negroes who knew how to read and write in Arabic, were imported to Brazil. And sexual selection had something to do with the importation of Africans from so fine a stock.[8]

The mixed-blood offspring of the sexual association between the two races enjoyed special privileges and were destined to play an important role in the history of Brazil. As the rural patriarchal organization disintegrated and urban communities began to dominate the political as well as the intellectual life of the country, the mixed-blood found an opportunity to compete on almost equal terms with the pure-blooded Portuguese. In a book describing the process by which the urban communities overcome the power of the rural patriarchal organization, Gilberto Freyre has devoted a chapter to the rise of the bachelor of arts and the

[8]   Freyre, "Some Aspects of the Social Development of Portuguese America" in *Concerning Latin American culture*, Charles C. Grifflin (ed.) (New York, 1940), pp. 83–84.

mulatto.[9] These two elements in Brazilian society were responsible for its political and economic transformation during the nineteenth century.

The abolition of slavery in Brazil did not occur until 1888, or nearly a quarter of a century after the Civil War in United States. Although, as Ramos points out, abolition came as "the result of a long process of evolution of public opinion,"[10] it was accompanied by heated controversies involving economic interests.[11] However, it was not accompanied by a violent civil war, as in the United States. There was no sharp boundary between free and slave territory, nor was there a well-defined conflict between an industrial and an agrarian economy. All classes were found in the abolition movement, some of the leaders being Negroes and persons of Negro descent. This was an indication of the extent to which Negroes and persons of Negro descent had already been assimilated into Brazilian society. One of the main consequences of abolition for the problem which we are considering is that it increased the mobility of the Negro population and facilitated the process of race mixture.

This brief account of the historical background of race relations in Brazil is sufficient to make apparent a number of important contrasts with the situation in the United States.

In a certain sense, one may not properly speak of race relations in Brazil. For, as Dr. Park has pointed out in an incisive essay, "The Nature of Race Relations," "Race Relations . . . are not so much the relations that exist between individuals of different races as between individuals conscious of these differences."[12] In Brazil, there is lacking, both on the part of the Portuguese and the

[9]   Gilberto Freyre, *Sobrados e Mucambos* (São Paulo, 1936). The title of this book may be translated as "Two-storied town houses and huts."
[10]   Arthur Ramos, *The Negro in Brazil* (Washington, D.C., 1939), p. 54.
[11]   João Dornas Filho, *A Escravidão no Brasil* (Rio de Janeiro, 1939), pp. 133 ff.
[12]   Robert E. Park, "The Nature of Race Relations," in Edgar T. Thompson (ed.), *Race Relations and the Race Problem* (Durham, N. C., 1939), p. 3.

"white" Brazilians and, on the part of the "black" or "colored" Brazilians, a consciousness of racial differences. In fact, it is impossible to secure accurate figures on the various racial elements in the Brazilian population. In 1830, it was estimated that about 71 per cent of the population was white and of mixed blood and 29 per cent Negroes.[13] Since the emancipation of slavery in 1888, there has been an unwillingness to separate the population on the basis of race. However, an examination of 30,000 soldiers by an army officer gave the following percentages: whites, 59; mulattoes, 30; Negroes, 10; and caboclos (Indian-white mixtures) 1 per cent. These percentages are different from those obtained by Professor Roquette Pinto who, after researches in the National Museum, arrived at the following percentages for the various ethnic elements: whites, 51; mulattoes, 22; caboclos, 11; Negroes, 11; and Indians, 2 per cent. During his recent study of the Negro in Brazil, Pierson undertook to secure statistical data on race mixture in the city of Bahia.[14] He made an examination of the photographs of the first five hundred persons listed in 1937 as "brancos" or whites in the files of the Gabinete de Identificação.[15] He identified 68 per cent as whites, 19 per cent as mulattoes, 7.8 per cent as of white and Indian ancestry, and the remaining 5.2 per cent of Indian-white-Negro blood. In 1936, he undertook to determine by inspection the racial origin of 5,000 participants in a festival in Bahia.[16] He classified 31.7 per cent as European, 18 per cent as Negro, 49.9 per cent as mulatto, and less than one per cent as of Negro-Indian ancestry. The figures are practically the same as those which were furnished me by Dr. Adolfo R. Leite, the statistician in the Department of Health of Bahia, who made his estimates on the basis of the school population and birth and death rates.[17] For the year 1938, he estimated the racial composition of Bahia to be as follows: whites, 32 per cent; colored, 49 per cent;

---

[13]   Ramos, *op. cit.*, pp. 9–10.
[14]   Donald Pierson, *Negroes in Brazil* (Chicago, 1942).
[15]   *Ibid.*, pp. 128–29.
[16]   *Ibid.*, pp. 131–32.
[17]   See E. Franklin Frazier, "The Negro family in Bahia, Brazil," *American Sociological Review*, 7 (August, 1942):467–68.

and Negro, 19 per cent. As we shall see, the racial classification has little significance from the standpoint of race relations as we conceive them in the United States. In fact, the figures just cited are not so much an index to the distribution of races in Brazil as an indication of the extent to which a new race is being formed.

In contrasting the racial situation in Brazil with that in the United States, much emphasis has been placed upon the difference in attitudes. This factor was of considerable importance in the early history of Brazil when compared with the traditional racial feeling in the United States. For, even during the early years of the seventeenth century, when Negroes had the same status as white indentured servants, distinctions based upon consciousness of racial differences existed.[18] As the importations of Negroes increased, this racial consciousness increased. This was not only true of the South where in many areas the Negroes outnumbered the whites and there were fears of insurrections. In fact, the intense racial feeling in the South has sometimes been attributed to fear of insurrections. However, in Brazil there were numerous slave insurrections which were attended by greater success than those in the United States. Pierson has suggested that the intense racial feeling in the South is due to the Civil War and, more especially, to the racial conflict during Reconstruction.[19] Undoubtedly, these various cultural and historical factors have played an important role in differentiating the course of the development of race relations in the two countries. They should not, however, be regarded as causative factors, but should be considered in relation to more fundamental ecological, economic and cultural factors.

The first fact of importance is the difference in the geography of the two countries. A large part of Brazil, especially the areas into which Negroes were imported, is in the tropics. Although the question has not been settled whether the white man can establish permanent settlements in the tropics, this factor has important consequences for race relations. The Portuguese, who have been regarded as "particularly fitted for tropical settlement by environ-

[18]   See Helen T. Catterall (ed.), *Judicial Cases Concerning American Slavery and the Negro* (Washington, D. C., 1926), 1:77.
[19]   See Pierson, *op. cit.*, p. 347.

mental experience and racial history,"[20] were confronted, as other white races, with the problem of adapting themselves to life in the tropics. The most successful white settlement, at first by the Portuguese and later by the Italians and Germans, were in the highlands of Brazil. In the northern part of Brazil, where large numbers of Negroes were imported, there was a struggle for existence in a geographical environment in which the Negro had the advantage. The Negro slaves found their new habitat very similar to their homeland, in regard to the climate and the vegetation. It has been suggested by some Brazilian scholars that the ability of the Portuguese to survive in the new environment was due to the admixture of Negro blood. Whether this is true or not, in the southern States the white man was not confronted with the problem of meeting the superior adaptation of the Negro to the geographic environment. If it is true that Negro slavery displaced white servitude because it was more economical, this only emphasizes the fact that social rather than biological factors were responsible for the growth of the Negro population in the South. Even in those States where the plantation system has flourished, there has been a decline in the relative numbers of Negroes during the present century.

The next factor of importance in comparing race relations in the two countries is the economic relations of the two races. In Brazil, as in the southern States, Negroes were introduced primarily to provide the labor needs of the plantation economy. But the role of the plantation system in the economy of the two countries was different. Up until the nineteenth century, Brazil was essentially a rural civilization resting upon the plantation economy. In the United States, despite the political powers of the planter class, only eighteen per cent of the farms in the South were classified as plantations. Because of the romance that has grown up about the planter class, the white gentry has been absorbed with the "poor whites." During the period of the plantation regime in Brazil, there was neither a white gentry nor a "poor white" class of any importance from the standpoint of numbers. Moreover, the plantations were more self-sufficient than those in the United States. The

[20]   A. Grenfall Price, *White Settlers in the Tropics* (New York, 1939), p. 15.

dependence of the Portuguese upon the labor of the Negro was greater. This dependence was not simply upon the physical strength of the Negro. The Portuguese were dependent upon the technical skills of the Negro. Many of the Negro slaves introduced into Brazil were not only highly skilled craftsmen but were often more literate than the Portuguese. This was especially true of those who had come under Mohammedan influences.

Writing of the "great house" in which the owner led a patriarchal existence, Gilberto Freyre states that it "came to symbolize not only an economic but a social and cultural system. It served not only as the residence of the plantation owner, but as fortress, school, guest house, church, hospital, bank and even harem."[21] This description calls to mind many of the characteristics of the plantation system in the ante-bellum South. However, in the South, the plantation culture did not dominate society to the extent that it did in Brazil, nor were these various characteristics as highly developed as in Brazil. Although there was a tendency in the South for the plantations to assume a patriarchal character, women were not subordinated to the extent that they were in Brazil, where they "were traded by their husbands in an almost oriental or Moorish way."[22] Moreover, it does not appear that under the partriarchal regime in the South, there developed the solidarity of feeling and sentiment that characterized the patriarchal household in Brazil. This was probably due partly to differences in racial attitudes, but it was also related to greater isolation of the Brazilian plantations. Even in regard to the racial mixture which occurred on a large scale in the ante-bellum South as in Brazil, there were important differences. It is likely, that because of Puritanical mores and the higher status of women, there was a sense of sin and greater protest against concubinage in the South. Attitudes toward racial mixture in Brazil had been influenced to some extent by the fact that many of the early settlers were men without families. They had mated with both Indian and Negro women, and the offspring of these alliances had provided wives for later settlers. On the other hand, the migration of family groups and white women

21   "Some aspects of the development of Portuguese America," p. 83.
22   *Ibid.*, p. 97.

to the colonies in North America tended to preserve the integrity of the white family.

As one studies the history of the relations between whites and Negroes during the plantation and slavery regime in the two countries, other important facts become apparent. In both countries, a class of free Negroes, among whom there were many mulattoes, grew up outside the slave system. In both countries these free Negroes and mulattoes had gained their freedom through purchasing it, through the humanitarianism of their owners and, more especially, because their white fathers had set them free. But here the similarity between the situation of the free Negroes in Brazil and the United States ends. The free Negro in the South, and even in the North, was an anomaly. There was no place for him in the economic or social organization. In the North, he led a precarious existence, because European labor was plentiful and could exclude him as a competitor. In the South, especially in the plantation area, the free Negro could find no place in the economic organization and was considered a threat to the slave regime. Hence, free Negroes were concentrated largely in cities which have always provided a refuge for those elements that cannot fit into the traditional social organization. In Charleston, South Carolina, and New Orleans, large and prosperous communities of free Negroes, largely of mulatto origin, grew up. Although, economically, they acquired a secure foothold in the economic organization, they constituted a distinct caste in society. Yet the continual sexual association between whites and the mixed-bloods tended to erase the color-line and nullify the attempt to maintain a pure white caste. In Maryland and Virginia, where the ecological basis of slavery had disappeared, a semi-free class of Negro laborers came into existence. Sexual relations between this class and the whites were likewise making it impossible to maintain a caste system based upon race purity. Moreover, it should not be overlooked that, despite the effort to maintain caste in the southern States, white fathers often gave their children a good education and left them property which enabled them to rise in the world.

Yet, slavery in the United States provided a form of accommodation between the two races that did not exist in Brazil. This was not due entirely to the absence of race feeling in the latter country but also to the existence of a large "poor white" class in the United States. Even during the slavery period, there were protests on the part of the non-slave-holding whites against the monopoly which the free blacks and mulatto artisans had in the economic organization. As long as slavery continued and political power was in the hands of the plantation owners, who often hired out their black mechanics, the protests of the "poor whites" were ineffectual. However, when the slaves were emancipated they were thrown into competition with the "poor whites," who, through organization and a system of apprenticeship, were able to exclude the Negroes from competition. Moreover, when the industrial revolution reached the South, the new forms of industry demanded skilled industrial workers and not workers possessing the skills required in the older handicrafts. The cotton mills, when symbolized the impact of the industrial revolution upon the South, became an exclusive field of labor for the "poor whites."

These economic, political, and social conditions did not exist in Brazil. The transition from slave to free labor caused, to be sure, some dislocations in the economy. However, the abolition of slavery dealt the final blow to the decaying plantation economy and the patriarchal regime. In the shift of political and economic power and cultural dominance to the towns, the educated mixed-bloods, as well as the educated whites, rose to positions of importance.[23] There was, undoubtedly, some prejudice against the mixed-bloods, but they were too numerous and too powerful for the relatively small number of pure whites to exclude them from competing for a place in the political and social organization. Many of the mixed-bloods were officers in the army, which comprised many blacks as well as mixed-bloods. Therefore, the entire structure of Brazilian society, both from a racial and an economic standpoint, was such as to preclude the possibility of a bi-racial organization. Moreover, whereas in the United States abolition and the emergence of the non-slave-holding whites tended to sever the sentimental ties that had existed between the two races during slavery, in the Brazilian abolition the bonds that had grown up between the whites and

[23]   Freyre, *Sobrados e Mucambos*, pp. 302 ff.

the blacks and the mixed-bloods were never broken. In fact, it was often the colored sons of the aristocracy who won the prizes in the competitive life of the new commercial urban economy.

There is one phase of the contrast in race relations in the two countries that has been neglected until recent years. That is the difference in the extent to which the African culture of the Negro slaves survived in Brazil and in the United States. Within recent years, Professor Herskovits has been engaged in discovering African survivals among the Negroes in the United States.[24] Although, in certain isolated areas as, for example, on the coast of South Carolina and Georgia, a number of linguistic survivals have been discovered,[25] there is practically no evidence that African survivals have influence the social development of the Negroes in the United States. Even Professor Herskovits, who makes the extreme claims for African survivals, states that "one can set off the United States from the rest of the New World as a region where departure from African modes of life were greatest, and where such Africanisms as persisted were carried through in generalized forms, almost never directly referable to a specific tribe or area."[26] On the other hand, in the case of Brazil, it is not necessary to engage in speculation concerning African survivals. First, it should be noted that the Negroes introduced into Brazil did not suffer the destruction of their social life nor experience the distintegration of their cultural heritage to the same extent as the slaves imported into the United States. Therefore, on the large plantations in northern Brazil and even in the region about Rio de Janeiro, it was possible for them to re-knit the threads of their social life and re-establish their traditional culture. In fact, because of the close commercial relations between Bahia, the chief port of entry for slaves, and Africa, diplomatic relations were established with Dahomey.[27] The most important African culture that took root in Brazil was the

[24]   Melville J. Herskovits, *The myth of the Negro past* (New York, 1941).
[25]   *Ibid.*, pp. 276–79.
[26]   *Ibid.*, p. 122.
[27]   Arthur Ramos, *Las Culturas Negros en el Nuevo Mundo*, Version española (Mexico, 1943), p. 265.

Yoruban, and it seems that it absorbed or displaced the Bantu and other cultures. For a time, however, the culture of the Islamized Negroes from the Sudan exercised considerable influence on the slaves and race relations in Bahia. It was the Islamized Negroes who were responsible for the recurrent insurrections in Bahia from 1807 to 1830 and the revolution in 1835.[28] The Islamized Negroes organized communities and established schools and, in fact, possessed more literacy and technical skill than the Portuguese adventurers, criminals, impoverished noblemen and gypsies who settled in Bahia.

During the last decade of the nineteenth century, Nina Rodrigues began his pioneer studies of African cultural survivals in the religious practices and the folklore of the Negroes in Bahia.[29] With the exception of Manuel Querino's study of African customs in Brazil, the scientific study of the Negro did not engage the attention of scholars for twenty years after Rodrigues' work. Around 1926, Brazilian scholars, among whom Arthur Ramos, Gilberto Freyre and Edison Carneiro played leading roles, took up the work of Rodrigues. In their work, they have directed their attention chiefly to African survivals in folklore and religion. However, Freyre has devoted his attention not so much to African survivals among Negroes as the influence of African culture upon Portuguese culture in America. Interest of Brazilian scholars in both of these aspects of the influence of African cultural survivals on Brazilian society indicates their importance in the assimilation of the Negro.

The Negro in Brazil, in contrast to the Negro in the United States, resisted the process of acculturation. The uprisings on the part of the Islamized Negroes were neither a racial conflict nor a revolt against the treatment of their white masters. These revolts were essentially a continuation of the wars of the Mohammedans against Christians. Resistance to Christianity has not been confined to the Islamized Negroes. Islamized survivals in the religious practices of Negroes have almost entirely disappeared, whereas the Yoruban religious conceptions and practices have persisted

[28]   *Ibid.*, pp. 277–79.
[29]   See Rodrigues, *Os Africanos* 2a. (São Paulo, 1935).

until the present day. In the candomblés of Bahia and the shangôs in the northeast, many of the African elements have been preserved, though they have become fused with Christian ideas and practices. Before the African communities were broken up, other phases of African traditions and social organization persisted, and the relations between these Negro communities and the Portuguese community were similar to those between immigrant communities in the United States and the larger society. On the other hand, because of the advantages that the Negro enjoyed in the struggle for survival in the tropical environment, the Portuguese took over from the Africans many elements of the culture of the latter. African influences are apparent in the language, the diet and music of the Brazilians. The influences are not regarded as quaint or exotic excrescenses but as an integral part of the culture of Brazilian society.

A rough index to the acculturation of the Negro and his assimilation into Brazilian society is provided in the study of the changing color of the population of Bahia and the relation of color to the occupational class structure. Whereas, according to the estimates of the statistician in the Department of Health, the proportion of whites in the population had remained about 33 per cent from 1897 to 1938, the black element had declined from 38 to 19 per cent and the colored element had increased from 29 to 47 per cent.[30] Just as we have seen that the designation "white" in the records of the Gabinete de Identificação did not mean pure white ancestry, the percentages for whites just cited include mixed-bloods. In fact, the term "white" is used so loosely in Bahia, which is called A Velha Mulatta or "The Old Mulatto Woman," that Brazilians often speak of the Bahian whites. The term "white" is closely tied up with the social status, as it has been in the case of mixed-bloods throughout the history of Brazil. Therefore, in considering Pierson's tables showing the proportion of whites, colored, and blacks in the various occupations, this fact should be kept in mind. According to Pierson, "The whites, as might be anticipated, are concentrated in the upper levels. Their numbers, both absolute

[30] See Diagram 1, in Frazier, "The Negro family in Bahia, Brazil," *loc. cit.*, p. 467.

and relative, diminish sharply as one descends the occupational scale, and they appear only in small percentages in the lower tiers."[31] For example, we find street-sweepers distributed as follows, as to color: mulatto, 62.7 per cent; black, 34.7 per cent; and white, 2.6 per cent. On the other hand, physicians show the following distribution: white, 63.0 per cent; mulatto, 20.0 per cent; black, 1 per cent; and branco da Bahia or Bahian white, 16 per cent. Pierson is correct, in my opinion, in ascribing the situation to the fact that the black have not been free as long as the mixed-bloods. By that statement, he means, of course, that because of their short period of freedom, their poverty, and their lack of education, the blacks as a group have not been able to compete with those of a lighter complexion.

But it would be wrong to assume that, during the process in which the Negro and the mixed-blood have been assimilated into Brazilian society, or even today, race and color consciousness on the part of the various racial elements has been entirely absent. I think the process of assimilation may be shown in a study of the lives of Machado de Assis and André Rebouças. The first was, perhaps, the greatest writer Brazil has produced, and the second, a distinguished engineer and an abolitionist. Machado was born in 1839 of poor mulatto parents, both of whom were free, his father being a house painter and his mother a laundress.[32] He was taught to read and write by his stepmother and later he secured a job in a printing office. When he went to Rio de Janeiro he entered upon the career of a journalist. For a brief period his creative efforts were in the field of poetry. But he soon turned his attention to the romantic novel, a field in which he established himself as a master of style and the author of the literary emancipation of Brazil from Portugal. Rebouças was born a year before Machado, of parents who had a small admixture of white blood.[33] His father was a lawyer and a provincial deputy who, because of his opposition to the smugglers of slaves in the State of Bahia, was forced to move to Rio de Janeiro. Young Rebouças, as well as his brother, received

---

[31]   Pierson, *op. cit.*, p. 178.
[32]   Lucia Miguel-Pereira, *Machado de Assis* (Rio de Janeiro, 1939).
[33]   Ignacio Jose Verissimo, *Andre Rebouças* (Rio de Janeiro, 1939).

a good education in engineering and was sent abroad by his father to complete his education. He served as an engineer in the army during the war with Paraguay and surveyed the ground for the first important railways in Brazil. After an active career as an abolitionist, he followed the royal family into exile.

The first fact that strikes us in the careers of these two men is that they were able to compete on almost equal terms with white Brazilians. I say "almost equal terms," because Rebouças complained in his biographical notes that he did not receive the traveling fellowship to study in Europe because of his color. Yet, Machado was given opportunity to participate in the literary movement of his day and Rebouças was given every opportunity to utilize his education and talents as an engineer. Both of these men thought of themselves as Brazilians, though both had some consciousness of their racial origin. Machado was conscious of his mulatto origin and disliked any reference to it. Moreover, when he began to court the daughter of an aristocratic Portuguese family, there was considerable opposition on the part of her family. Yet, after they were married, they were accepted into the highest social and literary circles in Brazil. Despite the consciousness of their racial origin, they were not "marginal" men or cultural hybrids in the sense in which Park defined the term.[34] The reason for this was doubtless that there was no segregated colored community with which they could be identified. This had important consequences for their work as well as their personalities. Neither of these men was concerned with the race or color problem. Their work was a part of the culture of the community and it was evaluated in terms of the standards of the Brazilian culture. These men were not considered a "Negro writer" and a "Negro engineer," but Brazilian workers in their various fields. This is quite different from the situation in the United States, where there are Negro writers, journalists, and even biologists and chemists and a different standard for evaluating their achievements.

There is, in Brazil, little discussion of the racial or the color situation. It appears that there is an unexpressed understanding among all elements in the population not to discuss the racial situa-

34   See Robert E. Park, "Human Migration and the Marginal Man," *The American Journal of Sociology*, 33 (1928) :881–93.

tion, at least as a contemporary phenomenon. Apparently, there is a general recognition that Brazil is essentially a country of mixed-bloods and that a new ethnic type is being formed. Oliveira Vianna is a rare exception among the scholars, in that he regards both Indians and Negroes as inferior races and believes that, through Aryanization or a whitening process, Brazil will become a white nation.[35] Although there is no race problem in Brazil, the upper classes are conscious of color differences and these color differences become the basis of social distances that are maintained by a subtle system of etiquette. In fact, these distinctions would escape the casual observer and, even when one discovers them, it is dangerous to generalize about them. If one should suggest an American situation analogous to the situation in Bahia, one might point to the colored community in Charleston and New Orleans, forty or fifty years ago. Bahia is essentially a mulatto community where persons of light complexion tend to dissociate themselves as much as possible from those of dark or black complexion. Of course, this does not preclude friendships between whites and blacks. According to a lawyer of pure Portuguese ancestry, members of his group are likely to be more free and friendly with blacks than the mixed-bloods. It is not unusual for whites or so-called whites to marry people of light-brown and brown complexion. In such cases, the brown-skin people are likely to become essentially white persons, or at least the children of such unions would be regarded as white. In fact, one of the reasons that it is impossible to draw a color line, not only in the north but in other parts of Brazil, is because it would cut across families.

The prejudice toward black persons seems to operate most strongly in intimate social relations involving marriage and in the new type of social life which is developing in clubs and hotels. For example, black persons do not attend the weekly dances at the large hotels patronized by Brazilian officials and business men as well as foreigners; nor are black men to be found at the tennis clubs and the yacht clubs. They may attend on some special occasion, but they do not move about freely and they would not be invited to become members. Of course, if they marry a white person, their

[35]   Oliveira Vianna, *Evoluçao do Povo Brasileiro* (Rio de Janeiro, 1933).

children would be eligible for membership provided their parents belonged to the upper economic classes. Since foreign whites frequent the hotels and the clubs, it may be asked, to what extent are they responsible for these attitudes toward the blacks? Undoubtedly, the British and the Americans would not care to have black people in these places and some Brazilians are sensitive to their attitudes in regard to blacks. But the foreigners are not entirely nor primarily responsible for the attitudes toward blacks. They reflect the attitudes of the mixed-bloods who seek to identify themselves with the whites. What has been said so far applies to the upper social and economic strata in Bahia. Color distinctions and prejudices against the blacks are seemingly absent on the whole from the mind of the masses. This is apparent not only in their everyday activities but in the numerous festivals where all colors mingle freely. In fact, it is among the laboring masses that race mixture is continuing on a large scale in Brazil.[36]

In the states São Paulo, Santa Catharina, and Paraná in southern Brazil, color prejudice is much more marked than in the north. These are the states to which have come large numbers of European immigrants—chiefly German and Italian—who have a different attitude toward the Negro from that of the Portuguese. In these areas, the Negro, especially the dark or black person of Negro descent, has become a conspicuous minority in a predominately white population. In this region, the attitude toward the Negro assumes often the character of race prejudice as opposed to color prejudice. Although there are no legal discriminations against persons of Negro blood, they are isolated and discriminated against in subtle ways. From conversations with some of the leaders among the blacks, it appeared that the Negro suffers chiefly from the economic competition of the European immigrant, especially the Italian. As the Negro is pushed down in the economic scale, he is unable to acquire the education and the skills which would enable him to compete successfully with other groups. The only escape for the Negro is to mingle his blood with that of the whites. This he is doing, though not as freely as in other parts of Brazil.

Because of the isolation of the Negro in the south, a number

[36]   Freyre, "Some aspects of the social development of the Portuguese in America," pp. 102–103.

of Negro organizations have come into existence to fight discrimination on the basis of color. Out of these various organizations has come *Frente Negra Brasileira*, which was started in 1931 as a movement to include all Negroes in Brazil.[37] In this year, the organization announced, at a meeting of over a thousand Negroes, its program for the improvement of the moral, educational, economical, and political status of the Negro. It was recognized by the government as a political party but, after the changes in the government in 1937, it retained only the cultural and social features of its program. Besides the *Frente Negra Brasileira*, a number of other Negro clubs and associations have been organized in the south and in other parts of Brazil. The organizations in the south are sharply differentiated from those in the north. In the south, they are fighting discrimination and are seeking to integrate themselves into the social and economic organization. On the other hand, in the north, they have cooperated with whites in studying the cultural contributions of the Negro and have fought for religious liberty for Negro cults, as well as the improvement of the social condition of blacks. It appears that the Negro organizations in Brazil lack the drive and motivation of similar organizations in the United States. This is doubtless due to the fact that racial discrimination is not as strong even in southern Brazil as in the United States. In São Paulo, where a number of these movements originated, there are two Negro professors on the law faculty of the University. It appears that amalgamation will constantly undermine these Negro movements unless outside influences affect present tendencies.

Outside influences certainly have had some effect upon attitudes toward colored and black people. Many Brazilians are conscious of being regarded as a colored nation by Argentina and other so-called white nations of South America. Then, in recent years, Nazi racial theories have had some influence among the Germans in the south who tended to intermarry with the Brazilians.[38] The most important source of outside influence has been the financial and

[37]   See Ramos, *The Negro in Brazil*, pp. 167–76, concerning the various Negro organizations and movements in Brazil.
[38]   Emilio Willems, *Assimilação e Populações Marginais no Brasil* (São Paulo, 1940), pp. 76–166.

industrial penetration of the country. The British and the Americans draw a color line, not only in their social contacts with Brazilians, but when their business houses employ Brazilians as white collar workers. Americans who have gone to Brazil as technical advisers have insisted that even distinguished black officials be ejected from hotels and, when their wishes were not respected, they have left the hotels. In spite of the "good neighbor" policy, it is likely that increasing financial and industrial penetration of Brazil by Americans will accentuate discrimination on the basis of color. Even at the present time, Brazilians are careful to select pictures of the right complexion for the American public.

In spite of these differences between the racial situation in Brazil and the United States, it should be pointed out by way of conclusion that the development of race relations in the two countries reveals some underlying similarities. In both countries, the close association of the whites and blacks produced a class of mixed-bloods. Although, in the United States, an attempt to maintain a caste system has prevented the identification of the mixed-bloods with the whites, through the process of "passing," persons with Negro blood have passed into the white race. With the increasing mobility of our population, it is likely that this will continue. It is hardly probable that the so-called "race purity" laws of Virginia and Georgia will stop the process. Race mixture in the United States, as in Brazil, has been one of the chief factors in the social differentiation of the non-white population, and it has facilitated the social mobility of colored individuals. The relation of color differences to occupational structure in Brazil closely parallels the same phenomenon in the segregated Negro community in the United States. Moreover, as in Brazil, this phenomenon in the United States is a rough index to the process of acculturation, though it does not lead to complete assimilation, because of the attempt to maintain a racial caste in the United States. As the attempt to maintain a caste system becomes less effectual because of urbanization and the general educational and cultural development of the Negro, it is likely that the racial situation will approximate the situation in Brazil.

7

RACIAL PROBLEMS IN
WORLD SOCIETY

1955

WHEN ONE views the problem of race in world perspective, one must face the inescapable fact that the peoples of the world are identified as members of the white or colored races.[1] This classification may appear to some people, especially scholars, as an oversimplification of the situation and it may even seem to be reminiscent of the naïve classification of the races of mankind on the basis of color before anthropologists and biologists attempted to classify races in terms of biology and genetics. It is more likely, however, that this dichotomous division of mankind will be regarded as a confusion of politics and race. There are, nevertheless, sound reasons—ideological, pragmatic, and sociological—for defining the problems of race in modern world society in terms of the relations of white and colored peoples. The racial ideology which has divided the peoples of the world into white and colored races

---

Read at the dedication of the Robert E. Park Building, Fisk University, March, 1955, and subsequently revised in 1961. Reprinted from *Race Relations Problems and Theory*, ed. J. Masuoka and Preston Valien (Chapel Hill: University of North Carolina Press, 1961), pp. 38–50.

1   See James Bryce, *The Relations of the Advanced and Backward Races of Mankind* (Oxford: Clarendon Press, 1902), pp. 6–7, where the author stated that one of the most pressing problems of the modern world was the relations of white and colored peoples, and W. E. B. DuBois, *The Souls of Black Folk* (Chicago: A. C. McClurg and Co., 1904), p. 383, where the Negro scholar stated: "The problem of the twentieth century is the problem of the color-line—the relation of the darker to the lighter races of man in Asia and Africa."

grew out of the economic, political, and social relations which were established between white and colored peoples.

The expansion of Europe which began in the fifteenth century brought the European peoples into contact first with the Negroid peoples of Africa, then with the Indians of the New World, and soon thereafter with the peoples of Asia. Their contacts with the Negroid peoples south of the Sahara led to the slave trade which lasted three centuries. The enslavement of Negroes was justified at first on the grounds that they were heathen, but when Christian baptism threatened the profit derived from trade in black human beings, the idea of racial inferiority was invoked as a justification. When the Europeans first encountered the people of Asia, they were inclined to acknowledge the superiority of the Asian in cultural attainments. It was only after Europeans had achieved political mastery over the countries of Asia that the doctrine of racialism was invoked to justify their domination.[2] European aggression against the peoples of Asia and their trade was declared first to be a war against the infidel Moors. But it was not long before it was justified on the basis that "common rights" to navigate the seas were restricted to European peoples.[3] Thus as Europeans extended their political domination over Asia and Africa, there developed a racial ideology which embodied the superiority of the white race.

The ideology of white superiority did not rest, however, solely upon political domination. In Europe the age of invention followed closely on the edge of discovery. The age of invention provided the Europeans with the technological superiority which enabled them to conquer the peoples of Asia and Africa. The technological superiority of the Europeans seemed to validate their claim to racial superiority, since it was assumed to be the result of intellectual superiority. It only needed some of the classical anthropologists and Herbert Spencer to establish a hierarchy of intellectual capacities among the races to give the final justification for the ideology of white supremacy.

Nevertheless, the extent and character of white domination was

[2]   See K. M. Panikkar, *Asia and Western Dominance* (New York: The John Day Co., n.d.), pp. 14 ff.
[3]   *Ibid.*, p. 42.

determined in the end by the geographic environment and demographic, economic, political, and social factors. As the result of these various factors certain fairly typical areas of contact between the white and colored races came into existence. These three types of what might be called racial frontiers are (1) the so-called multiracial communities in which Europeans and colored peoples live in the same community; (2) the tropical dependencies where European settlement has not been possible but white control exists; and (3) the older civilizations of Asia where European political and economic control has existed but the problem of personal relations between white and colored persons is of little consequence.

Having sketched briefly how the race problems on a world scale have come into existence, I shall say a few words about the frame of reference in which the problems will be discussed. The frame of reference is very similar to that of Park, which appeared in his article entitled, "Our Racial Frontier on the Pacific," published in the *Survey Graphic* in 1926.[4] In that article Park proposed to study race relations in relation to geography, world economy, world politics, the melting pot, and the race relations cycle. The frame of reference in which this present discussion will be presented is based upon a logical scheme which takes into account the dynamic aspects of race relations, or what is implied in Park's concept of the race relations cycle.[5] It should be pointed out, however, that in referring to stages or phases in the race relations cycle, it is not my intention to suggest that these stages represent a chronological order in the development of race relations.[6] Since these different stages in the race relations cycle may exist simultaneously, they represent logical steps in a systematic sociological analysis of the subject. My analysis will take account of the dynamic factors—demographic, economic, political, and social—in each stage which would rule out any notion of a unilinear evolutionary process.

[4]   Robert E. Park, *Survey Graphic*, 66 (May, 1926) :57–85.
[5]   See E. Franklin Frazier, "Theoretical Structure of Sociology and Sociological Research," *The British Journal of Sociology*, 4 (December, 1953) :293–311.
[6]   See E. Franklin Frazier, *Race and Culture Contacts in the Modern World* (New York: Alfred A. Knopf, 1957), p. 32.

As in Park's frame of reference, the biological and ecological aspects of race relations are regarded as the first phase of race relations. The next phase involves the development of economic relations between the white and colored races. The third aspect of race relations includes the various types of political systems which have been established in order to maintain control and resolve the conflicting interests of white and colored peoples. In the final stage, the racial problem becomes a problem of social organization in what are called multi-racial communities, and a problem of world organization involving European and colored peoples who have achieved political indepedence, or European states and colored peoples who are struggling to become independent nations. In the last phase of race relations are included such problems as culture conflicts and the personalities of those who are affected by racial conflicts in the world society which is struggling to be born. What follows, therefore, will be an attempt to analyze within this frame of reference the racial problems which arise within the three types of racial frontiers which have been defined.

The biological and ecological aspects of race relations or the struggle of white and colored peoples for survival and the symbiotic relations which develop between them are revealed under different aspects in the three types of racial frontiers. One might begin with the United States, especially the southern states, with its Negro population, which represents the multi-racial type of community. During the colonial period there were fears concerning the introduction of Negro slaves in large numbers because of the possibility that they would swamp the white population. But these fears subsided largely when slavery was firmly established on an institutional basis and perhaps because in the country as a whole the white population multiplied at a higher rate than the Negro population. At any rate, in the South the biological aspects of race relations tended to disappear as the result of the operation of economic and social forces. The latent biological aspects of race relations once more became apparent, however, during the social disorganization following emancipation and when the former slaves attempted to secure an equal status with the whites in the new social organization that was coming into existence.

Although after 1880 the proportion of Negroes in the population of the South declined sharply, the biological aspect of the
racial struggle not only did not disappear but became more acute.
This can be attributed to the fact that in the absence of a new
accommodation between the races, the economic, political, and
social aspects of the relation of white and Negroes were defined
in racial terms. It was a case of what Lord Bryce has discussed in
his well-known essay on the role of the sentiment of race in history.[7]
All of this tends to underline the fact that from the sociological
standpoint the biological struggle of races is not the result of the
mere biological differences existing between races but rather the
consequence of the manner in which these differences are defined
in the economic competition between races and their struggle for
power and status. It was not until the Negro was completely reduced
to a subordinate status in the southern states that the biological
aspecs of race relations (lynchings and other forms of violence)
tended to be modified. Although the proportion of Negroes in
the population of the southern states continued to decline, this
decline did not affect the subordinate status of Negroes. Therefore,
it would be misleading to attribute recent changes in race relations
to demographic factors.

The racial situation in Southern Africa provides another case
of the type of racial frontier which was created by a multi-racial
community. Unlike the situation in the southern states of the
United States, the majority of the non-European peoples in South
Africa not only outnumber the whites but the majority of them
are still more or less part of a traditional tribal organization and
preliterate culture. But here again one may see how the biological
competition of white and colored peoples is related to economic
and political forces. It has been the changes which are occurring
in the economic and industrial organization of the South African
community that have tended to accentuate the latent biological
struggle of the races. Although the proportion of non-Europeans
in the population of South Africa has scarcely increased 1 per cent
in a half-century, the biological phases of the relations between

[7]   James Bryce, *Race Sentiment as a Factor in History* (London:
Hodder and Stoughton, 1915).

white and non-white peoples have become more acute during the past decade.[8]

In South America the biological phase of race relations has never been important. As the result of the fusion of white and colored peoples—the Spaniards and Portuguese with Indians and Negroes—the doctrine of the purity of the white race has never become the basis of economic, political, and social ascendancy. Yet the ideology of white superiority has not been entirely absent since those who have approximated the whites in physical characteristics have been able to achieve a superior economic and social status and have wielded political power. In Australia, another area of white settlement, the biological struggle of European and non-white races was settled by the practical extermination of the native population and the exclusion of colored immigrants. In New Zealand the biological struggle between the white and colored races was terminated when the Europeans gained ascendancy but there are still problems which belong to later phases of the contacts of white and colored peoples.

In considering the biological aspects of the relations of the white and colored races in the tropical areas, the situation in the West Indies will provide a good transition. Although it was recognized from the beginning that the West Indies was not congenial to white settlement, white communities were established in that area. In Barbados, for example, the decline in the white population resulted from the large holdings and the plantation system with black labor.[9] Nevertheless, in the British West Indies the white community was able to subsist until the abolition of slavery and the plantation system.[10] In the French West Indies the whites have either been driven out as in the case of Haiti or the fusion of the races has resolved, as in South America, the biological struggle. When one turns to tropical Africa, Southeast Asia, and the islands

[8]   See Ellen Hellmann (ed.), *Handbook on Race Relations in South Africa* (New York: Oxford University Press, 1949), Table 3, p. 9.
[9]   See Vincent T. Harlow, *A History of Barbados* (Oxford: The Clarendon Press, 1926).
[10]   See Lowell J. Ragatz, *The Fall of the Planter Class in the British Caribbean, 1763–1833* (New York: The Century Co., 1928).

of the Pacific where white settlements have been impossible, the biological struggle between the white and colored races does not exist. If it exists at all it has become a part of the political and economic problems of the modern world. Likewise, the biological aspects of the relations of the white and colored races, so far as Asians are concerned, need not be discussed at this point because they have become a part of the political struggles in the modern world.

The economic relations between the white and colored peoples of the world began with barter, but the subsequent development of economic relations has varied in the three racial frontiers. In the United States the racial frontiers involving Negroes and whites were created by the importation of Africans to supply the demands of a capitalistic agricultural organization for cheap and servile labor. As the result of the westward advance of the Cotton Kingdom in search of more productive lands, in the areas no longer fitted for plantation agriculture, a considerable number of Negroes and mixed-bloods managed to become free and to find a place as skilled mechanics in the economic organization of the South. It was not until after emancipation that the competition of white and black labor or the economic aspects of the racial problem became acute. After emancipation only a fourth of the Negroes in the rural South ever succeeded in securing the ownership of even small parcels of the least desirable lands while the remainder continued an existence very similar to that of the slaves. The descendants of the landless whites pre-empted the jobs requiring skill, especially the new jobs created by the industrialization of the South. The confinement of the Negro to unskilled occupations and domestic service is an aspect of the political struggle in the South, not between the whites and Negroes but between the white propertied classes and white working classes. The changes which have occurred in the economic aspects of race relations have been caused by two world wars that sent Negroes to northern and western industrial areas. This movement resulted in political changes that have tended to lower the racial barriers against the employment of Negroes in skilled and white collar occupations.

At one time a small, skilled European labor force was superimposed in South Africa upon a mass of non-European labor force with a low standard of living.[11] But as Europeans have gradually entered unskilled occupations, competition has developed between white and colored labor. Then, too, as colored workers have become better educated and more efficient, they have demanded skilled positions. More important still is the fact that as the result of the industrial expansion in South Africa, the employers have been inclined to utilize colored labor in skilled positions since the color bar in employment tends to destroy the mobility of the labor force that is necessary in a community as it becomes industrialized and urbanized. The political forces that are in control in South Africa today are attempting to create and maintain a system of nineteenth-century colonialism in conjunction with a modern industrial community.

Turning to the tropical areas of the world, one finds that the characteristic system of exploitation of colored peoples by Europeans has been some form of forced labor. Africans became the source of forced labor for the new world and thus helped to create the capital that was necessary for the development of capitalism in the eighteenth and nineteenth centuries.[12] When the first investment of capital began in Africa, it was characterized by what Frankel calls the "terror economy" of the Belgians and the "Raubwirtschaft" of French Equatorial Africa which destroyed both the natural and human resources of these areas.[13] The subsequent development of a more humane system of exploitation was not the result so much of the growth of humanitarian sentiment as of the need for native labor.[14] In Java the Dutch introduced a disguised system of forced labor known as the "culture system."[15] The "culture system" was succeeded by a system of "credit bondage" which was similar to peonage in the South. It was not until 1930 that the

[11]   See S. Herbert Frankel, *Capital Investment in Africa* (New York: Oxford University Press, 1938), pp. 141–42.

[12]   See Eric Williams, *Capitalism and Slavery* (Chapel Hill: University of North Carolina Press, 1944).

[13]   Frankel, *Capital Investment in Africa*, p. 34.

[14]   *Ibid.*, p. 37.

[15]   See Clive Day, *The Policy and Administration of the Dutch in Java* (New York: Macmillan Co., 1904), chaps. 7, 8, and 9.

Forced Labor Convention was submitted by the League of Nations to its members.

The racial problems arising from the fact that the lands of the colored peoples of the world offer a field for capital investment by the white nations have become the most important problems in the modern world. Under the colonial regime the economic basis of white domination was often concealed by an administrative system which tended to emphasize the political aspects of colonialism. However, when the colored peoples began to achieve political power and to gain independence, the economic interests involved in colonialism became the source of conflict. As a result there ensued a struggle on the part of the colored peoples to secure a larger share of the wealth of their territories in order to achieve a higher standard of living. This struggle has threatened the very roots of the economic system of the white European nations. This phase of the racial problems has become increasingly acute because of the growth of communism, especially in the case of China, which has presented a challenge to the entire system of capitalistic exploitation of the colored peoples of the world. The great issue which has been raised in regard to the new nations of Africa is whether they will follow the example of China. This has been especially true in regard to Ghana and Guinea, but it also exists where other new nations of Africa have not decided upon what terms white capital will be used in the building of modern states in Africa.

As is indicated in the above statement, the economic aspects of race relations are closely involved with the political aspects. We might begin our consideration of the political aspects of race relations with the United States. In the United States this phase of race relations did not emerge until after the Civil War, when the question of the legal status of the Negro became an issue. Since the industrial North had triumphed in the struggle, it was in its interest to establish a political democracy which would prevent the return to power of the landholding class and at the same time would assure its own ascendancy in the nation. It was necessary, therefore, to enfranchise the Negro and support his political participation by armed force. As soon as industrial capitalism had assured its legal and political ascendancy in the nation, the Negro was abandoned and became the victim of Southern politics. When "white restoration," which became a shibboleth of Southern politicians, was first accomplished, the Negro was sometimes used by the planters to thwart the aspirations of the "poor whites." For a brief moment Negroes were recruited by the leaders of the agrarian unrest to aid the "poor whites." But as the result of the class struggle within the white community, the Negro became the scapegoat of the machinations of the demagogues. These demagogues, who offered no threat to the economic interests and political dominance of the white propertied classes, diverted public funds from Negro schools to white schools, disfranchised the Negro, and established a system of legal segregation. It was not until changes had occurred in the economic and political organization of American life that the political aspects of Negro-white relations once more became important.

What has occurred in the United States is indicative of the importance of the political factor in race relations. The racial accommodation which was established between 1890 and 1915 was achieved through violence and terror, but it has not provided a permanent solution of the problem. Although the relative number of Negroes in the population of the South has declined from one in three to about one in five, Negroes continue to be excluded from sharing in the governments of the southern states. Likewise, in Africa, except in those areas where white settlement has not been possible and colored peoples have gained independence, whites have refused to share real political power with the colored peoples.[16] Both in Kenya and in the Central African Federation every attempt has been made to work out a formula by which the African majority would be satisfied with the semblance of sharing in the government while real political power was retained by the whites. In South Africa today the dominant white numerical minor-

[16]   The British West Indies have recently been granted a large measure of political autonomy but the location of real political power is symbolized by the white British regiment in Jamaica. Moreover, there is a sullen resentment on the part of the black masses against the whites and near whites as they see white Americans, especially, buy up the beach fronts for estates and hotels from which blacks are excluded.

ity is using violence to prevent any political activity on the part of the non-Europeans. However, in view of the growing unrest among the non-Europeans, no one can predict how long the present power structure can be maintained without resort to violence on an unprecedented scale.

Confronted with the wave of nationalism which is sweeping Africa, the British have been forced to grant political independence to her former colonies in West Africa. Much of the resentment against British rule was created by the racial prejudice of the British against the educated elite.[17] However, it should be pointed out that although racial sentiment also played an important role in mobilizing the Africans in their struggle against colonialism, it has tended to disappear since Africans have gained independence in those areas of West Africa where there are no large white settlements. The racial violence which erupted in the Belgian Congo only tended to confirm what observers had noted concerning the latent racial conflict.[18] Beneath the apparent acceptance of the paternalistic regime of the Belgians there was smoldering racial hatred because of the psychological trauma that Africans had suffered as the result of white conquest. Moreover, in those areas of Africa where there was no opportunity for political development, the nationalistic movements which were highly tinged with racial feeling sought subterranean outlets in Messianic religious movements.[19]

In this connection a word should be said about the Africans who were once under French rule. Despite the fact that there was a disposition under colonialism for the African elite to identify with France and French culture, as the new African states have emerged on the ruins of the former French empire, the African leaders have ceased to be black Frenchmen and have become Africans who boast of their "negritude."

---

[17] See James S. Coleman, *Nigeria: Background to Nationalism* (Berkeley: University of California Press, 1958), pp. 145–66.
[18] Charles Pierce, S.J., "Le Traumatisme Noir," *Zaire*, 7 (May, 1953) :451–68.
[19] See Thomas Hodgkin, *Nationalism in Colonial Africa* (London: Frederick Muller, Ltd., 1956), chap. 3.

Racism or the desire to maintain white supremacy with its economic benefits was the chief factor responsible for the formation of the Federation of the Rhodesias and Nyasaland.[20] As a result there has been an intensification of racial feeling on the part of the Africans, and the whole theory of racial association in a multi-racial community has broken down in view of the struggle for status and power.

The problems arising from the contacts of white and colored peoples in the modern world are revealed most clearly in multiracial communities. For in such situations the problems of social organization or the difficulties of creating a single moral order are revealed most clearly. In the United States these problems were solved for a period by the existence of two separate social organizations. A Negro society, in the sociological meaning of the term, with its own institutions which duplicated the institutions of the white society, came into existence. Park saw in the evolution of this type of biracial organization an advance in race relations since it indicated that whites no longer looked down upon Negroes but looked across at them.[21] In fact, the idea of a biracial organization almost became the official policy of the United States since it was argued that Negroes, because of their peculiar racial traits, could not be integrated into American society. The "separate but equal" doctrine which was upheld by the Supreme Court in 1896 in regard to separate public schools for Negroes was an expression of the quasi-official policy. Despite the attempts to make such a policy conform to what Myrdal has called the "democratic creed," by arguing that separation did not imply an inferior status, the most illiterate Negro had enough sense to know that segregation implied that the Negro was unfit for normal human association. There have been changes in the official policy of the United States with reference to the Negro as the result of internal economic, political, and social changes and because of the new position of the United States in international relations. As the

[20]   See Thomas M. Franck, *Race and Nationalism: Struggle for Power in Rhodesia-Nyasaland* (New York: Fordham University Press, 1960), p. 35.
[21]   *The Annals*, 140 (November 28, 1928) :11–20.

result of the emergence of independent Asian and African nations whose support the United States is seeking in the struggle with the Soviet Union, the American people have been forced to modify their policy in regard to colored people. Nevertheless, the problem of the integration of the Negro into American society, especially in the South, has not been solved.

In South Africa the problem of creating a single social organization is even more difficult because of cultural differences, the numerical superiority of non-Europeans, and the doctrine of racial purity and white supremacy. Race may be man's most dangerous myth[22] as Ashley Montague has said, but for the Afrikaners it is a reality. Because of their fanatical belief that the separation of white and colored people or "total apartheid" is God's will, they would slaughter millions of colored people to have God's will prevail.[23] However, it is not certain that the Afrikaners with the most efficient instruments of mass destruction will make God's will, as they see it, prevail in a world where the colored peoples are gaining power. However, even "men of good will," who were no longer under the spell of the "racial fallacy" and were armed with the best social science knowledge, would find the problem of creating a single social organization in South Africa a most difficult problem.

The problem of integrating non-white people into the social organization of the countries of South America is not essentially a racial problem but rather an economic and social problem involving class relations. To be sure, there is some color snobbishness in these countries which often reflects the influence of the ideology of white superiority. But economic mobility has always resulted in social mobility and racial mixture, a fact which makes any pretense of pure white ancestry ridiculous. Even in the British West Indies the country clubs have ceased to be a refuge for white men and many people are inclined not to raise the question of racial purity. In the tropical areas generally, the question of social orga-

[22]   M. F. Ashley Montague, *Man's Most Dangerous Myth* (New York: Columbia University Press, 1945).
[23]   See Eugene P. Dvorin, *Racial Separation in South Africa* (Chicago: University of Chicago Press, 1952), pp. 38 ff.

nization is not a pressing problem, since colonial society is a transient affair and colonies are becoming dominions or new nations.

If one would think of the problem of social organization in terms of world society or a universal moral order, as contrasted with a world community arising out of the economic relations of the peoples of the world, it becomes apparent that the relations of white and colored peoples involve economic relations and the struggle for power. In the struggle to escape the economic and political domination of the whites, there is evidence that the colored peoples are beginning to reject the values of the West or the whites. This is true, not only of the peoples of Asia who have accepted communism, but of other Asians and of some Africans. Capitalism and Christianity are not only regarded as expressions of Western civilization but are regarded as the white man's outlook on life and manner of adjustment to the world. The extent to which such an attitude towards the West prevails among the colored peoples of the world is a measure of the importance of the racial question, that is, the relation of white and colored peoples in the world today.

III. Urbanization and Social Change

8

THE NEGRO FAMILY
IN CHICAGO

1964

THE PURPOSE of this chapter is twofold. The first is to give a summary review of *The Negro Family in Chicago*, indicating the sociological problem with which it is concerned, the general frame of reference of the study and the specific hypothesis which it tests, the sources and nature of the materials which are utilized, and the conclusions reached. The second is to assess the contribution of this study to urban sociology, especially in regard to the family and in view of the recent interest in sociological studies of cities in underdeveloped or preindustrial areas of the world.

The Problem

The problem with which this study was concerned was, broadly speaking, the demoralization of Negro family life but more specifically with the more acute manifestations of family disorganization in the cities to which Negroes had been migrating since emancipation. The explanations offered for the continued disorganization of Negro family life over the years ranged from such biological explanations as the compelling sexual appetite and the childlike mentality of the Negro to such anthropological and sociological explanations as the influence of the African cultural heritage and the lack of moral restraints in Negro life. All of these

Based on the author's Ph.D. dissertation of the same title, Sociology, 1931, and recent research. Reprinted from *Contributions to Urban Sociology*, ed. Ernest W. Burgess and Donald J. Bogue (Chicago: University of Chicago Press, 1964), pp. 404–18. © 1964 by The Univesity of Chicago.

explanations seemed inadequate, especially since a knowledge of the social history of Negroes in the United States was necessary for an understanding of family disorganization among them. The social history of the Negro reveals the fundamental distinction between the loose family organization, based upon habit and affection, which was characteristic of the family among the slaves and among the rural folk Negro and the well-organized institutional families which developed among the Negroes who were free before the Civil War and their descendants. The widespread and continued family disorganization among Negroes in cities which had attracted the attention of students and social workers and officials is one of the results of the impact of the urban environment upon the simple and loose family organization of the Negro folk.

The mistake, then, of the various explanations of the disorganization of Negro family life was to treat the Negro population as a homogeneous group. The differences in the culture and social development of various elements in the Negro population were obscured, for example, in the statistics on the marital status of the Negro population as well as on the trend in the rate of illegitimacy in the United States as a whole. Even statistics on Negro family life for cities obscure important social differences in the Negro population. The inadequacy of the statistical treatment of the Negro population as a homogeneous group may be seen in the case of the statistics on Negro illegitimacy in the District of Columbia, where the rate had shown little change over a period of more than half a century. This was often cited as the classic illustration of the failure of the Negro to achieve the standards of American civilization in familial and sexual behavior. An alternate but obvious sociological explanation was never advanced, namely, that the District of Columbia was one of the focal points of the migration of the Negro folk from the rural South and that the process of family disorganization was only repeating itself with each new wave of migrants. Moreover, in the District of Columbia as in other cities of the country, the disorganization of Negro family life was not characteristic of all elements of the Negro population and the impact of urban life on the Negro population was affected by differences in the social and cultural heritage of Negro families.

Hypothesis To Be Tested

The general hypothesis that gradually emerged from this view of the problem of family disorganization was that the disorganization and reorganization of Negro family life are part of the processes of selection and segregation of those elements in the Negro population which have become emancipated from the traditional status of the masses. A combination of circumstances made the Negro community in Chicago an ideal place in which to test the validity of this hypothesis. First, the Negro population of Chicago, which had increased rapidly along with the growth of the city, represented a cross-section of the Negro population of the United States. It included the descendants of both the slave and the free population and families accustomed to residence in northern and southern cities as well as those who had migrated recently from the plantations of the South. Still more important for the successful prosecution of this study were the research facilities and the resources provided by the local Community Research Laboratory at the University of Chicago. This laboratory provided statistical data on the Negro population for census tracts, thus making it possible to relate indexes of family life to the selection and segregation of socially and culturally significant elements in the Negro population. Moreover, studies that had been carried on in connection with the laboratory served as models and showed the fruitful results of the point of view and methods represented in this study.[1]

However, from the standpoint of testing the hypothesis, the most important factor was Burgess' theory concerning urban expansion which he demonstrated could be measured by rates of change in poverty, home ownership, and other variable conditions for unit areas along the main thoroughfares radiating from the cen-

---

[1]   Outstanding among these studies were Harvey W. Zorbaugh, *The Gold Coast and the Slum* (Chicago: University of Chicago Press, 1929) ; Ruth S. Cavan, *Suicide* (Chicago: University of Chicago Press, 1928) ; and papers edited by Robert E. Park and E. W. Burgess in *The City* (Chicago: University of Chicago Press, 1925) and *The Urban Community* (Chicago: University of Chicago Press, 1926), edited by Ernest W. Burgess.

ter of the city.[2] In the city of Chicago the Negro community, which had expanded southward from the center of the city along one of the main thoroughfares, State Street, had cut across several of the concentric zones marking the expansion of Chicago. Therefore, it was logical to assume that if the processes of selection and segregation operated according to Burgess' theory of urban expansion, the processes of selection and segregation should be reflected in the Negro community. Therefore, the first step in this study was to determine if this was true.

The Seven Zones of the Negro Community

The Negro community which extended from Twelfth Street southward to Sixty-third Street and was bounded on the west by Wentworth Avenue and on the east by Cottage Grove Avenue could be divided on the basis of census tracts into seven zones which marked the expansion of the Negro community. That these zones provided a means of measuring the process of selection and segregation of elements in the Negro population which were differentiated demographically and socially is indicated first by the character of the population in the seven zones (see Table 1). Although nearly four-fifths of the Negroes in Chicago in 1920 were adults, only the third zone or the bright light area and business center of the community showed a comparable preponderance of adults. The proportion of adults in the population was smaller in the first zone near the Loop in Chicago, where the poorer southern migrants settled, as well as in the areas of more stable community life, Zones VI and VII, where the higher occupational classes resided. A process of selection and segregation was likewise revealed in regard to the proportion of males in the seven zones. Although Chicago, because of the opportunities for industrial employment, had attracted more men than women, the preponderance

[2]   See Ernest W. Burgess, "The Growth of the City" in *The City*, Robert E. Park and Ernest W. Burgess (eds.) (Chicago: University of Chicago Press, 1925), and "The Determination of Gradients in the Growth of the City," *Publications of the American Sociological Society*, 26 (1927): 178–84.

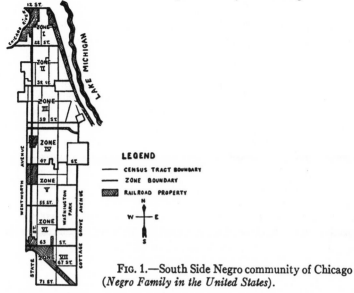

FIG. 1.—South Side Negro community of Chicago
(*Negro Family in the United States*).

of males appeared only in certain areas—the deteriorated areas near the center of the city. The proportion of males in the Negro population declined in the succeeding zones, and in the better areas in the southern section of the community women actually outnumbered men.

One of the most striking features of the process of selection and segregation was the variation in the percentage of mulattoes in the population of the different zones. In the two zones near the center of the city or the Loop about one Negro man out of five and one Negro woman out of four was a mulatto or mixed blood. In Zone III the proportion of mulatto men mounted suddenly to one out of three and the proportion of mulatto women rose to two out of five. In the next two zones the proportion of mulatto men and women in the population of these zones was about the same as in the first two zones. But in Zone VI the proportion of mulatto men and women increased to about a third, while in Zone VII practically a half of the Negro men and women were mulattoes.

We shall see how the concentration of mulattoes in Zone VII was related to the concentration of the higher occupational classes in this zone. However, a word needs to be said concerning the concentration of mulattoes in Zone III. This zone was a bright light area of the Negro community.

Through the heart of this zone ran Thirty-fifth Street, the brightlight area of the Negro community. Here were found the "black and tan" cabarets, pleasure gardens, gambling places, night clubs, hotels, and houses of prostitution. It was the headquarters of the famous "policy king;" the rendezvous of the "pretty" brownskinned boys, many of whom were former bellhops, who "worked" white and colored girls in hotels and on the streets; here the mulatto queen of the underworld ran the biggest poker game on the South Side; here the "gambler de luxe" ruled until he was killed by a brow-beaten waiter. In this world the mulatto girl from the South who, ever since she heard that she was "pretty enough to be an actress," had visions of the stage, realized her dream in one of the cheap theaters. To this same congenial environment the mulatto boy from Oklahoma, who danced in the role of the son of an Indian woman, had found his way. To this area were attracted the Bohemian, the disorganized, and the vicious elements of the Negro world.[3]

When we turn from the demographic to the social aspects of the Negro population of the seven zones, we find the same process of selection and segregation. We note first that Zone I or the area in which the poorer migrants first get a foothold has the highest proportion of heads of families who were born in the South. The proportion declines steadily from nearly four-fifths in Zone I to slightly less than two-thirds in Zone VII. This decline in the proportion of head of families who were born in the South is correlated with the decline in the proportion of illiterate Negroes in the seven zones. In Zone I the illiteracy rate among Negroes was about the same as it was in Houston and Dallas, Texas, and more than four times the rate for the Negro population as a whole in

---

[3]   *The Negro Family in Chicago* (Chicago: University of Chicago Press, 1932), p. 103. This quotation from the study will indicate how documentary materials gathered through uncontrolled observations during "field studies" in modern communities will illuminate or, perhaps better, will make it possible for statistics to have meaning in terms of social processes.

Chicago. The illiteracy rate declined rapidly after Zone I and in the three outermost zones it was less than 3 per cent.

The occupational status of the Negroes in the seven zones is of special interest because it reflects not only the social and cultural differences in the Negro population but provides an index to the class structure of the Negro Community. It will be seen in Table 1 that the proportion of railroad porters or Pullman porters among employed males increases in the seven zones marking the expan-

TABLE 1

Some Indexes to the Differences in the Demographic and Social Character
of the Population in the Seven Zones of the
Negro Community in Chicago

Characteristic (per cent)	Zones						
	I	II	III	IV	V	VI	VII
Persons 21 years and over..........	71.6	76.3	77.6	75.4	72.7	69.0	70.5
Males........................	55.6	54.7	52.0	50.2	48.5	49.8	47.1
Mulattoes: 15 years and over							
Male........................	19.2	19.0	33.5	19.2	22.8	31.3	49.7
Female......................	27.2	23.8	40.2	24.0	24.7	32.8	48.5
Heads of families							
Southern born.................	77.7	77.0	74.7	73.8	72.6	69.0	65.2
Persons illiterate							
10 years and over..............	13.4	4.6	3.2	2.3	3.3	2.9	2.7
Occupational classes: Males							
Professional and white collar.......	5.8	5.5	10.7	11.2	12.5	13.4	34.2
Skilled......................	6.2	10.8	12.3	13.6	11.1	14.4	13.0
Railroad porters*...............	1.4	3.4	6.7	6.5	7.5	7.7	10.7

* Presumably Pullman porters.

sion of the Negro community and that in Zone VII they constitute more than a tenth of the employed males. This is interesting because at one time Pullman porters were, on the whole, a group with comparatively good incomes and maintained a stable family life, and constituted an important element in the Negro upper class. But by the time this study was made in the late twenties they had been superseded by the professional and business classes in the Negro community. However, like the Pullman porters, the proportion of Negro men and women in professional and white-collar occupations, although the figures for women are not given in Table 1, increased regularly in the zones, marking the expansion of the

Negro population from the area of first settlement near the center of the city. For example, in Zone I one out of every sixteen employed Negro males is employed in professional, business, and white-collar occupations as compared with one out of three in Zone VII. The tendency for the Negro women in this occupational group to be concentrated in areas of the outermost expansion of the Negro community is even more marked. Likewise, both Negro men and women in skilled occupations are concentrated in the same zones as the professional and business classes. And contrariwise, although the figures are not given in Table 1, Negro men and women in semiskilled occupations, domestic service, and employed as laborers are concentrated in the zones where the poorer newcomers to the cities are concentrated.

The census data which provided information on the demographic and social characteristics of the Negroes in the seven zones were supplemented by case materials including uncontrolled observations on the behavior of peoples in the seven zones, on the physical character and on the nature of the institutions in the seven zones. Some of this information could be treated statistically as, for example, in enumerating the number of the various denominational churches and "storefront churches," houses of prostitution, saloons, billiard halls, gambling places, and cabarets.[4] Moreover, materials were collected on the social organization of the community though, as we shall see, this material was inadequate for a thoroughgoing analysis of the social changes in the urban environment.

Indexes to Character of the Family

On the basis of the federal census data for the census tracts it was possible to secure some indexes to the character and organization of Negro family life in the seven zones (see Table 2). First, it will be noted that there were important differences in the marital status of men in the zones. In Zone I, nearly 40 per cent of the men were single and only slightly more than a half of them were married.

[4]   See *The Negro Family in Chicago*, Appendix B., p. 276.

TABLE 2

SOME INDEXES TO THE CHARACTER OF FAMILY LIFE IN THE SEVEN
ZONES OF THE NEGRO COMMUNITY IN CHICAGO

CHARACTERISTIC (per cent)	ZONES						
	I	II	III	IV	V	VI	VII
Marital status of males:							
Single..........................	38.6	38.1	35.9	32.0	30.7	27.3	24.7
Married.........................	52.1	54.4	55.8	61.1	62.5	65.6	68.5
Widowed........................	6.3	6.3	7.2	4.9	5.5	6.1	5.5
Divorced........................	0.9	0.9	0.7	1.4	1.5	1.8	1.2
Families with female heads..........	22.0	23.1	20.8	20.4	20.5	15.2	11.9
Married females 15–19 years.........	2.8	2.5	2.1	2.1	1.8	2.1	0.7
House ownership..................	0	1.2	6.2	7.2	8.3	11.4	29.8

The proportion of single men declined for the successive zones to the point that in Zone VII only a fourth of them were single and more than two-thirds of them were married. The proportion of Negro men widowed did not show the some variation. However, there were variations in the proportion of divorced men which may have had some significance. In Zone VII, where the higher occupational classes were concentrated, there was a decidedly higher proportion of divorced males. The significance of this will be commented upon in relation to the marital status of Negro females.

It will be noted that the marital status of Negro females does not vary in the different zones as that of Negro males. An explanation of this difference can only be obtained from what is known of the social behavior of Negroes in case materials on the social and cultural life of Negroes. The census returns on the marital status of Negro women in the zones toward the outermost expansion of the Negro community are probably accurate or nearly accurate. But generally speaking, from what is known concerning the marital status of Negroes, one cannot accept what the women say when they say that they are widowed. Many of the so-called "widowed" Negro females are unmarried mothers or women whose husbands or men with whom they have been living have deserted them. It is interesting to note, however, that in the zones on the periphery of the community the proportion of Negro women who are divorced is significantly higher than in the zones inhabited by the newcomers to the city. This only tends to confirm what was said concerning the validity of statistics on the marital status of the women in the various zones.

The difference in the character of the family was revealed in the difference in the proportion of families with female heads in the seven zones. In Zone I, where we have seen the poorer southern migrants first gain a foothold, in more than a fifth of the families the woman is head of the family. The proportion of families with female heads declined to less than an eighth in Zone VII, where the higher occupational classes and mulattoes are concentrated. In this connection another fact of interest is that in Zone VII only a fourth as many Negro females between the age of fifteen and nineteen were married as in Zone I.

Perhaps the most important index to the progressive stabilization of family life in the seven zones was provided in the increase in the proportion of home-owning Negro families in the seven zones. In Zone I, there was no home ownership among Negroes and only slightly more than 1 per cent in Zone II. But in Zone III, it was a little more than 6 per cent, and in Zones IV and V it continued to increase. In Zone VI more than an eighth of the families owned their homes and in Zone VII three out of every ten Negro families were home-owners. In the study, the progressive increase in homeownership was related to the changes in the physical and social character of the neighbors of the different zones. Moreover, it should be noted that the changes in rates of homeownership were related to the gradual decline in the average number of families and persons per dwelling unit in the seven zones.

Another index to the variation in the character of family life in the seven zones was provided by the census data on the average size of the household and on the number of children under 15, under 5, and under one to Negro women of childbearing age.[5] The average size of household, which was 3.8 in Zone I, increased to 4.2, 4.4, 4.3 in the next three zones and declined to 4.0 and 3.7 in Zones VI and VII.[6] The increase in the size of the household was related to the increase in the number of households with lodgers.

[5]   See *ibid.*, Table XIII, p. 127.

[6]   The average size of household and number of children under five and under one are not given in Table 2.

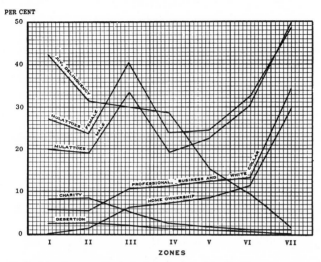

Fig. 2.—Rates of homeownership, charity, family desertion, and juvenile delinquency; percentage of mulattoes in the population; and percentage of males in professional, business, and white-collar occupations in the seven zones of the Negro community of Chicago.

But it is important to note that the size of the household in Zone VII was practically the same as the size in Zone I. The significance of this will become clear when considered in relation to the number of children to women of child-bearing age in the zones.

In Zone I there were 70.7 children under 15 to each 100 women of childbearing age. The number declined in the next four zones and only began to increase in Zone VI and reached 74.1 in Zone VII. The same trend can be observed in regard to the number of children under five (not shown in Table 2) where the number of children declined from 19.8 and increased again from 20 in Zone V to 27.6 in Zone VII. The decline in the number of children to women of childbearing age in Zones II, III, and IV was undoubtedly the result of the decline of the importance of the family in these zones. However, when we consider the number of children under one (not shown in Table 2), one may note that there is a slight increase in the number of children in Zone II but not in

Zone III and that the significant increases were in the next four zones, though the number is less in Zone VII than in Zone VI. The only explanation for the small number under one in Zone I is that since it is in this zone that the southern migrants first secured a foothold in the city, this was the area which would reflect the immediate effects of city life on the decline in the number of Negro births. Then it appears that among the more stable and more economically secure families in Zone VII, there are actually more children per family than in the poor and disorganized families in the other areas of the community.

Indexes to Family Disorganization

In order to secure indexes as measures of family disorganization in the seven zones, it was necessary to utilize the records of the United Charities, the Juvenile Court, the Court of Domestic Relations, the Cook County Hospital, and the Institute of Juvenile Research. The rates of various forms of family disorganization and dependency are given in Table 3. First, it will be noted that about 8 per cent of the families in Zone I and II came to the charities for aid. The rate of dependency as measured by the number of families applying for aid declined sharply in the successive zones

TABLE 3

SOME INDEXES OF SOCIAL DISORGANIZATION IN THE SEVEN
ZONES OF THE NEGRO COMMUNITY IN CHICAGO

SUBJECT	ZONES						
	I	II	III	IV	V	VI	VII
Charity cases...................	8.0	8.2	5.3	2.8	1.9	1.0	1.1
Warrants for non-support..........	2.5	2.0	2.3	2.3	1.5	0.5	0.4
Family desertion.................	2.5	2.6	2.1	1.5	1.1	0.4	0.2
Illegitimacy.....................	2.3	1.1	1.2	0.9	0.6	0.4	0.2
Juvenile delinquency..............	42.8	31.4	30.0	28.8	15.7	9.6	1.4
Adult delinquency................	9.4	6.7	3.8	2.5	2.9	3.2	1.2

until it was only about 1 per cent in the Zones VI and VII. A similar trend may be observed in regard to warrants for non-support and family desertion on the part of the men. In Zones VI and VII the rates for both of these forms of family disorganization declined to one-half of 1 per cent and even less. As one would expect, the decline in the rates of illegitimacy, based upon the number of unmarried mothers per 100 married women, 14 to 44 years of age, followed the same pattern of decline for the seven zones.

The decline in rate of adult delinquency but more especially juvenile delinquency in the seven zones is even more striking. In Zone I where the poorer migrants from the South are concentrated, the number of inmates in the county jail represented nearly a tenth of the adult Negro male population. The proportion declined rapidly for the successive zones until it amounted to scarcely more than one out of a hundred men in Zone VII. In the case of juvenile delinquency, more than two boys out of five had been arrested for delinquency in Zone I. In the next three zones the rates kept close to 30 per cent, but in the next three zones there was a sharp decline until it was only slightly more than 1 per cent in Zone VII.

The statistical materials were analyzed and interpreted on the basis of case materials, including family history documents, the results of interviews, and printed documents in order to throw light on the processes of social disorganization and reorganization in the seven zones. In the last section of the study an attempt was made to show how traditions have been built up in Negro families and how these traditions have been the means whereby the Negro has achieved social stability in a changing world and have taken over the patterns of family life similar to the American pattern.

Extension of Study to Other Areas

Before attempting an assessment of the study as a contribution to urban sociology, we shall indicate how the hypothesis in this study has been utilized in other studies carried on within the general frame of reference of this study. Since the publication of *The Negro Family in Chicago* nearly thirty years ago, I have engaged in the study of the Negro family on a larger scale, including field studies in Brazil and in the West Indies.[7] However, the most immediately relevant study I undertook was the study of the

[7]   See "The Negro Family in Bahia," *American Sociological Review*, 7 (August, 1942) :465–78.

Negro community in Harlem, New York City.[8] Although this study was undertaken to determine the economic and social causes of a race riot in 1935, during the course of the study I collected important materials on the ecological organization of the Negro community which permitted me to test my findings concerning the Negro community in Chicago, especially in regard to some aspects of family life.[9] The ecological organization of the Negro community in Harlem was found to differ in an important respect from the ecological organization of the Negro community in Chicago. As we have seen, the Negro community in Chicago and expanded along one of the main thoroughfares radiating from the center of the city and had cut across the concentric zones marking the expansion of the city as a whole. This was reflected in indexes to community life and in family organization and disorganization. In Harlem the Negro population had expanded from the center of the Negro community—Seventh Avenue and 135th Street—in all directions with the result that the ecological organization of the Negro community was similar to that of a self-contained city. It was possible to mark off on the basis of census tracts five concentric zones indicating the radial expansion of the Negro community in Harlem from its center. First, it was noted (see Table 4) that Negroes had taken over almost entirely Zone I or the center of the community and that the extent to which they had taken over the other four zones diminished as one went from the center to the periphery of the Negro community. Then, it may be observed also that the extent to which Negroes had taken over the successive zones corresponded with the decline in the percentage of non-residential structures in the five zones. The ecological organization of the Harlem Negro community showed in this respect the same relationship of the population to the physical habitat as the Chicago Negro community.

The differences in the social character of the Negro popula-

8   See "The Negro in Harlem, A Report on Social and Economic Conditions Responsible for the Outbreak on March 19, 1935," for the *Mayor's Commission on Conditions in Harlem*, New York, 1936. Unpublished.
9   "Negro Harlem: An Ecological Study," *American Journal of Sociology*, 43 (July, 1937) :72–88.

tion in the Harlem community was shown in the marital status of the population in the five zones. There was a gradual but marked decline in the proportion of single men and women in the successive zones. Associated with the decline in the proportion of single men was a corresponding increase in the proportion of men and women who were returned in the federal census as married. Likewise, paradoxical as it might seem, the increase in the proportion divorced from Zone I to Zone V was indicative of more conventional marital relations. In the case of both the "widowed" and "divorced" it was most likely that these terms represented more truly the marital status of men and women in the peripheral zones than in Zones I and II. These differences in the marital status of the population conformed to the problem of changes in the desertion rates and family dependence as measured by relief cases obtained from the social agencies. The desertion rate declined from 9 per 1000 families in Zone I to 4 per 1000 families in Zone V. This study was carried out during the depression years in the thir-

TABLE 4

SOME INDEXES TO THE HOUSING AND THE SOCIAL AND DEMOGRAPHIC CHARACTER OF
THE POPULATION OF THE FIVE ZONES OF THE HARLEM
NEGRO COMMUNITY IN NEW YORK CITY

CHARACTERISTIC	ZONES				
	I	II	III	IV	V
Percentage of population Negro in 1930....	99.8	87.8	41.4	22.7	6.2
Percentage of non-residential structures in 1934....................................	83.8	78.2	59.8	42.5	28.0
Marital status:					
Single {M...............................	42.6	38.5	35.3	34.0	31.1
{F...............................	30.9	27.6	26.3	25.6	23.5
Married {M...............................	49.8	56.0	60.3	62.3	64.2
{F...............................	50.5	54.8	57.6	59.8	60.1
Widowed {M...............................	7.3	4.7	3.6	2.9	3.8
{F...............................	17.6	16.4	15.0	13.0	14.4
Divorced {M...............................	0.2	0.5	0.4	0.6	0.5
{F...............................	0.6	0.8	0.7	1.1	1.6
Ratio of children under 5 to 1000 women 20–44 years of age: 1930...............	115	176	225	315	462
Births per 1000 married women 15–44 years of age: 1930........................	66.1	81.5	91.9	141.6	168.4
Desertion rate per 1000 families..........	9.0	5.2	4.8	3.5	4.0
Families on relief per 1000 families........	709	585	395	311	284
Boys arrested per 100 boys 10–16 years of age	5.5	4.5	5.7	4.8	4.3

ties, when large numbers of Negro families were dependent upon relief. But the incidence of relief declined considerably in the five zones. In Zone I seven out of ten Negro families were receiving relief and the rate declined in the four succeeding zones until it was less than three out of ten families in Zone V. The rates of juvenile delinquency tended to fluctuate rather than decline, though it was less in the outermost zone than in any of the other zones.

The statistics on births and on the number of children to women of child-bearing age were both related to the marital status of the population and to the character of family life. In Zone I, which was the center of the Harlem community, where there were relatively large numbers of single men and women, there was great dependence upon relief. In this same zone there were only 115 children under five years of age to 1000 women of child-bearing age. This indicated that not only did the family tend to disappear but the population did not reproduce itself. There was a progressive increase in the ratio of children and in the number of children born to women of childbearing age in the successive zones. In fact, in Zone V the ratio of 462 children to 1000 women of childbearing age and the birth rate of 16.8 equaled that of the rural Negro population.

Although there has been no systematic attempt to study the ecological organization of Washington, D.C., I was able to define on the basis of census tract materials five concentric zones which indicated the expansion of the city from the business center. It was found that the slum, concerning which there has been so much complaint, was within the shadow of the nation's Capitol, and fitted perfectly into the ecological organization of the city. However, more important for our interest here was the fact that the rate of home ownership for Negroes increased regularly from the central zone or Zone I to Zone V, and that it was practically the same as the rate of home ownership for white families in each of the five zones.[10]

It was pointed out at the beginning of this chapter that the important social and cultural differences in the Negro population

[10]   Unpublished materials in the Department of Sociology and Anthropology, Howard University.

provided the general frame of reference within which study of the Negro family in Chicago was carried out. The specific hypothesis which was being tested was that these important social and cultural differences were reflected in the traditions and patterns of Negro family life. On the basis of materials which were collected during a larger study of the Negro family in the United States, it was possible to define more precisely the differences in the social heritage and problems of family life.[11] It was possible to define four distinct types of traditional patterns of family life. An attempt has been made to describe and analyze the accommodations which these four types of families made to the urban environment.[12] Not only did these four types of families make different accommodations to the urban environment but the urban environment exercised a selective influence on these various family types. And it was out of this process that there emerged a new social and cultural organization of Negro life and in fact a new Negro personality. It was largely through the methods developed in these various studies that it was possible to organize and present in the general frame of reference the development of the Negro family as an institution.[13]

Assessment of the Study as a Contribution to Urban Sociology

In order to make a proper assessment of *The Negro Family in Chicago* as a contribution to urban sociology, it will be necessary to give some attention to recent discussions of the definition of the city or urbanism. These discussions are the result of urbanization in underdeveloped or non-industrial areas in the world. In fact, some of the studies of urbanization in these areas are concerned with the problems with which the study in Chicago deals. It is felt that a redefinition of the city is necessary because the defi-

[11] "Traditions and Patterns of Negro Family Life" in *Race and Culture Contacts*, Edward B. Reuter (ed.) (New York: McGraw-Hill Co., Inc., 1934).

[12] "The Impact of Urban Civilization upon Negro Family Life," *American Sociological Review*, 2 (October, 1937):609–18.

[13] *The Negro Family in the United States* (Chicago: University of Chicago Press, 1939).

nition of the city as a large and dense population aggregate in which the family loses its importance and that as the result of mobility the contacts of people are impersonal and there is much anomie is descriptive of a special type of city which has grown up in the Western world. Therefore, an attempt has been made to differentiate the pre-industrial city which has been characteristic of Asia and Africa from the Western industrial city.[14]

The problem of the definition of the city really concerns those features of social organization which are supposed to make urbanism a peculiar way of life.[15] In his article on "Urbanization among the Yoruba," Bascom contends that, while the distinction between pre-industrial and industrial cities is important, urbanization does not necessarily involve the decline in the importance of the family in the social organization and that primary forms of social control may still be effective in an urban environment.[16] The significance of Bascom's contention in this assessment of *The Negro Family in Chicago* becomes apparent when one views even casually the studies of social changes in the urban areas of Africa.[17]

The important factor, it seems to me, in differentiating the pre-industrial and industrial city concerns the difference in social organization. In the pre-industrial cities of Africa, kinship and lineages and primary forms of social control played the chief role in the social organization. But as these cities acquire the character of industrial cities, it is apparent in all the studies that these traditional forms of social organization are being dissolved. Then, too, as the Africans migrate to the new industrialized cities, despite their effort to maintain the traditional forms of social organization or create new forms of associations based upon the traditional culture, they are unable to do so. What is happening to the urbanized Afri-

[14]   Gideon Sjoberg, "The Preindustrial City," *American Journal of Sociology*, 9 (March, 1955) :438–45.
[15]   Louis Wirth, "Urbanism as a Way of Life," *American Journal of Sociology*, 44 (July, 1938) :1–8.
[16]   William R. Bascom, "Urbanization among the Yoruba," *American Journal of Sociology*, 50 (March, 1955) :446–53.
[17]   See, for example, J. Clyde Mitchell, *Africans in Industrial Towns in Northern Rhodesia* (H.R.H. The Duke of Edinburgh's Study Conference, 1956).

can is very similar to what happened and continues to happen to the southern Negro who with his background of folk culture migrates to the industrial cities of the United States. Of course, the African's culture may be more resistant to change because the folk culture of the American Negro is essentially a subculture, since even the folk Negro lives in the twilight of American civilization. But the disintegration of the American Negro's traditional folk culture and the reorganization of his social life in the urban environment is very similar to what is occurring in the urban areas of Africa.

In view of the nature of the problem with which *The Negro Family in Chicago* is concerned, namely, social change as it is effected in the urban environment, one must recognize the limitations of the ecological approach to the problem. Human ecology, at least as Park conceived it, "was not a branch of sociology but rather a perspective, a method, and a body of knowledge essential for the scientific study of social life, and hence, like social psychology, a general discipline basic to all the social sciences."[18] Ecological studies were focused originally upon the community which was differentiated theoretically and for purposes of analysis from society, behavior in the former being characterized by the impersonal powers of competition and in the latter by norms and values which govern human behavior. As human ecology has developed as a scientific discipline, it has revealed through empirical studies the relevance of the physical basis of social life to the understanding of social and cultural phenomena. Moreover, the ecological approach to social studies has helped social scientists to define social problems and to discover interrelationships among social phenomena. But the relations which are revealed between phenomena in ecological studies are not explanations of social phenomena but indicate the selection and segregation of certain elements in the population. Thus, ecological studies are not a substitute for sociological studies but supplement studies of human social life. For a complete understanding of social phenomena it is necessary to investigate

[18]   Louis Wirth, "Human Ecology," *American Journal of Sociology,* 50 (March, 1955) :484. This article is devoted to a systematic and critical analysis of the ecological approach to studies of social behavior.

the social organization and culture of a community and the attitudes of the people who constitute the community.

The hypothesis which *The Negro Family in Chicago* undertakes to test is narrowly defined; family disorganization among Negroes cate the selection and segregation of certain elements in the popu- was an aspect of the selective and segregative process of the urban community. The ecological approach to this study provided an adequate test of this hypothesis. However, the general frame of reference of the study was much broader. The study was really concerned with the fundamental social and cultural differences in the Negro population which determined the extent and nature of family disorganization and how these important social and cultural differences influenced the reorganization of life among Negroes on a different basis in the urban environment. Here we are brought face to face with the problem of the adequacy of the ecological approach to sociological problems involved in social changes resulting from urbanization. Quite aside from the question whether the new cities of Africa and Asia have the census materials for cities which would enable one to make an ecological study similar to the study which we are assessing, there is the more fundamental question of the adequacy of the ecological approach to this problem.[19] The sociological problem is essentially the problem of social organization.

The remainder of this chapter will be devoted to an assessment of the study as a contribution to the analysis and understanding of the processes of social organization or social reorganization which are involved in the social changes resulting from urbanization. It might be noted, first, that the study contains a description of the social organization of the Negro community which, it was stated, was shaped by the division of labor or occupational organization

[19]   In this connection reference should be made to the excellent ecological study by Leo Kuper, *Durban: A Study in Racial Ecology* (London: Jonathan Cape, 1958), which indicates what may be done in a South African city where statistics are available for census tracts. The study is restricted, however, to the relations of the races with reference to spatial distribution.

of the community.[20] This provided a sketchy description of the various types of associations and institutions in the Negro community. But there was no attempt to describe or analyze the social stratification of the Negro community which would have provided the most important frame of reference for studying social reorganization in the urban community.[21] Of course, in the social analysis which was designed to explain the process of selection and segregation, an attempt was made to analyze on the basis of case materials why, for example, there is more family stability and less family disorganization in the areas in which the higher occupational classes are concentrated. But this analysis is not specifically related to the new social stratification in the urban community nor is the analysis in terms of social processes. Such an analysis would be necessary, however, for an understanding of the processes of reorganization in the urban community. The ecological selection which the study revealed represented in fact changes which had occurred during two or more generations. Because of educational opportunities children acquired new skills and new ambitions and were able to rise in the new social stratification. It was because of the opportunity for this type of social mobility that they were able to escape from the condition of masses, that is, enter new occupations, become homeowners, maintain a conventional family life, and move to areas which were congenial to their way of life. It is only in the final chapter which deals with the manner in which traditions in the Negro family are built up that the social analysis deals with these processes of social change.

The study of social organization is especially important in the sociological studies which are being made among the urbanized Africans. The traditional forms of social stratification are being undermined or completely dissolved in the urban environment and

20   *The Negro Family in Chicago*, pp. 112–15.
21   In *The Negro Family in the United States*, I have devoted much attention to the analysis of the social processes by which new classes have come into existence among Negroes in the United States and the role of fundamental social and cultural differences in the formation of the new class structure as well as the new social distinctions.

a new and more complex type of social stratification is replacing them.[22] In this process the old social distinctions and prestige values are being supplanted by those which have meaning for the African in the new world of the city. This leads us to another aspect of the social reorganization of life in the city to which this study scarcely gives any attention but is especially important in areas like Africa. One of the most important phases of the reorganization of life among urbanized Africans is the development of new forms of associations. As the traditional African society dissolves or disintegrates the fabric of a new social life is coming into existence in the urban environment. These new forms of social life have a functional relationship to the needs of the new environment. Very often these new associations incorporate the attitudes and patterns of behavior of the traditional culture. But more often they represent adjustments to new situations for which the traditional culture does not provide solutions. There are, for example, new types of economic associations which approximate in form and purpose the labor unions of the Europeans and perhaps even more important the new political organizations with nationalistic aims. Then as the traditional religions disintegrate, there are all sorts of cults formed to meet the new conditions of city living. Although the situation of the American Negro in the city is not exactly the same, there are many parallels. The study fails to deal with this aspect of adjustment to the urban environment.

Although the study is concerned with the problem of the family in the city, it does not deal with its crucial role in the social organization or the social reorganization of life in the city. This is of primary importance not only in studying the American Negro but in studying the African in the city. In the case of the American Negro the family in the plantation areas lacked an institutional basis and owed its cohesion and continuity to habitual association in the same household and the emotions and sentiments that grew out of this association. On the other hand, the African who comes to the city has been part of a family and lineage group with an institutional basis and social sanctions deeply rooted in their cul-

[22]   See, for example, A. L. Epstein, *Politics in an Urban African Community* (Manchester: Manchester University Press, 1958).

ture. However, in both cases the family had a functional relationship to the conditions of life and played an indispensable role in the social organization. In destroying both types of family groups the impact of the urban environment has resulted in social disorganization and created a cultural crisis. In dealing with this crisis, whether the family is organized on a different pattern or new types of associations are formed, it is in the family that the new norms of behavior and new conceptions of life and new values will provide the basis of the new social organization. These important aspects of the role of the family in social organization are only touched upon or implicit in this ecological study of the Negro family in the city.

In concluding this chapter, we shall attempt to sum up our assessment of *The Negro Family in Chicago* after a period of nearly thirty years since its publication. From the standpoint of its significance for human ecology, the study demonstrates in an unmistakable manner the validity of the theory of human ecology in the approach to the study of the urban environment and contains a broader and more developed conception of human ecology than the more restricted spatial aspects of human ecology. Moreover, it makes a distinct contribution to the theory of the ecological organization of the city especially in the application of its methods to the Negro community in New York. There it shows that gradients are not only found in the growth of the city as a whole but that in cultural or racial communities within the city there are gradients similar to those in the city as a whole. Nevertheless, the study reveals the limitations of the ecological approach to the study of the important problem of social organization and social reorganization in the city. It fails to show the social stratification of the community which would provide the most important frame of reference for studying the social changes in the life of the Negro or any other urbanized group. Nor is there an analysis of the important role of the family in the social organization, although it is suggested in this study and carried out in the larger study of the Negro family. In brief this study in human ecology indicates and tends to define some of the sociological problems which need to be studied in the field of social disorganization and reorganization of life in the city.

9

NEGRO HARLEM:

AN ECOLOGICAL STUDY

1937

IN A STUDY published a few years ago, the writer was able to show, by means of an ecological analysis, that the organization and disorganization of Negro family life in the northern city were closely tied up with the economic and social structure of the Negro community.[1] Specifically, in the case of Chicago, it was found that, as a result of the selection and segregation incident to the expansion of population, the Negro community had assumed a definite spatial pattern. This spatial pattern bore the impress of the ecological organization of the larger community and could be represented by seven zones indicating the outward expansion of the community from the slum area about the central business district. On the basis of these seven zones it was possible to measure the selection and segregation, as revealed in the distribution of occupational classes, in the proportion of males, mulattoes, and illiterates in the population and other indexes to the economic and social structure of the community. Family disorganization—measured in terms of family dependency and desertion—nonsupport, illegitimacy, and juvenile delinquency were found to diminish in the successive zones marking the progressive stabilization of community life.

With the results of the Chicago study in mind, the writer undertook, on the basis of materials collected while making a survey of

---

Reprinted from the *American Journal of Sociology*, 43 (July, 1937) :72–88.

[1] See *The Negro Family in Chicago* (Chicago: University of Chicago Press, 1932).

Harlem for The Mayor's Commission on Conditions in Harlem, to determine to what extent the Negro community in Harlem had assumed a natural or ecological order during its expansion.[2] The results of this study are embodied in the present article.

I. *Origin, Growth, and Expansion of the Negro Community*

Reports differ concerning the historical events leading up to the settlement of the Negro in Harlem; but it seems fairly well established that Harlem had already deteriorated as a residential area when Negroes began finding homes there at the opening of the present century.[3] As is usually the case when Negroes first enter neighborhoods occupied by whites, the movement of Negroes into Harlem provoked a storm of protest. The *New York Herald* of July 10, 1906, reported indignation meetings "throughout the neighborhood of West 135th Street, where thirty-five white families" were to be ejected to make room for Negro tenants. The article ended with the following comment: "It is generally believed by the residents, however, that the establishment of the Negroes in 135th Street is only the nucleus of a Negro settlement that will extend over a very wide area of Harlem within the next few years."[4]

The prophecy contained in the concluding comment has been fulfilled by the subsequent growth of the Harlem Negro community. From the small settlement in the block referred to above, the Negro community has gradually spread out in all directions. While the expansion of the Negro community in Harlem has been governed largely by social and economic forces similar to those that have determined the growth of the Negro community in Chicago, an important difference in the growth of these two communities is observable. Whereas the growth of the Negro community in Chicago was dominated, as we have indicated, almost entirely by the

[2]   The Commission was appointed by Mayor LaGuardia following the outbreak in Harlem on March 19, 1935.
[3]   See Clyde Vernon Kiser, *Sea Island to City* (New York, 1932), pp. 19–20.
[4]   Quoted, *ibid.*, p. 21.

ecological organization of the city of Chicago, the Harlem Negro community has shown a large measure of autonomy in its growth and, as we shall see, has assumed the same pattern of zones as a self-contained city.

MAP I

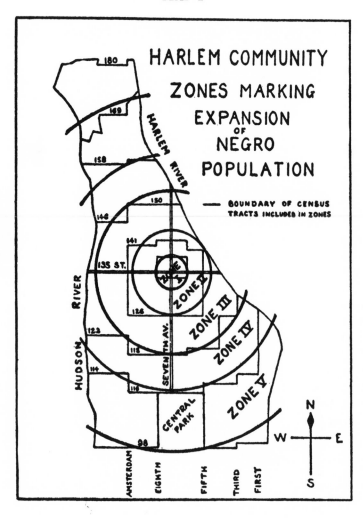

The radial expansion of the Negro population from the area about One Hundred and Thirty-fifth Street and Seventh Avenue may be represented ideally by drawing concentric circles about the census tract in which the intersection of these two main thoroughfares is located[5] (see Map I). In 1910 there were 15,028 Negroes or 54 per cent of the Negroes in the Harlem area concentrated in the first two zones (see Table 1). At that time Negroes comprised less than a fifth of the entire population of these two zones; while in

TABLE 1

NEGRO POPULATION IN THE FIVE ZONES OF THE HARLEM
COMMUNITY, NEW YORK CITY, 1910, 1920
1930, AND 1934

Zone	1910	1920	1930	1934*
I.....................	1,856	9,053	12,585	7,661
II....................	13,172	43,734	72,214	59,783
III...................	6,145	22,661	64,368	67,304
IV....................	1,879	2,058	40,312	55,337
V.....................	5,775	6,742	14,415	13,397
Total..........	27,827	83,248	203,894	203,482

* Census by the New York Housing Authority.

the three remaining zones marking the outward expansion of the Negro community, they became less and less significant in the population (see Diagram I). By 1920 Negroes constituted over three-fourths of the population of the first zone, over half of that of the second zone, and about a seventh of the population of the third. Up to 1920, whites in the two outlying zones still resisted the expanding Negro population. However, by 1930, the Negro had not only taken over almost the entire first zone and increased to seven-eighths and two-fifths of the populations of the second and

[5]   Statistical data from the federal census and other sources on the five zones are based on data for the census tracts which are included more or less in five zones represented ideally on Map I. Data on Zone I are drawn from statistics on one census tract, No. 228; while data on the other four zones are based on statistics on the successive groups of census tracts encircling this central census tract.

DIAGRAM I

PERCENTAGE DISTRIBUTION OF THE FOUR NATIVITY GROUPS IN THE POPULATION OF
EACH OF THE FIVE ZONES OF THE HARLEM COMMUNITY,
NEW YORK CITY, 1930, 1920, AND 1910

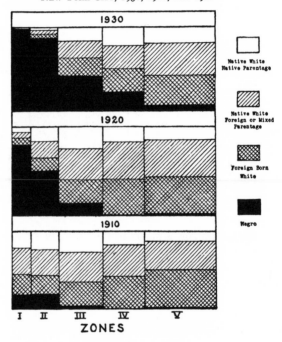

third zones, respectively, but had become a significant element—22.7 per cent—in the population of the fourth zone. Even in the fifth zone Negroes had increased from 2.5 to 6.2 per cent. This was due chiefly to the movement of Negroes into the area between Fifth Avenue and the Harlem River (see Map I). The bulk of the Negro population in the fifth zone had hitherto been concentrated in the neighborhood of Amsterdam Avenue and Ninety-eighth Street, this settlement being an extension of the West Side Negro community rather than an expansion of the Harlem community.

Although the five zones indicate the general tendency of the population to expand radially from the center of the community, the Negro population has not expanded to the same extent in all directions. Because of economic and social factors, the expansion of the Negro population has followed many tortuous paths. It has been held in check until residential areas have deteriorated and therefore have become accessible not only to Negroes but to Italians and Puerto Ricans who live in areas adjacent to those inhabited by Negroes. In some instances white residential areas, when almost surrounded by the expanding Negro population, have put up a long and stubborn resistance to the invasion of the Negro. This was the case with the area about Mount Morris Park; but when this area lost its purely residential character, and brownstone fronts became rooming-houses, the eventual entrance of the Negro was foreshadowed. Then, too, the advance of the Negro had been heralded by the location of light industries, as in the western section of Harlem where, after the establishment of a brewery doomed the area as a residential neighborhood for whites of foreign extraction, signs inviting Negro tenants began to appear on houses. But it seems that the westward expansion of the Negro population has been definitely halted at Amsterdam Avenue and will not be able to invade the exclusive residential area on Riverside Drive.[6]

We can get some idea of the relation between the expansion of the Negro population and the character of the areas into which it has spread by considering the predominant types of structures located in the five zones. First, we note in Table 2 that the Negro population predominates in those zones where the majority of the structures are nonresidential in character. Then, if we consider more closely the character of these nonresidential structures, we find

[6]   Since 1920 there has been a decrease in the number of Negroes west of Amsterdam Avenue.

TABLE 2

PERCENTAGE OF POPULATION NEGRO AND TYPES OF STRUCTURES IN FIVE
ZONES OF THE HARLEM COMMUNITY, NEW YORK CITY

	ZONES				
	I	II	III	IV	V
Percentage of population Negro in 1930..........................	99.0	87.8	41.4	22.7	6.2
Percentage of structures that were nonresidential in 1934...........	83.8	78.2	59.8	42.5	28.0
Percentage of nonresidential structures that were rooming- and lodging-houses in 1934*..............	34.2	32.0	31.5	23.0	18.5

* Rooming- and lodging-houses are classified as nonresidential structures.

that the Negro population is concentrated in those zones where rooming- and lodging-houses comprise a relatively large proportion of the non-residential structures. If further analysis were made of the various zones, it would probably reveal an even closer relationship between the expansion of the Negro population and the location of non-residential structures.

Further light on the relation between the expansion of the Negro community and the physical character of the areas into which Negroes have moved is afforded by data on the type, age, and condition of the residential structures in the five zones.[7] In respect to type of residential structures, the third zone showed a comparatively large proportion of one-family dwellings. This was due to the fact that the western section of the third zone (see Map I) includes a large part of the Riverside Drive area. The most noteworthy difference between the zones appeared in the proportion of hotels, boarding-houses, and institutions which were simply classified as "other." The proportion of this type of residential structure declined sharply from 51.7 per cent in the first zone to 14.9 per cent in the fifth. In the distribution of the residential structures according to their age, the differences in the physical character of the zones stand out more clearly. In the first and second zones, where

[7]   Space does not permit the inclusion of table containing this information.

99 and 87.8 per cent of the residents, respectively, were Negroes, 90 per cent of the residential structures were thirty-five years of age and over. For the remaining three zones the proportion of older structures declined significantly except in the fourth zone, which included a large number of deteriorated tenements in the eastern section. This is the very section of the fourth zone in which Negroes have settled. However, the relation between the condition of the residential structures in the various zones and the expansion of the Negro population is obscured by the fact that the zones are far from homogeneous in physical character. While the third and fifth zones showed the greatest proportion of first-class residential structures, the fourth zone had the highest proportion of fourth-class dwellings. Nevertheless, there was a smaller proportion of first- and second-class dwellings in the first zone than in any of the other four zones. This was true despite the fact that there was a higher proportion of first-class dwellings in the first zone than in either the second or the fourth zone. The comparatively large proportion of first-class structures in the first zone was due to the rehabilitation of this area.

II. *Age and Sex Distribution of the Population*

The selection and segregation which have taken place as the Negro population has expanded are seen, first, in the variations in the proportion of grown people in the five zones. Practically four out of five persons in the first zone were adults in 1930 (see Table 3). In the second zone the proportion of adults in the population declined to three out of four, and in the next three zones, from about seven to six out of ten persons in the population. The tendency on the part of older persons to become segregated toward the center of the community is reflected also in the relative number of children in the population of the various zones. In the first or central zone only 3.8 per cent of the entire population in 1930 was under five years of age. The proportion of children in this age group increased in each of the succesive zones until it reached 12.3 per cent in the fifth zone. There was also a slight increase in the proportion of females in the successive zones marking the outward expan-

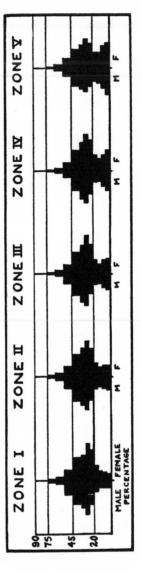

DIAGRAM II

AGE AND SEX PYRAMIDS SHOWING THE PERCENTAGE DISTRIBUTION OF MALES AND FEMALES IN THE NEGRO POPULATION OF EACH OF THE FIVE ZONES OF THE HARLEM COMMUNITY, NEW YORK CITY, ACCORDING TO THE FOLLOWING AGE PERIODS: UNDER FIVE; EACH FIVE-YEAR PERIOD FROM FIVE TO THIRTY-FOUR; EACH TEN-YEAR PERIOD FROM THIRTY-FIVE TO SEVENTY-FOUR; AND SEVENTY-FIVE YEARS AND OVER (1930)

TABLE 3

PERCENTAGE DISTRIBUTION OF MALES AND FEMALES IN THE NEGRO POPULATION OF EACH OF THE
FIVE ZONES OF THE HARLEM COMMUNITY, NEW YORK CITY, 1930

Age Period	Zone I		Zone II		Zone III		Zone IV		Zone V	
	M	F	M	F	M	F	M	F	M	F
75+...	0.1	0.2	0.0	0.2	0.0	0.2	0.0	0.2	0.0	0.2
65–74..	0.5	0.6	0.3	0.6	0.3	0.6	0.2	0.5	0.4	0.6
55–64..	1.6	1.7	1.4	1.6	1.2	1.4	0.9	1.2	1.3	1.5
45–54..	6.3	5.8	5.3	5.0	4.4	4.3	3.6	3.8	4.0	4.3
35–44..	11.4	11.2	11.0	10.7	10.0	10.0	8.8	8.5	8.5	8.7
30–34..	6.5	6.0	6.5	6.8	6.8	6.7	6.7	6.8	5.0	5.4
25–29..	8.0	8.6	7.5	8.4	7.4	9.0	7.6	8.5	5.5	6.9
20–24..	5.8	7.1	5.1	6.9	4.9	6.9	5.5	7.1	4.4	5.9
15–19..	2.7	3.6	2.6	3.4	2.6	3.5	2.9	3.8	3.2	3.7
10–14..	1.9	2.2	2.3	2.5	2.4	2.3	2.7	2.9	3.7	3.7
5–9...	1.9	2.0	2.8	2.9	3.3	3.6	3.8	3.9	4.8	5.4
–5...	1.9	1.9	2.9	2.9	3.7	3.7	4.9	4.8	6.3	6.0
Total	48.6	50.9	47.7	51.9	47.0	52.2	47.6	52.0	47.1	52.3

sion of the population. Here, too, the influence of selective factors was apparent. For, although there was an excess of females in the total population of the community, the excess of females in the first zone was counterbalanced by the tendency on the part of males to concentrate there. A graphic picture of the differences in the age and sex composition of the five zones is given in Diagram II.

III. *Marital Status of the Population*

The tendency on the part of family groups to move toward the periphery of the community was shown in the increasing proportion of married men and women in the successive zones.[8] In the first zone or center of the community only half of the men and women were married. From this zone outward the percentage of both men and women married increased until it amounted, in the fifth or outermost zone, to 64.2 per cent for the men and 60.1 per cent for the women. Correlated with the increase in the proportion of men and women married was the gradual decline not only in the

TABLE 4

PERCENTAGE OF NEGRO MALES AND FEMALES 15 YEARS OF AGE AND OVER SINGLE, MARRIED, WIDOWED, AND DIVORCED IN THE FIVE ZONES OF THE HARLEM NEGRO COMMUNITY, NEW YORK CITY, 1930

Marital Status	Sex	Zone I	Zone II	Zone III	Zone IV	Zone V
Single..................	M	42.6	38.5	35.3	34.0	31.1
	F	30.9	27.6	26.3	25.6	23.5
Married................	M	49.8	56.0	60.3	62.3	64.2
	F	50.5	54.8	57.6	59.8	60.1
Widowed................	M	7.3	4.7	3.6	2.9	3.8
	F	17.6	16.4	15.0	13.0	14.4
Divorced................	M	0.2	0.5	0.4	0.6	0.5
	F	0.6	0.8	0.7	1.1	1.6

[8]   The tendency on the part of foreign-born Negroes to move toward the periphery of the community was probably due to the fact that the foreign Negro population was comprised largely of family groups with children. The percentage of foreign-born Negroes in each of the five successive zones was as follows: 11.9, 15, 20, 22.6, and 15.6, respectively.

proportion of men and women single in the successive zones but also in the proportion of widowed persons in these five zones. Although these figures do not give an absolutely correct picture of the marital condition of the men and women in the community, it is interesting to note that the proportion of men and women widowed was highest in the center of the community where one would expect to find considerable family disorganization. The decline in the percentage of widowed among the males was even greater than among the females. At the same time there was an increase in the proportion of divorced persons in the successive zones as one left the center of the community. A possible explanation of the comparatively larger number of divorced persons in the outer zones is that it may indicate a greater regard for legal requirements in the breaking of marital ties.

IV. *Ratio of Children, Births, and Deaths*

The low fertility of Negroes in northern cities has been revealed in a number of important studies. For example, Thompson and Whelpton have shown that there has been a marked tendency for the ratio of children to Negro women of child-bearing age to vary inversely with size of city.[9] According to these same authors, Negroes in large cities, including Chicago and New York, "were not maintaining their numbers on a permanent basis in either 1920 or 1928."[10] The extremely low fertility of Negroes in Chicago has been clearly demonstrated by Phillip M. Hauser, of the University of Chicago, in an unpublished study. In the case of Chicago the present writer has shown in a study of the Negro family how selective factors within the Negro community affected the relative fertility of different sections of the Negro population.[11]

[9]   Warren S. Thompson and P. K. Whelpton, *Population Trends in the United States* (New York, 1933), p. 280.

[10]   *Ibid.*, p. 281.

[11]   See *The Negro Family in Chicago*, pp. 136–45. The highest ratio of children—276—to women of child-bearing age was found in the seventh zone which was farthest removed from the center of the city; while the lowest ratio—143—was in the third zone—an area distinguished by vice and other forms of social disorganization.

Lately, Kiser found in a study of Negro birth-rates in a health area of Harlem that the fertility of Negro women was lower than that of white women of a similar or even higher occupational level in Syracuse and two other urban communities.[12] Kiser indicated in his study that the low fertility of Negroes was "due partly to selective processes with reference to residence in Harlem as indicated by higher birth rates among the colored population in other parts of the city."[13] As a matter of fact, even within Harlem itself important differences are revealed if the fertility of Negro women is studied in relation to the selective processes within the community. These differences became apparent when the children under five to women of child-bearing age was calculated for the five zones by

TABLE 5

NUMBER OF CHILDREN UNDER 5 TO 1000 NEGRO WOMEN 20–44 YEARS OF
AGE IN FIVE ZONES OF THE HARLEM COMMUNITY, NEW
YORK CITY, 1920 AND 1930

ZONE	1930			1920		
	Women, Age 20–44	Children under 5	Ratio of Children to Women	Women, Age 20–44	Children under 5	Ratio of Children to Women
I..........	4,141	476	115	3,083	336	109
II..........	23,612	4,160	176	15,021	2,793	186
III..........	21,107	4,749	225	7,217	1,858	257
IV..........	12,498	3,940	315	805	173	214
V..........	3,872	1,790	462	2,262	621	274

which we have indicated the expansion of the Harlem Negro community. We find that both in 1920 and in 1930 there was, with one exception, a regular increase in the ration of children from the first to the fifth zone. In 1930 the ratio of children in the fifth zone was 462 or four times that in the first zone. The exception to the general trend, observable in the fourth zone in 1920, was probably due to the fact that at that time only a small number of economically

[12]   Clyde V. Kiser, "Fertility of Harlem Negroes," *Milbank Memorial Fund Quarterly*, 13 (July, 1935):273–85.
[13]   *Ibid.*, p. 284.

better-situated families had moved into this zone. On the other hand, the changes between 1920 and 1930 in the ratio of children in the three outer zones seem to indicate a movement toward or settlement in the peripheral zones by the more fertile groups.

TABLE 6

NUMBER OF CHILDREN BORN TO 1000 NEGRO MARRIED WOMEN, 15-44 YEARS OLD, AND RATIO OF CHILDREN UNDER 5 TO NEGRO WOMEN 15 AND OVER, MARRIED, WIDOWED, AND DIVORCED IN FIVE ZONES OF THE HARLEM COMMUNITY, NEW YORK CITY, 1930

Zone	Married Women, Age 15–44 (Estimated)	Number of Births	Births Per 1000 Married Women, Age 15–44	Women, Age 15 and Over, Married, Widowed, and Divorced	Children under 5	Ratio of Children to Women, Age 15 and Over, Married, Widowed, and Divorced
I..........	2,495	165	66.1	3,883	476	123
II..........	15,087	1,230	81.5	22,670	4,160	184
III..........	13,883	1,276	91.9	20,246	4,749	234
IV..........	8,552	1,211	141.6	12,120	3,940	325
V..........	2,833	477	168.4	4,104	1,790	436
Total....	42,850	4,359	101.7	63,023	15,115	240

We can get further light on the relation between the fertility of Negro women and residence in the various areas of the community by studying the ratio of children to women fifteen years of age and over who were married, widowed, and divorced and the number of births to married women fifteen to forty-four years of age. Here, again, we find the ratio of children increasing regularly in the successive zones marking the expansion of the Negro community. The same trend was apparent in regard to birth-rates in 1930. In the first zone there were only 66.1 births per one thousand Negro married women fifteen to forty-four years of age. But, as in the case of the ratio of children, the fertility of the women in the successive zones increased according to their distance from the center of the community. The fertility of the women in the fifth zone was slightly over two and one-half times as great is it was in the first.

Because of the differences in the age and sex composition of the five zones, the crude death-rates were not significant. However, when the ratio of births to deaths was calculated, important differences appeared. In the first zone deaths were in excess of births, while in the second zone they almost balanced the births. In the next three zones the number of births per one hundred deaths increased from 149 to 225 and declined to 167 in the outermost zone. In respect to infant mortality there was little difference between the zones, the highest infant death rate—10.8—being in the second zone, and the lowest—7.8—being in the fourth zone.

V. *Crime, Delinquency, and Dependency*

When we study such phenomena as crime and delinquency in their relation to the ecological organization of the Harlem Negro community, it appears that economic and cultural factors affect their distribution to a far greater extent than the distribution of the population with respect to age, sex, marital condition, and fertility.[14] First, we note (Table 7) that, during the first six months of 1930, the highest number of arrests in proportion to men in the

TABLE 7

CRIME AND DELINQUENCY RATES IN THE FIVE ZONES OF THE
HARLEM NEGRO COMMUNITY, NEW YORK CITY

Zone	Number of Males 17 Years and Over, 1930*	Number of Arrests of Males First Six Months, 1930	Arrests Per 100 Males 17 Years and Over	Number of Boys 10–16 Years of Age, 1930*	Number of Boys Arrested, 1930	Number of Boys Arrested Per 100 Boys, Age 10–16
I	5,329	333	6.2	329	18	5.5
II	28,256	2,264	8.0	2,326	105	4.5
III	23,065	1,350	5.8	2,088	120	5.7
IV	14,274	597	4.2	1,462	70	4.8
V	4,508	284	6.2	716	31	4.3

* Number of men and boys seventeen and sixteen years of age, respectively, estimated.

[14]   In a recent article Park has pointed out the fact that in human society the natural or ecological social order is limited and modified by institutional and cultural factors; see Robert Ezra Park, "Human Ecology," *American Journal of Sociology*, 42:12–15.

population occurred in the second zone just outside of the center of Negro Harlem's economic and cultural life. The rate of adult delinquency measured in terms of arrests declined gradually in the next two zones. But we find that the rate in the outermost zone equaled that in the center of the community. As we have already indicated, the southern portion of this outermost zone included a slum section and therefore manifested many of the characteristics of a slum area. The juvenile delinquency rates for the five zones were even more difficult to explain on the basis of the general community pattern without a knowledge of the variations in the character of these zones. In 1930—and the same held true for the five-year period from 1930 to 1934—the juvenile delinquency rate, measured in terms of boys arrested in proportion to boys ten to sixteen years of age, was practically as low in the second zone as in the outermost zone.[15]

Although dependency as represented in the comparatively few cases handled by the Charity Organization Society in 1930–31 did not indicate the influence of selective factors in the ecological organization of the Negro community, selection was apparent in the desertion rates and more especially in the proportion of families on Home Relief in the five zones (see Table 8). Desertion rates, based upon desertion cases handled by the Charity Organization Society, declined from 9.0 per one thousand families in the first zone to 4.0 in the fifth. On the basis of the census made by the New York City Housing Authority in 1934, the number of families on Home Relief declined from 709 per one thousand in the first zone to 284 in the fifth zone. However, it should be noted that the highest percentage—91.2—of families on relief was found in a census tract in the second zone, south of the census tract which constitutes the first zone in our scheme. But, in spite of this variation from the general pattern, the percentage of families on Home Relief in the poorer sections of the fifth zone varied slightly from the average for the entire zone. In view of what our statistics indicate concerning the nature of group life in these various zones, it seems reasonable to

[15] It might be mentioned in this connection that adult and juvenile delinquency in Chicago fitted into the much simpler ecological pattern of the Negro community; see *The Negro Family in Chicago*, chap. 10.

TABLE 8

DEPENDENCY AND DESERTION IN THE FIVE ZONES OF THE HARLEM
NEGRO COMMUNITY, NEW YORK CITY

ZONE	TOTAL NEGRO FAMILIES 1930	C.O.S. UNDER CARE FAMILIES				TOTAL NEGRO FAMILIES 1934	FAMILIES ON HOME RELIEF SEPT., 1935	
		All Cases		Desertion Cases				
		Number	Rate Per 1,000 Families	Number	Rate Per 1,000 Families		Number	Rate Per 1,000 Families
I.....	2,221	80	36	20	9.0	2,110	1,497	709
II.....	15,793	448	28	83	5.2	16,321	9,560	585
III.....	16,145	533	33	78	4.8	18,875	7,473	395
IV.....	9,558	343	35	34	3.5	14,945	4,658	311
V.....	3,717	140	37	15	4.0	3,886	1,104	284

conclude that the large number of families on relief in the zones close to the center of the community was associated with the breakdown of group life as represented by normal family life in these areas.

VI. *Distribution of Institutions*

The distribution of institutions in the Harlem Negro community reflects in a visible form the general community pattern. The concentration of institutions in the first zone was vividly portrayed by Rudolph Fisher in a story of Negro life there. "In a fraction of a mile of 135th Street," he wrote, "there occurs every institution necessary to civilization from a Carnegie Library opposite a public school at one point to a police station beside an undertaker's parlor at another."[16] A recent survey of this area revealed the extent to which the economic life of the Negro community, especially with respect to Negro business enterprises, is centered about One Hundred and Thirty-fifth Street and Seventh Avenue. There were in this area, in 1935, 321 business establishments, two-thirds of which were conducted by Negroes, in addition to 53 offices of

[16]   "Blades of Steel," *Anthology of American Negro Literature*, V. F. Calverton (ed.) (New York, 1929), p. 53.

Negro professional men and women. Because of the economic dependence of the community, whites owned the bank and more than 80 per cent of the retail food stores, while Negroes controlled practically all the businesses providing personal services and other types of enterprises not requiring large outlays of capital. In this area were also located the two principal Negro newspapers in Harlem and the offices of four Negro insurance companies.

As the center of Negro Harlem has come to play a specialized role in the organization of the community, the area affected by the process has extended beyond the limits of the single census tract which constitutes the first zone. For example, as an indication of this process, since 1930 the population of the second zone has declined as well as that of the first zone. Hence, in our consideration of the distribution of institutions with reference to zones, we shall regard as a single area Zones I and II, which have a total population about equal to that in each of the two next zones, III and IV (see Table 1). In 1935 there were in the central area seventy-five churches, not including spiritualists, psychologists, and Father Divine's "Kingdoms." Forty-two of the churches were of the "store-front" type, three so-called "spiritualist" churches, and the remaining thirty were denominational churches housed in regular edifices. The number of all types of religious institutions declined in the three zones outside of this central area. For example, in Zone V, there were only one regular church edifice and nine "storefront" churches. As the focus of the political life of the community, the central area contained ten of the eighteen political clubs in the community, while Zone III had six such clubs. Although about 40 per cent of the recreational institutions serving primarily Negro Harlem were located in the central area, they were more widely distributed in the five zones than other types of institutions. This fact is of special interest because it indicates how, in regard to the cultural superstructure, the main arteries of travel—Lenox, Seventh, and Eighth avenues—running the entire length of the community, and the "satellite loops" at One Hundred and Sixteenth, One Hundred and Twenty-fifth, and One Hundred and Forty-fifth streets tend to mar the symmetry of the community pattern.

However, this does not affect in any important manner the conclusion to which our study of the Harlem Negro community leads. Although our analysis provides additional substantiation of the general ecological hypothesis that the distribution of human activities resulting from competition assumes an orderly form, it introduces at the same time an important extension of the theory. It appears that, where a racial or cultural group is stringently segregated and carries on a more or less independent community life, such local communities may develop the same pattern of zones as the larger urban community.

10

THE IMPACT OF URBAN
CIVILIZATION UPON
NEGRO FAMILY LIFE

1936

Introduction

THE URBANIZATION of the Negro population during the present century has effected the most momentous change in the life of the Negro since his emancipation. During the first three decades of the century, nearly two and a half million Negroes moved from the rural South into the urban areas of the North and the South.[1] Public attention has been directed to the northward movements because they were dramatized by the mass migrations to northern industrial centers during the World War; whereas, the million or more Negroes who drifted into southern cities attracted little or no attention.[2] However, the shift from country to city in both the North and the South has been accompanied by profound changes in the Negro's behavior and general outlook on life. Be-

---

This article is an adaptation of a paper read before the annual meeting of the American Sociological Society at Chicago, Illinois, December, 1936. Reprinted from the *American Sociological Review*, 2 (August, 1937) : 609–18, by permission of the American Sociological Association.

[1]   Frank A. Ross, "Urbanization of the Negro," *Publications of the American Sociological Society*, 26:118.
[2]   *Ibid.*, p. 21. For literature on the movement of the Negro to northern cities one should consult Louise V. Kennedy, *The Negro Peasant Turns Cityward*, New York, 1930. This study lists books, articles, and editorials by 159 authors and organizations.

cause of the fundamental role of the family in social organization, the study of the Negro family offers the most fruitful approach to an understanding of these important changes in the social and cultural life of the Negro.

I

Although the great majority of Negroes who have migrated to urban areas have been simple peasant folk, the economic and cultural differences among the migrants as a whole have determined largely the kinds of accommodation which they have made to their new environment. Therefore, on the basis of a large body of documentary material we shall undertake first to describe four fairly distinct types of traditional patterns of family life found among the Negroes who make up communities in American cities.[3] [There is first the maternal family pattern which is found in its purest and most primitive form in the rural South. By a maternal pattern of family organization we mean a family that is based primarily upon the affectional ties and common interests existing between the offspring and the mother who is the head of the family. As one would expect, many of these families owe their origin to illegitimacy, often involving several men. In such cases the man's or father's function generally ceases after impregnation; and if he continues to show interest in the woman and the offspring, his contacts are casual and his contributions to the household are of the nature of gifts. But he has no authority in the family and the children may not even be aware of his relationship to them. This type of family pattern has existed since the days of slavery when the mother was the dominant and most stable element in the Negro family. Even after emancipation, which resulted in a general loosening of social bonds, the Negro mother continued in her accustomed role unless perchance the father acquired some interest in his family. The high rate of illegitimacy among southern Negroes represents family

[3]   A detailed discussion of these four types may be found in the author's "Traditions and Patterns of Negro Family Life in the United States," in *Race and Culture Contacts*, E. B. Reuter (ed.) (New York, 1934), pp. 191–207.

mores and folkways that have their roots in a natural maternal family organization that flourished during slavery.

The second type of family pattern shows many of the characteristics of the traditional family pattern of the American whites. In fact, the histories of the families of this type provide the source materials for studying the genesis of the traditional family type. It is possible to trace in the histories of some Negro families the actual process whereby the father's interest in the family became consolidated with the common interests of the various members of the family group of which he was the recognized head. In some cases traditions in these families go back to the time when the family was still in slavery. Where conditions were favorable to stable family life, the father's interest in his family was often bound up with his status among the slaves, as well as his trusted position in relation to the whites. The moralization of his behavior was further facilitated by incorporation into the household and church of his master or the Negro's own church. Under such circumstances the transition from serfdom to freedom did not result in a breakdown of family relations. In fact, when the father began working as a free man his authority was undisputed in his family. It has been upon such families that the development of the race as a whole in respect to character and culture has depended.

The third type of family pattern is sharply differentiated in regard to social heritage from the great mass of the Negro population. These families originated in the communities of free Negroes, usually of white and Negro and sometimes Indian ancestry, that existed in various parts of the country during pre-Civil War times. Many of these families not only achieved stability but also assumed an institutional character. The founder of these families inherited in some cases wealth from their white ancestors and generally showed the advantages of educational opportunities and white contacts. The families were as a rule patriarchal in organization with the female members playing roles similar to those of the slave-holding class in the ante-bellum South. Pride in white ancestry exercised considerable influence on their conception of themselves and their role in relation to the Negroes of unmixed blood and of slave origin. Many of the old established families in the North sprang from this group, families which were often forced to migrate before as well as after the Civil War in order to maintain their self-respect and secure advantages for their children.

We come finally to the fourth class of families who have been relatively isolated from the main currents of Negro life. These families originated in isolated communities of persons of Negro, white and Indian ancestry, and branches and remnants of these families may still be found in these communities, which are located in Alabama, North Carolina, Ohio, New Jersey, and New York. They are not a homogeneous group but are classified together because they show certain common characteristics. Usually they regard themselves as a distinct race from the Negroes and show in their behavior the clannishness of an isolated group. Their family organization is sternly patriarchal and is usually closely tied up with the religious organization of the community. Negro families that have their roots in such communities generally show in their behavior the influence of their peculiar cultural heritage.

II

Before considering the significance of these various patterns of family life in the accommodations which the Negro family has made to the urban environment, let us turn our attention to the sex behavior and familial life of the thousands of solitary men and women who have found their way into the towns and cities of the North and South. It is necessary to distinguish this group from the great body of black migrants, because their attitudes towards sex and family life have resulted from their mobility and emancipation from the most elementary forms of social control. Such a group of men and women have formed a part of the Negro population since the confusion and disorder following the Civil War. Although after emancipation the great mass of the Negro population settled down under a modified form of the plantation system, a fairly large number of Negro men and to a less extent Negro women continued to wander about in search of work and new experience. The size and character of this migratory element has been continually affected by the condition of southern agriculture and industry. On the other hand, when mass migrations were set in motion by demands of northern industries during and following the World War, many unattached men and women were among the migrants.

When the present economic crisis disrupted the economic life of the rural South, as well as that of industrial areas, the number of these unattached migrants was greatly augmented. A study by the Works Progress Administration showed that for the country as a whole, unattached Negro transients constituted 7 to 12 per cent of the total during the nine-month period August 1934 through April 1935.[4] In Chicago, during the first six months of 1934, 1,712 of the 10,962 unattached persons registered with the Cook County Bureau for Transients were Negro men and women. In the Harlem area of New York City, during the period from December 1931 to January 1936, there were 7,560 unattached Negro men registered with the Emergency Relief Bureau.[5] However, these figures include only those unattached Negro men and women who have sought relief; they leave out of account the thousands of roving men and homeless women who support themselves by both lawful and unlawful means.

Although we cannot describe in detail the various types of sexual unions which these migratory men and women form in the course of their wanderings from city to city, we may safely draw some conclusions concerning the general character of their sex behavior and mating. In a sense, one may say that the "Blues," those distinctive creations of the black troubadours in our industrial civilization, eqitomize the sex and family behavior of this class. In these songs the homeless, wandering, intermittent black workers sing of their disappointments and disillusionment in the city. An oft-repeated cause of this disillusionment is the uncertainty and instability of romantic love, if one might apply the term to the emotions of these migratory men and women. Yet, in a very real sense, one might say that in these songs one can discover the origin of romantic sentiments among the great masses of the Negro population. These songs record the spontaneous responses of strange

[4] *The Transient Unemployed*, Research Monograph III (Washington, 1935), p. 33.
[5] From the records of the Unattached and Transient Division.

men and women to each other in an unfamiliar environment. More important still, they reveal an awakening imagination that furnishes a sharp contract to the unromantic matings of Negroes in the isolated peasant communities of the rural South.

It is not our purpose to give the impression that the "Blues" furnish historical data on the sex and familial behavior of this migratory group. Through life history documents we have been able to distill from these songs their true significance. We find that in many cases these men begin their migratory careers by going first to nearby sawmills or turpentine camps, in order to supplement the landlord's allowances to their families. In fact, if one goes to one of the "quarters" near a sawmill in the South, one may find these foot-loose men and women living out the stories of their loves and disappointments which have become fixed in the "Blues." On the whole, their sexual unions and matings are characterized by impulsive behavior. However, just as their natural impulses urge them to all forms of anti-social behavior, spontaneous sympathy and tender emotions create the temporary unions which these men and women often form. In this connection one should not overlook the fact that a recurring theme of these songs is the longing for the intimate association of kinfolk, or wife and children, who have been left behind. Although the temporary unions which these men and women form are often characterized by fighting and quarreling, they supply a need which these wanderers feel for warm and intimate human association.

If the sawmill closes or the man feels the "itch" to travel, or some "Black Ulysses" from the outside world lures him by stories of a more exciting existence or a tale of fabulous wages in a nearby city, he takes to the road. In some cases, the girl may follow to the next city; but in the end she loses her temporary lover. During the course of their wanderings, these men may pick up lonely Negro women in domestic service who gratify their sexual longings and provide them with temporary lodging and food. While these men are acquiring sophistication in the ways of the city, they are becoming thoroughly individuated men. By the time they reach Chicago, Detroit, or New York, they have learned how to survive without support. Girls who have run away from their homes in the South and sought adventure in these large cities often become, in spite of their callousness and boasted toughness, the tools of these men. However, these same women sometimes during their sentimental reflections disclose a hidden longing for the security and affection of their families, or betray an abiding attachment to an illegitmate child that they have left with a parent or relative during their wanderings.

III

From this migratory group of men and women, we turn now to the great mass of the Negro migrants who have come to the city in family groups or in remnants of family groups. This movement was at its peak during the World War when not only whole families but entire communities picked up their meagre possessions and joined the flight from the semifeudal conditions of the South to the modern industrial centers of the North. One can get some notion of the volume of the tide of black humanity that overwhelmed the comparatively small Negro communities in northern cities by considering the increases in the Negro population of the four principal cities to which these migrants were attracted. Between 1910 and 1920, the Negro population of Detroit increased 611.13 per cent; that of Chicago 148.2 per cent; that of the Borough of Manhattan in New York City 80.3 per cent; and that of Philadelphia 58.9 per cent. The immediate effect of the inundation of Negro communities in northern cities was conflict with the white population in contiguous areas. However, the subsequent expansion of the Negro communities proceeded in accordance with the natural growth of these cities.

What especially interests us in regard to the expansion of these Negro communities is that, through selection, various elements of the population have become segregated, thus causing the spatial organization of these communities to reflect their economic and cultural organization. In the case of Chicago, it was possible to divide the Negro community into seven zones of about a mile in length indicating its southward expansion along and parallel to one of the arterial highways radiating from the center of the city.[6] The selection which had taken place during the expansion of the Negro population was indicated by the decline in the percentage of southern-born Negroes and illiteracy, the decrease in the proportion of persons engaged in unskilled labor and domestic service and the percentage of women employed, and a corresponding increase in the percentage of mulattoes in the population and of persons in professional and public service in the successive zones. A similar selection was found in the Harlem Negro community in New York City. However, whereas the Chicago Negro community in its expansion has cut across the concentric zones of the larger community and shows the impress of the larger community, the Harlem Negro community has expanded radially from the area where Negroes first settled and has assumed the same pattern of zones as a self-contained city.[7]

When the Negro family is studied in relation to the economic and cultural organization of these communities, we are able to obtain a rough measure, at least, of the Negro's success in the struggle to support himself or family and attain a normal family life. Therefore, let us consider first the question of family dependency. From the records of the United Charities it appears that under normal conditions between eight and nine per cent of the families in the poorer areas of Chicago are dependent upon charity. However, the rate of family dependency showed a progressive decline in the successive zones marking the expansion of the community. In the seventh zone only one per cent of the families were dependent.[8] Although we do not possess comparable data for Harlem, we know that prior to the crash in 1929 between 25 and 30 per cent of the "under care" families handled by the Charity Organization Society in an area in New York City including a part of Harlem were

[6]   See the author's *The Negro Family in Chicago* (Chicago, 1932), chap. 6, for detailed information on the character of these zones as well as the method used in defining them.
[7]   See the author's article, "Negro Harlem: An Ecological Study," *American Journal of Sociology*, July 1937.
[8]   See *The Negro Family in Chicago*, pp. 150 ff.

Negro cases. The present economic crisis has tended to emphasize the precarious economic situation of a large percentage of Negro families in our cities. According to the 1933 report of the Federal Emergency Relief Administration, as high as 85 per cent of the Negro families in some cities were receiving relief. The percentage of Negro families receiving relief was highest in such highly industrialized areas as Toledo, Akron, and Pittsburgh, where large numbers of Negroes are employed in unskilled labor; the percentage in Chicago and New York was around 46 per cent and 30 per cent, respectively.

In the case of the Harlem community, we are able to study the incidence of relief in relation to the spatial organization of the Negro area. During the first week of September 1935, there were 24,292 Negro families on Home Relief, this being 43.2 per cent of the 56,137 Negro families in this area. However, the incidence of relief varied considerably in the zones marking the outward expansion of the community from its center. The percentage of families receiving relief declined rapidly from 70.9 per cent in the central zone to 28.4 per cent in the outermost zone. This is of special interest because, although in some areas of the peripheral zone were found some of the poorest Negro families in the entire community, the incidence in these areas did not vary greatly from the average for the zone as a whole. The only explanation that occurs to us is that the family groups that tended to be segregated in the peripheral zones were better able to meet collectively the economic crisis than the single, unattached, separated and widowed men and women who tended to congregate in the center of the community. This selection was shown in the marital status of the population in the various zones. The percentage of single men declined in the successive zones outward from 42.6 to 31.1 per cent and that of single women from 30.9 to 23.5 per cent. On the other hand, the proportion of men and women married increased from about 50 per cent each to 64 per cent for the men and to 60 per cent for the women.[9] A similar tendency was discovered in the case of the Negro community in Chicago.[10]

9   See "Negro Harlem: An Ecological Study."
10   See *The Negro Family in Chicago*, chap. 7.

The selection and segregation of the population with reference to marital status coincides with other processes of organization and disorganization of Negro family life in the city. In Chicago, home ownership was closely correlated with family stability, whereas, in Harlem, with its apartments and multiple dwellings, it was not significant. Similarly, the relationship between family organization and disorganization and the spatial organization of the Negro community was more evident in Chicago with its relatively simple pattern than in Harlem with its more complex pattern. For example, the desertion and non-support rates declined regularly from two and a half per cent of the total families in the poorer zone near the Chicago loop to less than one half of one per cent in the outermost zone. Although a similar tendency in regard to desertions was discernible in the Harlem Negro community, the various zones did not show the same degree of cultural homogeneity as the Chicago zones. Thus, in Chicago the delinquency rate declined from 42.8 per cent in the zone of considerable family and community disorganization near the center of the city to 1.4 per cent in the outermost zone of stable family life and home ownership. However, in Harlem, no such decline in the successive zones of population expansion was discernible in regard to juvenile delinquency. It would require a more intimate study of the character and culture of the various zones in order to determine the relationship between community factors and juvenile delinquency. Nevertheless, it is apparent that as a result of competition, various elements of the Negro population in both cities are selected and segregated in a way which enables the student to get some measure of the processes of organization and disorganization.

This is seen most clearly in regard to the question of the survival of the Negro in the city. The low fertility of Negro women in cities has been shown in a number of studies. According to Thompson and Whelpton, Negroes in large cities, including Chicago and New York, "were not maintaining their numbers on a permanent basis in either 1920 or 1928."[11] Lately, Clyde Kiser has found that the fertility of Negro women in a health area in New

[11]   Warren S. Thompson and P. K. Whelpton, *Population Trends in the United States* (New York, 1933), p. 280.

York was lower than that of white women of similar and higher occupational status in several urban communities.[12] However, if we study the fertility of Negro women in relation to the organization of the Negro community, some important facts are revealed. For example, in Chicago in 1920, the highest ratio of children under five to women of child-bearing age, i.e., 15 to 44, was found in the two peripheral zones, or the areas of stable family life and home ownership. The ratio was higher in these zones than in the zones where the poorer migrant families settled and almost twice as high as the ratio in the bright light area with its cabarets, saloons, and houses of prostitution.[13]

Harlem offers even more striking evidence of the influence of selective factors on the survival of the Negro in the city. In 1920, the ratio of children under 5 to 1,000 women 20 to 44 years of age increased in the successive zones outward from the center of the community from 109 in the first to 274 in the fifth, with a slight variation in the fourth. However, in 1930, the ratio of children increased regularly from 115 in the first to 462 in the outermost zone. This latter figure is about the same as the ratio in towns with from 2,500 to 10,000 population. Differential survival rates were revealed also in the ratio of deaths to births in 1930 in the various zones. In the central zone, the population was dying out, there being 112 deaths to each 100 births. However, the ratio of deaths to births declined in the successive zones until it reached less than 50 to 100 in the areas near the periphery of the community. Looking at the situation from the standpoint of births alone, we find that in 1930 there was one child born to each 25 women, 20 to 44 years of age, in the central zone. From this zone outward, the number of women of child-bearing age per child born declined regularly until it reached eight in the outermost zone. Thus the survival of the Negro in the city seems to be influenced by the same selective factors which determine the spatial organization and social structure of the Negro community.

Let us return now to the four traditional patterns of family life

[12]   Clyde V. Kiser, "Fertility of Harlem Negroes," *The Milbank Memorial Fund Quarterly*, 13 (July, 1935) :273–85.
[13]   See *The Negro Family in Chicago*, pp. 136–44.

described above and consider them in relation to the selective process at work in these communities. The first or maternal type of family offers little resistance to the disintegrating forces in the urban environment. Because of their poverty, these families are forced to seek homes in the poorer sections of the Negro community. Moreover, since these families are supported solely by the mother, who is generally employed in domestic service or at unskilled labor, they easily slip into ranks of those dependent upon charity. The children suffer not only for the lack of parental control but are subjected to the vicious environment of disorganized areas. Consequently, many of the boys become members of delinquent gangs, while the girls are guilty of sex delinquency, which often leads to unmarried motherhood.

In these same areas may be found the poorer families of the paternal type. In these families, as well as those of the maternal type, a large percentage of the mothers are forced to be wage earners. Whether they maintain their paternal organization depends upon a number of factors, including the vitality of family traditions, the security and regularity of employment of the father, the development of common interests, and the degree to which these families are integrated into the institutions of the Negro community. But it often happens that the father's interest in his family rests upon some immediate interest, or is based upon mere sympathy and habit. Under such circumstances, if the father loses his job or if he develops new interests in the urban environment that are antagonistic to the common interests of his family, he may easily join the ranks of the large number of Negro deserters. In this connection, it should be pointed out that the families inhabiting these blighted areas are free from the censure of public opinion, as well as other types of communal control. On the other hand, those families that succeed in maintaining a community of interest or develop new ambitions for their children generally move, if their economic resources permit, towards the periphery of the Negro community. Their movement at first may be just beyond the area of extreme deterioration and poverty.

It may take another generation for these families to reach the periphery of the Negro community where one finds the families of the third type—those having a background of several generations of stable family life and firmly rooted traditions. It was old mulatto families of the third type who sometimes fled before the onrush of the uncouth Negroes from the South to areas beyond the borders of the Negro community. But as a rule they sought the periphery of the Negro community as is shown in the case of the seventh zone in Chicago, where half of the inhabitants were mulattoes.[14] Then, too, sometimes these old established families have isolated themselves and have regarded with mixed feelings of contempt and envy the rise of the ambitious elements in the lower and, on the whole, darker elements in the Negro population. But, just as in the rigorous competitive life of the northern city, the poor and illiterate Negroes with no other resources but their folk culture are ground down by disease, vice, and poverty, those possessing intelligence and skill and a fund of family traditions find a chance to rise beyond the caste restrictions of the South. Thus, there has come into existence in these cities a fairly large middle-class element comprised of the more ambitious elements of the second type of families and representatives of the third type with a few descendants of the fourth type of families. Their pattern of family life approaches that of the white middle class. It is the emergence of this class which accounts largely for those orderly and stable areas on the periphery of the Negro communities in our cities. In between such areas and the areas of extreme deterioration where family disorganization is highest, there are areas of a mixed character in which the more stable and better paid industrial workers find homes.

In view of the process described here, it is not surprising that, in the area occupied by the middle-class families, there may be on the average more children, as for example in Chicago, than in the areas of extreme poverty and family disorganization. In the case of the Harlem community which resembles in its spatial organization a self-contained city, relatively large family groups of working-class as well as middle-class status tend to become segregated on

[14]   See *The Negro Family in Chicago*, pp. 101–105.

the periphery, though they occupy different areas. In the center of the Harlem community, which is essentially a non-family area, one may find the emancipated from all classes and elements.

IV

Our discussion points to a number of conclusions which may be stated briefly as follows. First, it seems inevitable that, as long as the bankrupt and semifeudal agricultural system in the South continues to throw off men and women who lose the restraints imposed by a simple folk culture, there will be a class of roving Negroes who will live a lawless sex and quasi-family life. Secondly, the great mass of migrants who, as a rule, manage to preserve remnants of their family organization must face in the competitive life of the city a severe struggle for survival and, at the same time, be subjected to the disintegrating forces in the urban environment. The fate and fortunes of these families will depend upon both their economic and their cultural resources. Many of the poorer families that are held together solely by the affectional ties between mother and children, will be ground down by poverty and the children will be scattered and are likely to become delinquent. Those families in which the father's interest rests upon no firmer basis than some passing attachment, or mere sympathy and habit, may suffer a similar fate. But, if such families succeed in becoming integrated into the institutional life of the community and have sufficient income to avoid dependence upon charity, they may achieve a fair degree of stabilization. On the other hand, the economically better situated families, in which the father's interest is supported by tradition and tied up with the common interests of the family, may resist the disintegrating effects of the city, and some of the children will enter the middle class. The traditions of these families will become merged with the traditions of mulatto families, many of free origin, who once formed an upper social class. The economic and cultural organization of the Negro community which emerges as the result of competition indicates the selective influence of the urban environment on these various family heritages.

11

URBANIZATION AND ITS EFFECTS UPON THE TASK OF NATION-BUILDING IN AFRICA SOUTH OF THE SAHARA

1961

Introduction

THE IMPORTANT role of cities in nation building has generally been recognized. According to Spengler, "nations are *the true city-building peoples*. In the strongholds they arose, with the cities they ripen to the full height of their world-consciousness, and in the world-cities they dissolve."[1] In his latest book, Mumford points out that the Roman Empire was "the product of a single expanding urban power-center" and was itself " a vast city-building enterprise."[2] In Africa cities have played a similar role in nation building and empires as in other parts of the world.[3] The kingdoms

---

Reprinted from the *Journal of Negro Education*, 30 (Summer, 1961): 214–22.

[1]   Oswald Spengler, *The Decline of the West* (New York: Alfred A. Knopf, 1939), 2:171.
[2]   Lewis Mumford, *The City in History* (New York: Harcourt, Brace and World, 1961), p. 205.
[3]   See Basil Davidson, *The Lost Cities of Africa* (Boston: Little, Brown and Co., 1959).

of the Old Sudan—Ghana, Mali, and Songhay—were all the result of expanding urban power centers which, because of their superior iron technology, were able to control the flow of gold to the Mediterranean. Despite the distortions of the history of Africa by Europeans, the early Portuguese explorers reported that they found Benin, the capital of the city-state of the same name, prosperous, peaceful and orderly and devoted to the working of metals and wood.[4] The ruins of Zimbabwe are the mute evidence of a vast tribal-feudal kingdom in Southern Rhodesia.

Nature and Extent of Urbanization

There can be no question concerning the existence of cities in Africa before the coming of the European.[5] But we are not interested in the role of these cities in nation building. Although some of the African cities played some role in the slave trade, they finally succumbed in the devastation of Africa, both demographic and social, resulting from the slave trade. We are interested in the role of the new cities of Africa—the cities which are the product of the impact of industrialization and urbanization upon the traditional social organization and culture of Africa. It should be made clear here that the new cities of Africa are different from the cities which existed before the coming of the Europeans. I need only to repeat here what I have written in a previous article on the important difference between the preindustrial cities and the new cities of Africa.[6]

The preindustrial African city was a market place and the seat of feudal power, and often the center of a religious cult. It lacked the dynamism of the modern industrial city, a fact which is of primary importance in considering urbanization in relation to social change in Africa. The absence of the dynamic quality, which is characteristic of the modern industrial city, is manifested in the relationship of men

---

[4]   See *ibid.*, pp. 134 ff.

[5]   William Bascom, "Urbanization Among the Yoruba," *The American Journal of Sociology*, 60 (March, 1955) :446–54.

[6]   "Urbanization and Social Change in Africa," *AIS Review*, 3 (Winter, 1959) :3–9.

and institutions to the environment, in the organization of its economic life, and in the type of social organization which was adequate for a collective life. In the preindustrial city there was no specialization in land usage, and land had no exchange value in the market. There was no orderly arrangement of dwellings and no provisions for sanitation. People made their way through the narrow streets on foot or on beasts, and men as well as beasts provided the sole means of transporting goods. The economic life of the preindustrial city was in the hands of craftsmen who were kinsmen and organized in guilds. In fact, the important role of the guilds in the preindustrial city provides a clue to the nature of the social organization of these urban agglomerations. Kinship provided the basis of the social organization and played the most important role in the social stratification and in the power structure. The governing élite consisted of kinship groups whose monopoly of power was often partly maintained by the fact that they were literate and thus had a knowledge of the sacred texts of the cult which gave cohesion to urban life.

The emergence of modern industrial cities in Africa is the result of the impact of European technology and science. European technology has both transformed the physical and ecological organization of the preindustrial cities and given birth to new modern industrial cities. As a consequence there has been a specialization of land usage and land has acquired an economic value. New types of building structures have appeared and even the location as well as the construction of dwelling houses fits into the pattern of the economy of the industrial cities. Moreover, the ecology of the modern industrial city as contrasted with the preindustrial city is indicated in the laying out of streets according to some rational plan and the introduction of sanitary arrangements. All of this tends to encourage a rationalization and secularization of life which will become apparent when we consider the new type of social organization which has emerged in response to the new modes of production and consumption.

In the modern industrial city in Africa, men do not depend for a living upon their services to some feudal lord or upon their skill altogether to transform the raw materials from the surrounding area into finished goods for the local market. In West Africa, for example, the concentration of wage-earners in cities has been about the ports which provide an outlet for raw materials to the industrialized nations. More than a half million Africans have been drawn out of tribal communities to live under urban conditions in the Belgian Congo where western enterprise has been characterized by mining and large plantations. As the result of the industrial revolution in the Union of South Africa more than 25 per cent of the Bantu are in the cities of the Union. Although the introduction of cash crops and scientific agriculture is bringing about social changes in Africa, it is rather in the urban areas, brought into existence by industrialization, that the most important social changes are occurring. In these cities there is a division of labor which did not exist in the traditional African societies or in the pre-industrial cities. The new division of labor is partly the result of the skills which are required by the introduction of European technology and partly the result of the secondary industries which have come into existence to supply the new wants and needs of urbanized Africans. It is also in the cities that the social consequences of a money economy are most clearly revealed. The money economy has not only introduced a new set of evaluations but it has also tended to dissolve or secularize the social bonds of the traditional society.[7]

Our main task, then, is to analyze the social processes involved in urbanization in order to determine how they contribute to nation building.[8] It will help the reader to understand the importance of the new cities if we indicate the extent of urbanization in Africa, though it should be kept in mind that some of these new cities of Africa have grown up upon the foundation of older cities. Nonetheless, as I have shown, cities are new types of social organization and this fact is important for an analysis.

There are 35 cities in Africa South of the Sahara with a population of 100,000 or more. It is natural that the largest number of such cities in any single country would be in the Union of South Africa, which is the most highly industrialized area in Africa. In the Union there are ten cities with a 100,000 or more population, with Johannesburg leading with over 1,000,000 and Capetown with over 700,000 and Durban with over 600,000.

The country with the next largest number of cities with 100,000 or more population is Nigeria with seven such cities. The largest

[7]   *Ibid.*, pp. 3–5.

[8]   For the social processes involved in urbanization in West Africa, see Kenneth Little, "West African Urbanization as a Social Process," *Cahiers d'Etudes Africaines*, no. 3 (October, 1960), pp. 90–102.

of these cities is Ibadan with a population of nearly 500,000. The modern city of Ibadan is emerging from the traditional city which was comprised of enclaves of communities of kinship groups. On the other hand, Lagos, with a population of 350,000, is an outgrowth of the impact of Western industry and commerce.

Accra, one of the four cities of 100,000 population or more in Ghana, with nearly 400,000 owes its development along with Sekondi-Takoradi to industry and commerce.

There are no cities of 100,000 or more population in Northern Rhodesia but in Southern Rhodesia there are two cities in this category, Bulawayo with nearly 200,000 and Salisbury with nearly 300,000 population.

There are two cities also in the Belgian Congo in this category, Leopoldville with nearly 400,000 population and Elizabethville with nearly 200,000 population.

The remaining ten cities with 100,000 or more population include Luanda, Angola, with 190,000; Nairobi with 230,000 and Mombassa with 150,000 in Kenya; Abijan, Ivory Coast, with 127,-000; Lorenco Marques, 100,000, Mozambique; Bamako, 168,000, in Republic of Mali; Brazzaville, 100,000, Congo Republic; Dakar, 250,000, Senegal; Omdurman, 114,000, in Sudan; and Dar es-Salaam, 130,000 in Tanganyika.

Urbanization and Nation-Building

Having acquired some idea of the nature and extent of urbanization in Africa, we are prepared to consider specifically the manner in which the social processes involved in urbanization contribute to nation building. We shall begin with the city as a physical mechanism from which the new means of transportation and communication radiate. A glance at a map of Africa will show to what extent the railways which supplanted the waterways as the main means of access to the interior radiate from the developing cities of Africa.[9] Today, however, the new cities are not only railway terminals but are also the location of airfields, since trans-

[9]   See map opposite p. 1598 in Lord Hailey, *An African Survey*, rev. ed. (New York: Oxford University Press, 1957).

portation by air has become the chief means of access to all parts of Africa. As centers of new means of transportation and communication, these cities are also playing an important role in providing the economic basis of national integration.

As we have seen, in West Africa the cities with their concentrations of wage-earning populations have grown up around the ports.[10] As the result of mining and commerce and as administrative centers, the older cities are not only being transformed physically but, what is more important, as centers of a new economic life, the cities have repercussions upon the economic life of the hinterland. One measure of the ever widening influence of the new economy which is centered in cities may be found in the enlargement of the money economy.[11] In order to maintain the urban concentrations of wage-earning populations, a reorganization of indigenous agricultural production has become necessary, and there has been a commercialization of agriculture generally in order to enable cities to perform their specialized function in relation to the outside world.

The new African cities, like the cities of the Western world, are characterized by their heterogeneous population. By heterogeneous populations we mean that people of different racial and cultural backgrounds are drawn into the cities. In the case of African cities it is not so much a question of different races but of peoples drawn from different tribal or cultural backgrounds. In his survey of Sekondi-Takoradi, Busia states that 62 tribal divisions, including Europeans and other foreigners as one tribal division, are represented in that city.[12] Other cities of Africa, more especially the new cities, exhibit a similar ethnic and tribal heterogeneity. In the traditional cities the section settled by the newer ethnic and tribal elements are sometimes marked off from the older

[10]   See Daryll Forde, "Introductory Survey" in *Social Implications of Industrialization and Urbanization in Africa South of the Sahara* (Paris: UNESCO, 1956), pp. 26–27.
[11]   *Enlargement of the Exchange Economy in Tropical Africa* (UNESCO, 1954).
[12]   K. A. Busia, *Report on a Social Survey of Sekondi-Takoradi* (London: Crown Agents for the Colonies, 1951), p. 3.

sections inhabited by lineage or kinship groups.[13] The increasing heterogeneity of urban centers is very important in nation building because only as the Africans escape from their lineage or kinship attachments and become free of tribal particularisms can they develop a national consciousness. For example, as long as an African thinks of himself as a Yoruba or an Ibo or a Hausa and maintains his loyalty to one or the other of these people it will be impossible for a Nigerian nation to develop. As Coleman has pointed out, it is the stranger sectors of the cities of Nigeria that have become centers of nationalist activity, while the attachment of Africans to lineage groups in the tradition-bound older centers of the cities has been an obstacle to the emergence of a nationalist outlook.[14]

The most powerful factor in the new urban environment that is bringing about a dissolution of the traditional kinship ties and tribal loyalties is the new division of labor. In the traditional social organization and culture, the division of labor was determined mainly by sex and age. Certain occupations were limited to particular lineages and the traditional crafts were passed on from father to son. In the new industries, on the other had, men are recruited who have never been craftsmen and they belong to different lineages. There is no blood tie between men who engage in the various new occupations, and each man works as an individual, receiving money in return for his labor.

The new division of labor in the urban areas does not result simply in the atomization of African life. In the Yoruba towns, for example, new guilds were formed to perform many of the same functions as the traditional guilds, but with the important difference that the labor group was no longer composed of father and sons but of a master and journeymen and apprentices.[15] In other words, the workers were united on the basis of common interests. This leads us to emphasize a very important point in regard to the role of the city in nation building. New nations are not being

13   See James S. Coleman, *Nigeria: Background to Nationalism* (Berkeley: University of California Press, 1958), pp. 78–79.
14   *Ibid.*, p. 79.
15   Peter Lloyd, "Craft Organization in Yoruba Towns," *Africa*, 23 (January, 1953):30–44.

formed out of uprooted men and women without any common interests and social ties. They are being formed out of the new forms of associated life which are coming into existence. These new forms of social life will provide the social fabric of the new nations and thus make national integration possible.

As in the case of the new guilds in the Yoruba towns, the new forms of social life will embody some of the traditional culture and undertake to perform many of the traditional functions. The influence of the traditional social organization and traditional culture is apparent in the tribal associations which are formed in cities. These tribal associations, according to Busia, were concerned with economic as well as social obligations of kinship.[16] They represent a new form of mutual aid in the city, providing for assistance for funerals, marriages, and divorces. Little, in his studies of social change in West Africa, has noted similar developments in other areas.[17] Since these tribal associations have become the focus of political interests and political loyalties, Busia regards them as opposed to the development of a true civic spirit. If this were the entire story they would be a negative force in nation building.

But Wallerstein sees these ethnic associations as making a positive contribution to national integration in West Africa.[18] His position is that in the urban environment there is a tendency for African social life to be disorganized and that individuals become atomized. The first step in the reintegration of urbanized Africans into new social groupings and a new social order is the formation of these new ethnic or tribal associations. As he shows, these tribal or ethnic associations in the cities are in fact new social formations which are designed to meet the new needs of urban living. Moreover, to quote him, "in a modern nation-state, loyalties to ethnic groups interfere less with national integration than loyalties to the extended family."[19] The three other principal ways, according to Wallerstein, in which ethnic groups aid national integration are

[16]   Busia, *op. cit.*, p. 73.
[17]   Kenneth Little, "The Study of 'Social Change' in British West Africa," *Africa*, 23 (1953) : 274–84.
[18]   See I. Wallerstein, "Ethnicity and National Integration in West Africa," *Cahiers d'Etudes Africaines* (October, 1960), pp. 129–39.
[19]   *Ibid.*, p. 134.

the resocialization of the African which we have mentioned; the maintenance of a fluid class system concerning which we shall have something to say; and as an outlet for political tensions until the new nation has secured the full loyalty of its citizens.[20]

The ethnic or tribal associations which are formed in the urban environment represent, then, the first step in the creation of new forms of social life. However, because of the very nature of urban life, they cannot continue long to provide all the forms of organized social life which living in cities requires. Balandier in his study of Brazzaville has emphasized the fact that ethnic ties and the kinship bonds can only provide a temporary solution of the needs of the urban environment.[21] The new types of groupings in the city of Brazzaville included recreational associations which played an important role in orienting the African to the new type of social organization which is found in the city. There were also women's organizations, including even those of women who were engaged in prostitution, a new phenomenon in African life. This only underscored the extent to which the city was giving birth to a new organization of African society. However, the most important associations were those which were concerned with the economic life of the people in the city, such as savings associations and associations of workers.

In fact, it is the new economic life centered in the cities that is bringing about the most fundamental reorganization of African society and is thereby laying the foundation for national states. The manner in which fundamental changes in the constitution of African society is being accomplished has been made the subject of a study of a city in the copperbelt in Northern Rhodesia.[22] The

---

[20]   Thomas Hodgkin, *Nationalism in Colonial Africa* (London: Frederick Muller, Ltd., 1956), p. 86, points out three ways in which tribal associations contribute to the development of African nationalism: (1) by providing a network of communications under African control through which ideas can be diffused from the great towns to the bush; (2) through keeping alive African culture; and (3) by assisting in the evolution of an African elite.

[21]   Georges Balandier, *Sociologie des Brazzavilles Noires* (Paris: Librairie Armand Colin, 1955), p. 135.

[22]   A. L. Epstein, *Politics in an Urban African Community* (Manchester: University of Manchester Press, 1958).

author of this study points out in the introduction that "In a copperbelt town, the mine itself, the local Municipal Council, and the Office of the District Commissioner provide between them the fixed points in the social framework."[23] The Europeans in control of the mine were concerned with the problem of maintaining order and discipline among its African laborers. The Municipal Council, which was composed of Europeans, represented the European community. It operated on the assumption that the African worker would not become a permanent resident of the town. However, an African community did emerge in the town and this created a new problem of urban administration within the African community. Concerning the development of the African community, Epstein writes: ". . . forces were already at work making for social and economic differentiation amongst African urban dwellers. Africans in the towns were now beginning to group themselves, and thus distinguish themselves from their fellows in terms of their relative skills, their degree of education, and their general social values. Gradually new associations came into being to express these different interests and clashed for power within the existing administrative order."[24]

The District Commissioner, who functioned originally among the non-urbanized Africans and whose general orientation was towards the traditional culture of the African, formed for a time a connecting link between the Africans and the Municipal Council and the mines. But his position was precarious since he was divested of his traditional functions in both the urban area and the mining community. Moreover, rioting on the part of the African workers in 1935 and the strike on the part of African workers which followed a strike on the part of European workers in 1940 only tended to emphasize the fact that his traditional functions had no relation to the changing conditions of African life.

In dealing with the African workers the mining administration and the municipal authorities had set up a system of Elders or Tribal Representatives. At the time this seemed to be a logical and realistic approach to the problem of maintaining order and discipline since it seemed to take account of the traditional social

23   *Ibid.*, p. xiv.
24   *Ibid.*, p. xv.

organization and culture of the African workers. But the system of appointing Tribal Representatives turned out to be inadequate to deal with the relations of the African workers in the mining area or with their changing economic status in the African community. They could not represent effectively the workers in matters concerning wages and working conditions before the European Administration in the mine. A Boss Boys' Committee composed of Africans who had charge of groups of African laborers, which came into existence, provided a more effective system of representation. Likewise in the town itself similar changes were occurring. At first an Urban Advisory Council consisting of Tribal Elders who were appointed to represent the interests of the Africans was set up.[25] But soon the Africans organized their own welfare and recreational associations to represent their interests.

The development of welfare societies in the town and the organization of the workers in the mining location along occupational lines were indicative of important changes which were occurring in social organization of African life. In the town the representatives of the various occupations and professions who were forming the welfare societies "were actively pressing forward into a new form of society where clan affiliation or attachment to village headman and chief were no longer mechanisms of primary significance in ordering social relations."[26] It marked the defeat and disappearance of Tribal Representatives as the Africans prepared to participate in the political life of the new industrial society while "their final defeat and abolition on the mines came with the emergence of the African Mine Workers' Union."[27]

The change in social organization which we have just described suggests an important role of urbanization in nation building in Africa, namely, the creation of a new system of social stratification.

[25]   We cannot treat in this paper the peculiar conditions in the cities of the Union of South Africa where the system of native advisory boards proved ineffective and there has been an attempt on the part of the government to maintain tribal separateness and tribal particularisms by segregating the Africans according to ethnic or tribal origins. See South African Institute of Race Relations, *The Urban African in Local Government* (Johannesburg, 1960).

[26]   Epstein, *op. cit.*, p. 84.

[27]   *Ibid.*, p. 85.

The new system of social stratification results from the new occupational specialization and division of labor in the city. It cuts across traditional kinship loyalties and tribal identifications. The new social stratification is based upon one's education, which generally means a Western education, one's income and occupation, and the role which one plays in the new social organization in the city. In fact, in the changing conditions of urban life two systems of social hierarchies may coexist. The old scale of prestige values which determined the social status of Africans in the traditional society may continue along with the prestige values which are attached to the new occupations. This has been revealed in studies which have been made of the changing scale of prestige values in African cities. But as the African populations of the cities become stabilized, there is abundant evidence that the new prestige values are supplanting the traditional prestige values and that social prestige and social status are being determined by the new social stratification of the African population. The leader in the labor organization, the leader in politics, or one who holds a high position in the African National Congress is supplanting the chief as the person possessing the greatest prestige in the eyes of the urbanized Africans. It might appear on the surface that the new social stratification of the African population in the new cities has introduced a cleavage among Africans which may be opposed to national integration. But a closer analysis of the situation indicates that the new system of stratification in cities is actually contributing to national integration. It is not only cutting across kinship loyalties and tribal provincialisms, but it is developing a community of interests and outlook among people beyond the limits of the city. If classes emerge in the new African nations similar to those in Europe and in the United States, they will undoubtedly create a horizontal cleavage in African societies but that will be different from the kinship and tribal loyalties which are opposed to the creation of national states. At the present time, however, the new strata that are emerging have not reached the stage where they are creating an obstacle to nation building.

The new stratification of the African cities has brought into existence an intellectual élite which is indicative of the special role of the intellectual life of the city in nation building. Most of the educational institutions, especially the institutions of higher education, have been located in the cities and there has been a tendency for the Western educated élite to settle in the cities where they could find an outlet for their special talents and abilities and engage in a way of life that was free from the controls of the traditional African society. In his study of Brazzaville, Balandier estimated that about ten per cent of the migrants came to the city in order to move up in the social scale and another ten per cent came there in order to find an escape from the requirements of the traditional society.[28] It has been the intellectual élite of the cities who have been the leaders of the nationalistic movements and the leaders of the political parties. Dr. Nkrumah left his native village where he had begun preparing to become a teacher and went to Accra to continue his studies. It seems very likely that the relatively large number of Ibos who have played a prominent role in the Nationalist movement in Nigeria is the result of the rapid urbanization of the Ibo peoples in the Eastern region and the large proportion of Ibos in the population of non-Ibo cities.[29]

The intellectual leaders who represent the mentality of the new cities of Africa are creating the new ideologies and the new culture of the nations which are coming into existence in Africa. They are the men who are creating the new literature of Africa. They are men who are writing the history of a people who have long been called by Europeans a people without a history. Some of the ideologies which they are creating is response to a need to rationalize and to justify the political awakening in Africa and the new political organization that is taking form. The political parties which these leaders are organizing throughout their lands are contributing to national integration. They are destroying the autonomy of chiefs and they are supplanting the kinship loyalties. However, within the political parties, as in the case of other new elements of social organization in nation building, there are conflicting loyalties.[30]

---

[28]   Balandier, *op. cit.*, pp. 41–42.

[29]   See Coleman, *op. cit.*, pp. 76–77.

[30]   A study in Ivory Coast has revealed that where local branches of a political party have become centers of vested interests associated with

But in the final analysis the success in building new nations in Africa will depend upon the extent to which the new social fabric which is being woven in the life of the new cities of Africa becomes the social fabric of the nations as a whole.

Conclusion

By the way of summary and conclusion, it is only necessary to point out that the new cities of Africa have the same influence in nation building as cities have had in other parts of the world. They are centers of the new type of economies which provide the necessary material basis for the integration of modern nation-states. It is in these new cities that a market economy based upon exchange and money is developing and transforming the economic life of the hinterland. Moreover, it is in these cities that a new social organization is coming into existence. This new social organization is supplanting the traditional social organization which rested principally upon kinship or the extended family and tribal loyalties. Whether the new types of associations are formed for economic or social or political purposes, they are enabling the African to escape from the barriers to a national consciousness found in the extended family and the tribal loyalties. An important phase of this social transformation is the emergence of a new class structure based upon the new occupations and division of labor in the cities. Finally, these new cities are the centers of a new intellectual or mental life which is important for nation building. It is in the cities that a new intellectual élite—artists and thinkers—has come into existence. These artists and thinkers are creating the new ideologies and the new African culture which with its base in the traditional culture of Africa is providing the soul of the new African nations.

---

tribal loyalties, the political party may become a barrier to national integration. See A. R. Zolberg, "Effets de la Structure d'un Parti Politique sur l'Integration Nationale," *Cahiers d'Etudes Africaines* (October, 1960), pp. 140–49.

IV. The Negro Family

12

THE NEGRO FAMILY
IN AMERICA

1948

THE EVOLUTION of the Negro family in the United States
has a special significance for the science of culture. Within the
short space of 150 years, the Negro family has telescoped the age-
long evolution of the human family.[1] On the basis of concrete
factual materials it is possible to trace the evolution of the Negro
family from its roots in human nature to a highly institutionalized
form of human association. During the course of its evolution, the
Negro family has been forced to adjust itself to different forms of
social organization and to the stresses and strains of modern civilization. In studying the adjustments which the Negro family has
made to these changes, it is possible to gain a clearer understanding
of the relation of human motivations to culture. Moreover, the evolution of Negro family life not only has provided additional evidence of the primary importance of the family in the transmission
of culture, but also has shown the role of the family in the building
of new cultures.

Under the Institution of Slavery

As a result of the manner in which the Negro was enslaved,
the Negro's African cultural heritage has had practically no effect

Reprinted from *The Family: Its Function and Destiny*, Revised Edition,
ed. Ruth Anshen (New York: Harper & Brothers, 1959), pp. 65–84, by
permission of Harper & Row, Publishers. Copyright 1949 by Harper &
Brothers; 1959 by Ruth Nanda Anshen.

[1]   See the writer's *The Negro Family in the United States* (Chicago:
University of Chicago Press, 1939).

on the evolution of his family life in the United States. The slave traders along the coast of Africa who were primarily interested in healthy young Negroes—generally males—had no regard for family relationships. In fact, the human cargo which they collected were the remnants of various tribes and clan organizations. The manner in which men and women were packed indiscriminately in slave ships during the Middle Passage tended to destroy social bonds and tribal distinctions. Then the process of "breaking" the Negroes into the slave system in the West Indies, where they often landed before shipment to the colonies and the United States, tended to efface the memories of their traditional culture. In the colonies and later in the southern United States, the slaves were widely scattered on comparatively small plantations where there was little opportunity to reknit social bonds or regenerate the African culture.

Doubtless memories of African culture regarding mating survived, but these memories became meaningless in the New World. The mating or sexual associations which Negroes formed on American soil were largely in response to their natural impulses and the conditions of the new environment. There was, first, a lack of females in the slave population until the 1830's, and this caused the slaves in some sections to seek satisfaction of their sexual hunger among Indian women. Then there was the discipline of the plantation or the arbitrary will of the masters which regulated sexual association and the selection of mates among the slaves. Thus it came about that sexual selection and mating were no longer culturally defined or regulated by African mores.

Nevertheless, there was selection of mates on the basis of spontaneous impulses and mutual attraction. There was the wooing of females by males who attempted to win their favor by gifts and expressions of affection. The stability of these matings was dependent largely upon the temperaments of the mates and the strength of the mutual attraction and affection. Where the mates were inclined or were permitted to live together as husband and wife, mutual sympathies and understanding developed as the result of habitual association. Pregnancy and offspring sometimes resulted in the brekaing of bonds, but they often provided a new bond of sympathy and common interest. A common interest in the relationship was more likely to develop where there were mutual services and the sharing of benefits, as for example in the cultivation of a garden. Under such conditions the Negro family acquired the character of a natural organization in that it was based primarily upon human impulses and individual wishes rather than upon law and the mores.

Under favorable conditions the family as a natural organization developed considerable stability during slavery. The first requirement for stable family life among the slaves was, of course, that the family groups should not be broken up through sale or arbitrary action on the part of the masters. Where the plantation became a settled way of life and a social as well as an economic institution, the integrity of the slave family was generally respected by the masters. Moreover, the social relations which grew up facilitated the process by which the Negro took over the culture of the whites. The close association between whites and Negroes, often from childhood, enabled the slaves to take over the language, manners, and ideas of the masters. These close contacts were enjoyed by the slaves who worked in and about the master's house. On many plantations the masters provided religious and moral instruction for the slaves. The moral supervision included, in some cases at least, the chaperonage of the female slaves. It was through those channels that the white man's ideas and sentiments in regard to sex and family relations were communicated to the slaves. These cultural advantages, which were restricted mainly to the house servant, became the basis of social distinctions among the slaves. The house servants enjoyed a certain prestige in the slave society which grew up about the Negro quarters.

In the division of labor on the plantation there was some opportunity for the expression of talents and intelligence. This was especially true in regard to the black mechanics who were so necessary to the maintenance of self-sufficiency on the plantation. Often it was the son of a favored house servant who was apprenticed to a craftsman to learn a trade. In becoming a skilled craftsman or mechanic the intellectual powers as well as the manual dexterity of the slave were improved. In addition, because of his skill he was accorded recognition by the master and acquired a higher status among the slaves. The recognition which was accorded the personality of the skilled craftsman was reflected in his pride in his workmanship. What was more important was that it was a moralizing influence which was reflected in the family life of the skilled artisans. The skilled mechanic often assumed the conventional role of husband and father and was recognized as the head of his family. The fruits of his skill, so far as a premium was placed upon good performance, were often shared with his family. Consequently, these family groups, which were without the support of law, often achieved the solidarity and stability of a legally sanctioned family.

The development of family life described above represents the development of the slave family under the most favorable conditions. Among the vast majority of slaves, the Negro mother remained the most stable and dependable element during the entire period of slavery. Despite a benevolent master, the slave family was often dispersed when the plantation was sold or an estate was settled. With indifferent or cruel masters the slave family was constantly being broken up and its members scattered. But in either case some regard had to be shown for the bond between Negro mother and her children. The masters' economic interest in the survival of the children caused them to recognize the dependence of the young children upon the mother. Then, too, the master, whether out of humanity or self-interest, was compelled to respect the mother's often fierce attachment to her children. Wherever the charge that slave mothers were indifferent to their offspring has any factual support it can be explained by the forced pregnancies and harsh experiences attending motherhood. Most of the evidence indicates that the slave mother was devoted to her children and made tremendous sacrifices for their welfare. She was generally the recognized head of the family group. She was the mistress of the cabin, to which the "husband" or father often made only weekly visits. Under such circumstances a maternal family group took form and the tradition of the Negro woman's responsibility for her family took root.

The development of the maternal family among the slaves was

further encouraged by the sexual association between blacks and whites. In the cities, where slaves moved about freely and there were many free Negroes, the sexual relations between Negro women and white men were casual and often of a debased character. But it was not only in the cities that the races mixed. Although there is no way of measuring the extent of the sexual association between slaveholders and slaves, there is abundant evidence of concubinage and polygamy on the part of the masters. The character of the sexual associations between the two races ran the gamut of human relationships. At one extreme the slave woman or Negro woman was used to satisfy a fleeting impulse. At the other extreme the sexual association was supported by personal attachment and deep sentiment. In the latter case, the white father in rare instances might assume the role of a father which lacked only a legal sanction. Nevertheless, because of the ideas and sentiments embodied in the institution of slavery, the Negro or mulatto mother remained the responsible and stable head of the family group. On the other hand, it was from such associations that the free Negro population continued to increase until the Civil War.

The Family Among the Free Negroes

The free Negro population increased steadily from the time when Negroes were first introduced into the Virginia colony in 1619. For three or four decades the servitude of the Negroes was limited to seven years, as in the case of white servants. Even after the status of the Negro servants became one of perpetual servitude, or slavery, the free Negro population continued to increase. The increase in the free Negro population came from five sources: (1) children born of free colored parents; (2) mulatto children born of free colored mothers; (3) mulatto children born of white servants and of free white women; (4) children of free Negro and Indian parentage; and (5) manumitted slaves.[2] Although it is not possible to know the increase in the free Negro population through each of these sources, it appears that the manumission of slaves

[2]   John H. Russell, *The Free Negro in Virginia* (Baltimore: Johns Hopkins University Press, 1913), pp. 40–41.

was relatively the most important source. Slaves achieved freedom through manumission both because of the action of their owners and because of their own efforts. A large number of the white fathers emancipated their mulatto offspring; as a result about three-eighths of the free Negroes were mulattoes, as compared with only one-twelfth of the slave population. In numerous cases the white fathers provided for the economic welfare and education of their colored offspring. Slaves were able to become free through their own efforts, especially in Maryland, Virginia, and North Carolina, where the economic basis of slavery was being undermined. In these areas skilled artisans were permitted to hire out their time and save enough money to buy their freedom. Whether they were freed because of their relation to their white masters or because of their own efforts, the free Negroes possessed certain cultural advantages which were reflected in their family life.

It was among the free Negroes that the family first acquired an institutional character. This was possible primarily because the free Negroes were able to establish family life on a secure economic foundation. In the southern cities the free Negroes had a secure position in the economic organization. Partly on the basis of wealth and occupation, a class system emerged among the free Negroes. Among the wealthier free colored families in Louisiana and in Charleston, some of whom were themselves slaveholders, the family was similar to that of the white slaveholders. It was patriarchal in organization and the status of women was similar to that of the women among the white slaveholding class. Moreover, these families were founded upon traditions which had been built up over several generations. Those traditions were a measure, in a sense, of the extent to which the Negro had assimilated the American cultural heritage.

It has already been pointed out how the house servants and the slave artisans had been able because of their favored position to take over American culture. Here it should be pointed out how the free Negroes, who had come largely from these groups, incorporated the American culture and transmitted it through their families to succeeding generations. Because of their relationship to the white race the mulattoes generally had a conception of themselves different from that of the pure-blooded Negro. Where they were favored by their white fathers, the close association with their fathers or their position in the household enabled them to take over the attitudes and sentiments as well as the overt behavior of the father. As freedmen with some economic competence or with a mechanical skill which afforded a good income, they were able to maintain a way of life that accorded with their conception of themselves and with the patterns of behavior taken over from the whites. This led to the beginning of an institutional life within the free colored communities similar to that in the white communities. The free Negroes established schools, churches, literary societies, and organizations for mutual aid. The families with traditions formed the core of the organized social life in the free Negro communities. Not only did these families give support to the institutional life, but they were supported in turn by the institutions of the community. Although it is true that because of social isolation the culture of the free Negroes became provincial and ingrown, it nevertheless provided a heritage for their children.

Civil War and Emancipation

The Civil War and emancipation created a crisis in the family life of the Negro. This crisis affected the free Negro family as well as the slave family. It tended to destroy whatever stability the slave family had achieved under the slave regime. It tore the free Negro family from its moorings in a society where it occupied a privileged position. The distinction between slave and free was wiped out. How did the Negro family meet this crisis? How was its organization and stability influenced by its new relation to American culture? How, specifically, was its role or function in mediating American culture to the Negro affected by the Negro's new relation to American life? These are some of the questions which we shall attempt to answer in the present chapter.

As the Union armies penetrated the South, the plantation regime was disrupted and the slaves were uprooted from their customary way of life. Thousands of Negroes flocked to army camps and to the cities; thousands joined the march of Sherman to the sea. The disorder and confusion were a test of the strength and character of family ties. In many cases the family ties which were supported only by habit and custom were broken. Negro men deserted their families and even some Negro mothers deserted their children. On the other hand, many fathers took their families with them when they went in search of freedom. Many Negroes went in search of relatives from whom they had been separated through sale while they were slaves. Throughout this chaotic situation, the Negro mother held the family group together and supported her children. This devotion was based partly upon her traditional role and partly upon the deep emotional attachment to her young that was evoked in the face of danger.

The northern missionaries who went south to establish schools and hospitals and to assist the Negro during his first steps in freedom were faced with the problems of the Negro family. They encouraged the Negro to get a legal sanction for his marital relations and to settle down to orderly monogamous marriage. They had to contend with the confusion which slavery had caused by the selling away of "husbands" who returned to claim "wives" who had "married" other men. Then there was the problem of giving the Negro husband and father a status in family relations which he had not enjoyed during slavery. The missionaries depended chiefly upon exhortation and moralizing to establish conventional marital and familial relations among the freedmen. These methods had some effect, but they did not determine the future development of the Negro family. The course of that development was determined by the dominant economic and social forces in the South as well as by the social heritage of the freedmen.

When conditions became settled in the South the landless and illiterate freedman had to secure a living on a modified form of the plantation system. Concessions had to be made to the freedman in view of his new status. One of the concessions affected the family organization. The slave quarters were broken up and the Negroes were no longer forced to work in gangs. Each family group moved off by itself to a place where it could lead a separate existence. In the contracts which the Negroes made with their landlords, the Negro father and husband found a substantial support for his new status in family relations. Sometimes the wife as well as the husband made her cross for her signature to the contract, but more often it was the husband who assumed responsibility for the new economic relation with the white landlord. Masculine authority in the family was even more firmly established when the Negro undertook to buy a farm. Moreover, his new economic relationship to the land created a marterial interest in his family. As the head of the family he directed the labor of his wife and children and became concerned with the discipline of his children, who were to succeed him as owners of the land.

As the result of emancipation the Negro was thrown into competition with the poor whites. At the same time he became estranged from the former slaveholding class, and the sympathetic relations which had been built up during slavery were destroyed. Since the nature of the contacts between whites and blacks was changed, the character of the process of acculturation was changed. The estrangement between the whites and blacks was inevitable when the color caste was established in the South. If the democratic aims set up during the Reconstruction Period had been achieved, this estrangement would not have occurred. But where race was made the basis of status the Negroes, in defense, withdrew from the whites and suspected even their attempts to help the freedmen. Consequently, there came into existence two separate social worlds and, as far as spatial separation permitted, two separate communities. Since the Negro's personal life was oriented toward the separate Negro world, he derived his values from that world. The patterns of behavior and ideals which he took over from the white man were acquired generally through formal imitation of people outside his social world. In their social isolation the majority of Negroes were forced to draw upon the meager social heritage which they had acquired during slavery.

In the world of the Negro folk in the rural areas of the South, there grew up a family system that met the needs of the environment. Many of the ideas concerning sex relations and mating were carried over from slavery. Consequently, the family lacked an institutional character, since legal marriage and family traditions did not exist among a large section of the population. The family groups originated in the mating of young people who regarded sex relations outside of marriage as normal behavior. When pregnancy resulted, the child was taken into the mother's family group. Generally the family group to which the mother belonged had originated in a similar fashion. During the disorder following slavery a woman after becoming pregnant would assume the responsibility of motherhood. From time to time other children were added to the family group through more or less permanent "marriage" with one or more men. Sometimes the man might bring his child or children to the family group, or some orphaned child or the child of a relative might be included. Thus the family among a large section of the Negro population became a sort of amorphous group held together by the feelings and common interests that might develop in the same household during the struggle for existence.

From the standpoint of marriage statistics the rural Negro population has shown a large percentage of illegitimacy. But these statistics have little meaning if they are not related to the folkways regarding sex and marriage relations which have grown up in those isolated rural areas. The type of sex and marital relations which have been described does not indicate that sex relations have been promiscuous and free from controls. There has been, in the first place, the general recognition of the obligation of the mother to her children. In fact, pregnancy has been regarded as a phase of the maturing or fulfillment of the function of a woman. On the other hand, marriage meant subordination to a man or the formation of a new type of relationship. Often, therefore, when a girl became pregnant and the man wanted to marry her, the girl's mother objected. Later the girl might marry the father of her child or some other man. But this meant forming a partnership in working a farm together and assuming other obligations. In a society of this type the mother continued to occupy a dominant position in the family. The grandmother enjoyed an even more important position and has always been a leading figure in the Negro family.

Statistics have always shown a large number of Negro families with women as heads. These statistics have reflected the conditions described above. It appears that about 10 per cent of the Negro families in the rural areas, as compared with about 30 per cent in urban areas, have had women as heads. This difference is doubtless due to the fact that in the rural areas of the South the Negro man and the woman with her children need each other more in the struggle for existence than do those in the city. In fact, the stability of these family groups in the rural areas has depended largely upon the coöperation of man and woman in the struggle for a livelihood. As the result of this coöperation, deep sentiments and attachments have developed not only between spouses but also between the fathers and their children. This has caused these family groups to have on the whole the stability of conventional family groups.

Not all rural Negro communities in the South have been characterized by the simple mores described above. The rural Negro communities have differed greatly, the differences being dependent upon both economic and cultural factors. Where, outside the plantation area, the Negro has been able to acquire land and a higher economic status, the family has achieved an organization closely resembling the American pattern. The economic factor, however, has not been the sole determinant of this difference. In the areas outside the plantation region the Negro has never been so isolated biologically, mentally, and socially as in that section. Dating from the time of slavery, the Negro in those outside areas, as we have pointed out, has lived in closer association with the whites and has enjoyed some opportunity for self-development. When the Negro began his career as a freedman, therefore, he had a richer cultural heritage as well as a greater opportunity for economic development than the Negro in the plantation South. Nevertheless, the high percentage of landownership among the families outside the plantation area has provided a basis for a stable family life. As we have seen, it has encouraged the growth of patriarchal family system. Moreover, the church and other institutions in these communities have supported conventional family mores. Illegitimacy and unlegalized marriage relations have not been tolerated as among the isolated plantation folk.

The progressive stabilization of Negro family life continued throughout the nineteenth century and during the first decade of the twentieth. This process was associated with a gradual increase in home and landownership and has involved the intermarriage of the stable elements among the descendants of free Negroes with the more ambitious and successful freedmen with a background of slavery. The descendants of the free Negroes brought to these unions a rich cultural heritage, and the ambitious descendants of slaves brought new aspirations and a new outlook on life. Out of this process there emerged a class stratification of the Negro population which was based largely upon social distinctions, the principal one of which was the tradition of a stable and conventional family life. In placing a high value upon a stable and conventional family life, these elements in the Negro population were safeguarding the chief means through which the gains of the Negro in civilization were preserved and transmitted to future generations.

Urbanization and Family Life

So far the discussion of the Negro family has been concerned mainly with the family in the agricultural South, where nine-tenths of the Negro population was concentrated until the first decade of the present century. Around the opening of the century the drift of rural Negroes to southern cities had begun to attract attention. Then came the mass migrations to northern cities during and following the First World War, and these dramatized the accelerated urbanization of the Negro population.

In the hundreds of towns and cities of the South, the Negro family had taken shape and the rural folk culture was attempting to adjust itself to new conditions. Many Negro women had been attracted to these urban areas because of the chance to gain a living in domestic service. Sometimes they carried their illegitimate as well as their legitimate offspring with them. The freedom from familial and community controls sometimes meant the sloughing off of the responsibilities of motherhood, and the sexual freedom of the rural areas lost much of its harmless character. Sex expression tended to become a purely individualistic affair in which the hedonistic element became the chief end. Yet the family continued to survive among the majority of the population in these towns and cities. Here its maternal character was even more conspicuous than among the rural folk, not only as a result of the high rate of illegitimacy but also because of desertion on the part of the male head of the family. Amid the general demoralization of family life in these urban areas, there were enclaves of families which because of deeply rooted traditions maintained conventional family life and held themselves aloof from the masses.

The effects of an urban environment upon the Negro family were accentuated among the masses who migrated to the metropolitan areas of the North. The inadequacy of the sex and familial folkways and mores which had given stability to life in the rural South was revealed in the problems of the Negro family in the city. First, there was the problem of illegitimacy. As we have seen, illegitimacy was not necessarily a social problem among the isolated folk in the rural South. It did not violate the mores and the ideal of motherhood, for there women enjoyed a certain social sanction in any case. In an urban environment sex and motherhood were given a new social definition. The bearing of children was an economic burden which placed a handicap upon the mother as well as upon the family group in the severe struggle for existence. Then, too, the community, through neighbors, schoolteachers, social workers, and others, frowned upon unmarried motherhood and defined it as immoral. As a consequence the unmarried mother's behavior lost its naïve character. Her growing sophistication with the ways of city life, together with the economic burden of childbearing and the moral disapproval of the community, changed her attitude toward motherhood. Although this resulted in much demoralization, it should not be overlooked that the new stimuli of the city awakened the imagination of men and women, and the romantic element became involved in the sex experience.

Desertion on the part of the husband and father has been another serious problem of the Negro family in the city. In the rural South fathers had often deserted their families when they had gone to work in turpentine and lumber camps or in the cities. When Negroes began migrating to the North, it was sometimes the man who went first, with the idea of sending for his wife and children. Once in the environment of the city, however, the father or husband developed new interests and formed new sexual associations. Even when the husband or father brought his wife or family to the city, he often deserted them. Though in many cases of desertion the couple had not been legally married, nevertheless desertion on the part of the man was equivalent to the breaking of marital ties. Desertion meant that the community of interests and the sympathies which had held families together in the rural South were dissolved in the cities. Moreover, the social control exercised by the church and lodge and neighborhood opinion no longer existed in the city. Desertion revealed one of the chief weaknesses of this type of family: the absence of family traditions deeply rooted in the mores of the group. The informal breaking of legal marriage ties and the confused notions concerning the marital status and divorce tended to emphasize how much the family folkways of the migrants differed from the American mores governing marital relations.

The inadequacy of the type of family organization to which the migrant was accustomed resulted in much juvenile delinquency. Although juvenile delinquency in our cities is primarily a community problem, the widespread juvenile delinquency among the children of Negro migrants has resulted largely from the failure of the family. The poverty of the Negro has required many mothers to seek employment outside the home. As we have pointed out, in a third of the Negro families in the cities the mother has been the sole head of the family. Consequently, Negro children have been denied the supervision of their parents. Even in families where the father has been present, there has been no cultural heritage that could be communicated to the children. The folk culture, which these families have brought from the South, lost its meaning in the cities of the North. However much these families attempted to isolate their children from the influences of the cities, they could not prevent them from being affected by the public school.

Although the public school has contributed to the disorganization of the Negro folk culture in the city, it has also brought the Negro into contact with the larger American culture and thereby helped in the reorganization of his family life. The reorganization of family life, however, has not been achieved merely by the acquisition of new ideas concerning family life. The new ideas have only become effective in behavior when they were related to changed economic and social conditions. In the northern metropolis the occupational differentiation of the Negro population has been accelerated. As the Negro man has become an industrial worker and has no longer been dependent entirely upon domestic service and casual unskilled labor, he has become subject to a discipline that has affected his home life. The fact that he has received a higher and a more steady remuneration has enabled him to assume full responsibility for the support of his family. As a consequence, he has received more recognition as the head of the family and as such has taken more interest in his children, whom he has wanted to see "get ahead" as a result of greater educational opportunities.

The occupational differentiation of the Negro population was accelerated as the result of the changes in the economic organization of American life and important changes in the racial policy of the American government during and following World War II. Before the war, the increasing occupational differentiation of the Negro population had become the basis of a new class structure. Before the mass migration to northern cities which began with World War I, there had been small enclaves of Negro families— generally of free ancestry and mixed blood—that constituted an upper social class. The social position of these families was not determined so much by their occupation and income as by their cultural heritage and tradition of conventional family life. Sometimes when confronted by the onrush of southern migrants who threatened their way of life, they retreated into an isolated circle of friends. On the other hand, the migrants with their new economic, political, and educational opportunities and their awakened ambitions competed for a place in the Negro communities. In the fierce competition of urban life many of the old social distinctions lost their meaning and new standards of behavior and symbols of status came into existence. Such new marks of distinction as money, education, and power were essentially the same as those in the larger American culture, but the isolation of the Negro had given them relatively a different value.

Three fairly well defined socioeconomic classes began to emerge in the Negro communities in the larger cities.[3] At the

[3] See St. Clair Drake and Horace R. Clayton, *Black Metropolis* (New York: Harcourt, Brace and Company, 1945), pp. 494–715.

bottom of the social pyramid was the lower class. Among this class family life was a precarious affair, having no roots either in a fixed habitation and a secure income or in a traditional culture. The lower-class families were usually concentrated in slum areas and depended upon incomes derived from casual employment in the least desirable occupations. Because of the uncertain employment of the men, the women, who found less difficulty in securing employment, occupied a dominant position in the family. The marital relations among this class were unstable even when there had been legal marriage. When no children were involved the women were as mobile as the men, but when there were children the mother struggled to hold the family together. It was in this class that the socialization of the child had been based mainly upon the exigencies of daily living involving the interaction of the parents and their child. This interaction consisted mainly in the expression of emotional reactions and in the impulsive behavior of the members of the unstable household toward each other. These reactions were generally uninfluenced by a cultural tradition or by the cultural patterns of the American community.

As the result of improved economic and educational opportunities a middle class became differentiated from the lower class. The stable and conventional families forming this class were the core of the institutional life of the Negro community. Because of their attempt to maintain a conventional family life, these families placed much emphasis upon respectability. Some of these families had escaped from the lower-class status; thus they became the source of a tradition of conventional familial relations which was passed on to their children. Often, however, these middle-class families had a tradition of conventional family life which had its roots in the South. In fact, it was the families with some social heritage and with traditions of a stable family life which were most able to withstand the disintegrating effects of the urban environment.

The middle class has continued to expand in size and in influence as the Negro population has continued to become urbanized.[4] In the country as a whole about the same proportion—five-eighths —of Negroes as of whites live in cities. In the North and in the

[4]   See E. Franklin Frazier, *Black Bourgeoisie* (Glencoe, Ill.: The Free Press, 1957).

West where the Negro enjoys larger economic opportunities and political rights, about a fourth of the Negro families are able to maintain middle-class standards. On the other hand, in the South where there are racial barriers to the employment of Negroes in white-collared and professional occupations and Negroes lack political power, only an eighth of the Negro families are able to support a middle-class way of life. The emergence of a new middle class among Negroes which has been the result of urbanization and the improvement in the economic status of Negroes has had important social consequences in the development of the Negro family. Above all it has meant that a large section of the Negro population has broken with the two really vital cultural traditions in the social history of the Negro. On the one hand, the genteel tradition which flourished among the mulattoes who were free before the Civil War and their descendants has ceased to determine the character of the familial behavior of upper-class Negroes. On the other hand, it has resulted in the rejection of the familial behavior of the Negro folk. Although the disintegration of the genteel tradition has created greater instability in family relations, the rejection of the familial patterns of the Negro folk has brought about the institutionalization of marriage and family life.

The emergence of a relatively large and influential middle class which has been uprooted from its "racial" traditions has influenced in other ways the form and functioning of the Negro family. The Negro family has become largely oriented to the values of the American culture. This has tended to reduce the size of the Negro family and bring about a sense of equality among its members. Moreover, the Negro family has developed a new style of life and new goals for its members. One phase of this new orientation toward the values of American culture is seen in the great emphasis which the middle class places upon conspicuous consumption. The emphasis upon conspicuous consumption represents both an attempt to consolidate its superior status within the Negro community and to achieve identification with the white American community. This does not mean, however, that middle-class Negro families have discarded altogether their social heritage. In fact, the persistence of the genteel tradition and the folk tradition often creates a confusion of values and goals. This becomes evident in the behavior and general outlook of the so-called upper class which has tended to become differentiated from the middle class despite the fact that the so-called upper-class Negroes derive their incomes from professional and white-collar occupations and a comparatively few small businesses. Since this "upper-class" sector of the new middle class sets the patterns of behavior and aspirations of the new middle class, it has tended to create a "world of make believe" in view of the Negro's economic and social position in American life.

The Negro Family and Modern Civilization

Although this discussion has been concerned with the Negro family in American civilization, it has a broader significance. The problems which the Negro family has encountered in its development involve problems of acculturation and assimilation which other peoples as well as Negroes must face today as a result of the impact of Western civilization. In the United States Negroes are placed in a peculiar position with reference to Western civilization because they were practically stripped of their traditional culture. Consequently, there was scarcely any opportunity for cultural conflicts to develop in the United States as in other parts of the world.[5] However, as the result of the emergence of a new middle class among American Negroes, their changing relation to American society involves problems of culture and personality which are related to the family.

The character of the Negro family during the various stages of its development has been affected by the social isolation of Negroes in American society. The lack of opportunity for the Negro male to participate freely in the economic organization and his subordination to whites as well as the general exclusion of Negroes from political activities have all affected the organization and the functioning of the Negro family. This has entailed a waste of human life and human energy. It represents in a sense the price which the Negro has been forced to pay in order to survive in American

[5]   See, for example, I. Schapera, *Western Civilization and the Natives of South Africa* (London: George Routledge & Sons, 1934).

society. But this survival has not been the survival of a biological group but of a sociologically defined group. And it has been the family which has assured the survival of the Negro in American society.

The emergence of a new middle class is evidence of the increasing integration of the Negro in American society. However, the increasing integration of the Negro has brought into relief problems of culture and personality. The new middle class is without roots because it is increasingly cutting itself loose from its roots in the segregated Negro community. Moreover, it still has no social roots in the white community since it has not become identified with the white middle class. Consequently, middle-class Negroes are experiencing considerable conflict and frustration, and this is being reflected in Negro families. What social heritage can Negro parents pass on to their children? What group identification can they provide their children? Sociologically, these conflicts and frustrations are manifesting themselves in social disorganization and personal disorganization. Formerly, social and personal disorganization was confined almost exclusively to lower-class Negroes but increasingly the problems resulting from disorganization are manifesting themselves among middle-class Negroes.

The survival of the Negro in American civilization is a measure, in a sense, of his success in adopting the culture of the whites or an indication of the fact that the Negro has found within the white man's culture a satisfying life and a faith in his future. His future survival in a highly mobile and urbanized society will be on a different basis. In the large metropolitan communities of the North, Negroes are increasingly intermarrying with whites. Thus the Negro family is incorporating new traditions, and the children of mixed marriages have a new view on American life. As the result of these developments the Negro will have to face greater stresses in his personal life, and the segregated groups and institutions will no longer provide an adequate refuge in the white man's world. During all these changes and crises the family will continue to play an important role in transmitting the new conception which the Negro will acquire of himself and of his place in American society.

13

CERTAIN ASPECTS OF CONFLICT IN THE NEGRO FAMILY

1931

A RECENT novel, *Not Without Laughter*, by Langston Hughes presents a vivid and authentic picture of the conflicts in a migrant Negro family in a western city which grew out of the struggles of the members of this family to achieve a place for themselves in the small Negro community. The conflicts in this family were between the mother, who represented the traditions and conceptions of life acquired by the older generation in the South, and her three daughters who had broken more or less with these traditions as the result of education and residence in a northern city. Equally significant were the conflicts between the sisters themselves which arose as the result of their different educational and social status in the Negro group and their antagonistic conceptions of life. This literary account of conflicts in a Negro family focused attention upon the cultural factors in family conflicts among Negroes, which are generally overlooked in formal studies. There are, however, two other types of family conflict that are bound up with the development of the Negro group and reflect the influence of cultural factors. The first type of conflict is due to the absence of well defined social and economic classes with established traditions in the Negro population, and the second to the differences in color among Negroes, a fact which tends to determine status not only in the Negro group but also participation in the life of the larger commu-

Reprinted from *Social Forces*, 10 (October, 1931) : 76–84.

nity. While some attention will be given to those conflicts which arise between the older and the younger generations, and members of the same generation because of differences in social status, this paper will be concerned chiefly with those conflicts which are due to the absence of well defined classes with established traditions, and those conflicts which are due to the influence of color differences in the determination of social status and development of personality.

One of the most conspicuous and important features in Negro life is the rapid and fundamental change which education produces in social status. The children of poor, ignorant, and often almost primitive parents, who succeed in making their way through college and professional schools on account of their own efforts and through philanthropy, are raised thereby to the top of the Negro group. Some measure of the change in social and economic status which education produces was given in a study of the occupations of the fathers of 305 professional and business men and women listed in a directory of prominent Negroes in the country. Of these 305 persons who replied to questionnaires, 90 had fathers who were in business and professional pursuits. The same proportion of fathers with a similar background was found in the case of 123 graduates of a Negro college replying to the same questionnaire. The majority of the fathers of the remainder in both groups were in domestic and personal service, common labor, and agriculture.

Education as a rule means a complete break with the traditions, ideals, and customs of the masses from which educated Negroes have sprung. The change in social status places the educated person in a new world of ideas and values, and causes him to sever membership with all the old community organizations that are identified with traditional beliefs and customs of the masses of Negroes. The young Negro man or woman who succeeds, for example, in securing enough education to become a public school teacher often changes his membership from the Baptist and Methodist denominations to the Episcopal or Congregational Church. The conflict between the ideals and values of the parents and children begins often while the children are still under the authority of the parents. A typical case is that of a girl who through association in high school with the daughter of a professional man whose family belonged to the Episcopal church refused to refrain from dancing and card playing, which were forbidden by her parents who were Baptists.

The extent to which education produces a break with the older generation is shown in the case of a school principal who had married into one of the first families of a Negro community. He attempted to conceal his humble origin by clandestine visits to his mother and refused to acknowledge his relationship to his sister because she was ignorant. And when his mother died he went to her funeral in the role of a stranger. The same break with the older generation is seen in the case of a school teacher, whose mother washed clothes and lost her home through a mortgage in order to pay her daughter's way through college. This teacher moved from her mother's home because she was embarrassed in the presence of her "society" friends by her mother's ignorance. These cases show in a general way how changes in social status through education not only divorce the person from the traditions and outlook on life of the older generation, but often destroy the sympathetic relationships between parents and children.

Probably the most important factor that has produced rapid and fundamental changes in the social and economic status of the Negro has been the migrations to cities. The migration of large numbers of Negroes to northern cities during and since the World War has only accelerated and brought into prominence the urbanization of the Negro population which has been taking place since the opening of the present century. During the first decade the urban Negro population increased 34.1 per cent or one and a half per cent more than in the decade of the War. But in the first decade the increase was chiefly in Southern cities while in the second decade northern cities received most of the increase. Migrations to northern cities amounted to a second emancipation of the plantation Negro. It meant the breakdown of all the traditional and customary modes of behavior, the throwing off of the forms of accommodations to the white man's world in the South, and the birth of new ambitions, hopes, and ideals. Rudolph Fisher in a story, *The City of Refuge,* has given a vivid description of the effect of the sight of a Negro policeman on the mind of a newly arrived migrant in New York City. It is in the northern city that one sees the far-reaching effects that the city environment has on the young. The break with the attitudes and conceptions of life of the older generation is similar to that which one finds in second generation immigrant families. Time and space will permit the presentation of only one document that shows the conflict between the older and younger generation. This document was secured from a girl, about to graduate from high school, who had come with her family from Mississippi to Chicago.

My mother and all of us belonged to the Baptist Church. But my mother hardly ever went to church or any place but we always went. I would go to Sunday School and then I would come home and go to the Methodist church down in Mississippi—that is the only place you can go is church. I would stay in church most all of the time. My mother has prayer meeting every Wednesday morning by herself here. Sometimes we come in. But in Jackson all of us would be there for prayer. Now we hardly ever go. Sometime when we feel sick we go in and let mamma pray, you know. My mother doesn't work. My father is a porter on the West side in the saloon. Seemingly all of them work at saloons. I haven't joined church since I been here. My mother belongs to Pilgrim. But I go to Bethel. She doesn't go any place much. My father goes to church when I carry him. The boys you know how they are, they hardly ever go. Well, I will tell you about myself. I joined the same church my mother did in Mississippi. They was having a revival and so I didn't have no religion. I didn't know what I was doing, I was about eight or ten years old. I go to shows and the Savoy. I go to the Regal every week and the Metropolitan. I go to school parties. I tell you, I like to go on Sunday to the Savoy. Whenever I go I have to slip off and go. You see, mamma doesn't want us to go to show on Sunday, nor play cards or dance. I have a beau. You know how it is, you have about two or three. But you have a main one to fall back on, you know. I always went to dances at home but I would have to have a chaperone. I can hardly get out anywhere. Mamma's got to know the people, you see, and if she hear anything about their parents she won't let me go around with those girls. Nowadays, you know, every place you go everybody is selling liquor. So now, I hardly have but two or three girl friends. If my girl friends people have liquor, I don't know nothing about it, for they never let me see it. My mother is very strict with me. Last night the people in the first floor were out in the sun parlor playing cards and mamma thought it was awful. Like it was at the Regal the other evening, I went and didn't know the show was going to last so long so I had to go out and call my mother and let her know because she would have been wondering, you know. She thinks Chicago is awful. All men will try to get fly with you, but I know what to say to them. Mamma always wants me to hurry back home before night.

In the above document one sees clearly the process by which the control exercised by the primary organization in the rural southern community, as well as that of the family, tends to break down in the northern city. In the urban environment the traditional and customary forms of behavior are destroyed and the new conceptions of right and wrong acquired by the children through education, literature, and association with other emancipated groups come into conflict with the conceptions of life held by the parents. In the case of this high school girl from Mississippi it should be noted in this connection that she said concerning her reading: "I read True Love, Love Story, and those physical culture books. My mother says it ain't nothing to them love stories. I like them."

Sufficient has been presented to show how conflicts arise between the older and the younger generations. Something should be said concerning the conflicts which arise in Negro families between members of the same generation. The process by which individuals in the Negro group break away from the customs and traditions of the masses tends to create among the children themselves wide differences in culture. Sometimes one son in the family or the girls through sacrifices of their brothers succeed in acquiring a college or normal school education. The educated member or members of the family enter a different world with ideals and forms of behavior that are antagonistic to the old associations from which they have escaped. This often leads to conflicts in the same family which end sometimes in the disintegration of family life. There are numerous cases in real life to match the sister in Hughes' novel, who after marrying a postal clerk gained entrance into the society of the small colored elite. She paid only formal visits to the house of her mother and clashed constantly with one sister who became a singer of the blues and used dialect, and with the other sister because she was apparently satisfied to remain a servant in white people's homes and represented everything that was reminiscent of the status from which the Negro should, in the mind of the more favored sister, try to escape.

The small social elite in Negro communities is drawn from many occupational classes. They represent on the whole the first generation that has escaped from the widely divergent social condition of the masses. In most cases the social differentiation of the Negro community is not built upon occupational differentiation of the population, but represents the efforts of those who have achieved some culture and education to enforce standards and recognize distinctions in behavior. In the case of the 428 professional and business people mentioned above, less than a score represented the third generation in the upper social and economic classes. Therefore, the traditions of the small upper class group among Negroes have not grown out of the diverse occupational groups. In a southern city, for example, the small elite will be composed of a few school teachers, a couple of physicians, a dentist, postal employees, and one or two other families who have acquired a superior status because of family, property or sometimes because of some unique position in the white community. The composition of this class will vary according to the size, general culture, and history of the Negro community. What needs particular emphasis is the fact that occupations in the Negro group do not have the same connotations, and do not give the same social status as similar occupations in the white community. The standard of living and the modes of behavior are derived from their relative position in the Negro community. This explains the surprise of a white social worker that her Negro colleague was a "society" leader.

The absence to a large extent of class differentiation built upon differences in occupational status in the Negro group tends to divide the Negro community, especially in small southern cities, into two classes. The upper class is a rather heterogeneous group of people drawn from many diverse occupations who have one principal characteristic in common—they have escaped from the ignorance, the primitiveness, and economic dependence, as a rule, of the masses. But since this class, as a rule, has no established traditions to define behavior, its behavior is determined to a large extent by suggestion and imitation. As a rule the sources of suggestion and the models are in the wealthy white class. The absence of established class traditions helps to explain the observation of Dr. Robert E. Park about twenty some years ago that the children of well-to-do Negroes were, as a rule, spoiled. The dean of women in a Negro college, where some students represent the second and third generations of families in attendance, said that over eighty per cent of the students were living beyond their parents' income in an effort to copy the behavior of students in exclusive white colleges.

In the absence of social gradations, each with its own traditions, in the upper class Negro group, there is a struggle among the members of this class to maintain standards of living set up by the wealthiest members of this class. This often produces a conflict situation in families where the husband's income is not sufficient to support the requirements of his wife, who attempts to maintain her status in this class. A woman who finally separated from her husband, an insurance agent, writes:

I came from a family that people call rather "well-to-do"; I had been accustomed to have everything I wanted as a child, and all thru my school days I was accustomed to many elaborate social affairs and lovely clothes, as well as extensive travel.

Against my parents wishes, I married a fellow who was earning a small salary and could not give me the home, the lovely furniture, a pretty car, pretty clothes, etc., that I had always had.

We moved into a neat little home and he began buying; our furniture was very nice but not what I wanted; later we got a Ford but I wanted a Dodge. Gradually, I became more and more dissatisfied with the things which he could not give and as I look back over it now I see that I was constantly nagging about not being able to entertain, to travel, to dress, to "put on the show" that my friends did.

One day my husband said to me "I love you better than I do my own life and from now on I am going to see if I can't give you everything you want." I did not know then the real import of these words. About a month afterwards he told me that he wanted me to have my own car and that he would keep the Ford. I was delighted when he sent out a pretty Dodge coupe—all for me. I did not question how he got it but was satisfied that he knew what he was doing. When we had been married about two years he said he wanted to re-furnish our little love nest. I was overjoyed when I saw the lovely furniture brought in and the old furniture carried out. Still I did not question. My next desire was a new home; he felt that he could not give me just what I wanted, so I continued to "nag." For a good while I was dissatisfied—wanting the home which he said he could not afford. Spats occurred frequently—conflicts continuously. Finally he said "I'll give you the home you want—just give me time." It was during this "time" that I heard that he was gambling and had been gambling for some time. The home was being built when I asked him if he ever gambled. Truthfully and frankly, he told me that my wants had been so many and so heavy that it was for that reason that he started it.

There are developing among Negroes, especially in the large northern cities, different social and economic classes with their own set of traditions and modes of behavior that are related to their occupational status. The wife of a professional man who had migrated to a northern city remarked that she was able to become identified with her own proper class and was relieved of the struggle to maintain the standard of living that was required by her membership in the upper class in a southern city, whose standards were dictated by a few people with much higher incomes than her own. Here and there even in southern communities there are families, whose status does not depend upon their copying the behavior of the elite, who maintain modes of behavior that are traditional in their small group.

A form of family conflict that arises out of the Negro's status in American life is due to color differences in the same family. These color differences tend to define the Negro's status not only in his own group but in the white community. A fair skin permits a degree of participation in the white world that often destroys the solidarity of the family, when fair skinned members of the family pass over completely into the white world. Even in those cases where there is not a complete break with the family, conflicts arise over diversity of interests and differences in attitudes towards the Negro group. Dr. Park in his writings has called attention to the conflicts within the mulatto's mind because he becomes a cultural hybrid. The cultural conflict is reflected in family conflicts where different colors in the same family tend to destroy mutual sympathies and common interests. The form of this conflict is shown in the case of a Negro family where the father was fair enough to be taken for a white man and his wife and children were unmistakably colored. A daughter in this northern family has written of the conflict as follows:

Awareness of conflict within our family, due to the difference of color, came first to me when I noticed preferential treatment by my father of white guests as over against the courtesies accorded our Negro friends. How much of this observation was original or how much was transmitted to me by my elder brother and sister is hard to say.

Father always greeted white people more effusively than Negroes. And very often he offered them refreshments when it was rare that Negro men were invited to eat at our table. The older children were coldly polite on the occasions when white guests were with us. The two older than I, who were then ten and twelve, used to slyly giggle and I was prone to wonder first why there was a difference made between what seemed to me to be equal quantities—white and Negro people. In school the one Negro boy, whom I thoroughly detested because he pulled at my braids, I consciously treated with a good deal more consideration than I was wont to do because I was beginning to feel that Negroes were not treated the same as whites and I linked up the attitude expressed by my father toward Negroes with the white teachers' and pupils' attitude to this black boy. Father often paraded the musical talents of his daughter before the seeming admiration of his white friends, but on the occasions when Negro men visited us, he often called the young ladies into the living room. The girls so resented this parade that there came a time when they refused to play for certain guests and mother would always have a convenient errand for them to do.

My sisters and I discussed father's attitude among ourselves and finally when the older girls refused any information as to the reason, I determined to ask mother. Mother never permitted any criticism of her husband and so I had to be contented with my own solution of the problem. I noticed, however, that both white and Negro guests were treated with the same courtesy when my mother was in evidence. The second observation which tended to reenforce the first belief that father preferred the society of white people and definitely sought their company came when I was old enough to take his Saturday's dinner pail to him. Almost always he fraternized with his white workmen more than with his Negro employees and upon returning from work, he was almost always with white men, although very often the Negroes were forced to pass through our section of the town to go to the Southside.

School offered opportunities a-plenty for parents' visitations, and when parents, Negro and white, came together, I often wondered why my parents never appeared at the same program. Either mother came alone or else Dad appeared in company with other men—invariably white. . . .

Papa never did in all the years that I can remember even take mother out publicly to social functions, concerts, etc. The children used to talk about it to themselves and E— would say, "oh well, you know what papa thinks." To mother we never mentioned this omission because we were careful of her feelings; to Dad, we didn't because we were too proud, and the sense of filial respect was too great. However, each of us was conscious of the slight and V. often said the very light men needn't call upon her, for she didn't like them. She married a handsome black man in spite of the numerous fair men who paid her court. My brother never would even consider a fair girl for a friend and I have often seen him discourage their attentions. . . .

One sister says to this day that she has no respect for my Dad because of his treatment of mother. When my brother came home on furlough from camp and wanted a snap of Dad and mother together, mother said, "oh, no, Dad doesn't want his picture with me" in a deprecatory manner. My brother said, "he ought to be proud to have the picture with you." The picture was taken. We all felt embarrassed for the unspeakable had been expressed and by mother. I have always been sorry that mother married a person who obviously regarded her as an inferior and my dislike and disrespect for Dad has grown during the years as tangible evidences of this sense of inferiority unfolded themselves. This knowledge, a sense of conflict, has operated to restrict to formal-relationship my own acquaintances with very fair men and white men. Even in Europe my sense of race loyalty forbade an affirmative answer to a proposal of marriage from a white man of high status.

Once returning from college for vacation, the household got embroiled in a deep discussion on race. Mother was silent but the rest of us arguing more or less heatedly the problems surrounding Negro youth. Papa remarked, "I know no color." Immediately I said, "you can say that when your son and daughters can't, because they are colored, get the jobs they are fitted for. Isn't D— reputed the best bricklayer in town and don't you know they discriminate against him. You just can't understand these problems; you don't know what it is to be a Negro." "There is no use talking about them to you." Father and I didn't speak for a month. We have never discussed those problems since then, and it was only out of respect for mother that we didn't go further and tell him he must know color else his attitude toward mother all these years would have been different, and all the other evidences of his racial discriminations would not have been. None of us have ever respected and loved our father as we did our mother. And even now we never discuss those questions and problems that lie most closely to us with him.

Other documents could be cited to show how color differences in the same families become the basis of similar conflicts. I will quote excerpts from one other in which the northern born wife of a Negro teacher describes the family conflct, which arose in her home when she was a child, because of color differences.

He (my father) adored my mother but seemed to feel inferior to her because of the difference in color. He showed this when they quarrelled. He often caller her an "Irish Mick" or "poor white trash" or said that she came from low parentage. These things always hurt mother and daddy would do everything he possibly could to make up with her. He would bring her little trinkets or candy or flowers to help her to forget what he had said. Mother always felt that she and Daddy would be forced to separate.

Daddy always preferred light Negroes to darker ones. He never cared for anyone darker than himself. Mother on the other hand made friends with any one and one of her dearest friends to this day is a dark woman. Their first child, who died in infancy, would have been the fairest of the children. He had light eyes and dark hair.

As we became older and I started to receive company, Daddy began to drill me, that he did not want me to marry a dark man. If a dark friend came to the house he made it very uncomfortable for them, even though they were friends of the family. It happened that I liked three boys who were all real brown. Daddy liked them personally but he did not really encourage our friendship to any great extent. My brother, Jack, would tease me about my three "blackies" as he called them.

I distinctly remember one day that daddy and mother quarrelled over something which mother did not understand thoroughly. Daddy became exasperated and called mother a "half white nit wit." Mother cried and then daddy apologized and said he had merely lost his temper. I told him he was a "living devil" to hurt mother so and that a "half white" was better than a "nigger" like him! . . .

Mother told me sometime, years later, that I had hurt Daddy terribly in calling him a "nigger." She said he told her that he guessed after all he was just a "nigger" and he believed that she felt that way about him too. He told her that she could not help it; that it was her white blood.

Before concluding this paper I would like to call your attention to two other forms of family conflict, one of which has practically disappeared and the other is of slight importance at present, because of the few cases of intermarriage between Negroes and foreign peoples. In both cases, however, the family conflicts reflect the cultural conflicts in the Negro group. The first form of conflicts was due to the distinction that was prominent especially after Emancipation between Negroes of free ancestry and those of slave origin. It is now a well known fact that a class of free Negroes have existed in this country since their introduction into America. In Charleston, S.C., and New Orleans, especially, the free mulatto class constituted a distinct caste. They held a secure place in the economic system and acquired considerable education and culture. The traditions of this class were entirely different from the masses of Negroes on the plantation and under domestic slavery. After Emancipation members of this class, often even the most indigent in the rural sections of the South, looked down upon the newly emancipated blacks. In the competition for political offices and control of church organizations in some localities, those of free ancestry in some cases attempted to ostracize and eliminate the new "ishy," as they were called in North Carolina. The influence of the cultural differences between these two groups of the Negro family is shown in the case of a father who banished his daughter from his home because she married a man of slave ancestry. This case was one of several in a small community in North Carolina where there was a community of free mulatto families who boasted of their free ancestry and held themselves aloof from those of slave origin.

A similar care of family conflict arising out of the distinctions between the free mulattoes in New Orleans and the descendants of slaves is furnished in a family history of a woman who was the offspring of a marriage between representatives of these two classes. Her mother descended from an old family of free mulattoes in New Orleans who owned slaves. One of the cherished memories in the family is the refusal of a grandmother to marry a Union soldier or to salute the American flag because they symbolized the loss of her slaves. "And until her death," this granddaughter wrote, "she regarded Abraham Lincoln as her enemy." She continued, "Grandmother strenuously objected to my father's marrying her daughter because he was a descendant of slaves." The conflict in this family arose over this woman's education when her mother opposed her father's desire to have her attend a Negro college.

When I was about eleven years old, I completed what was known as my spiritual education. I had gone to a private school where I was taught French, English, and the cathechism. I had received my first Holy Communion, and been confirmed. This meant that I could either continue in a convent or get a higher education. At this time my father jogged in and insisted that I attend a colored school because all of his interests were with colored people. My mother objected most strenuously for she never considered herself a colored woman. But father finally won and gave me my choice of the state school or private college.

This document indicates how the different set of traditions became the cause of family conflict. As one follows the history of this family, one sees two conflicting attitudes toward the Negro influencing not only the attitude of this woman toward matters pertaining to race but also her attitude towards religion, morals, and life in general.

The second minor form of family conflict arising from diverse cultural backgrounds is found often in cases of marriages between West Indian men and American Negro women. Although the West Indian element is small in this country and there is some prejudice on the part of American Negroes against them, the educated men from the islands seek unions with American Negro women because they represent on the whole a higher level of culture than most of the West Indian women who come to this country. The following excerpt it taken from a family document written by a woman who divorced her West Indian husband.

In 1922 I was married to a young Jamaican who at that time was a chiropodist. A boy was born after a year. We lived together two years and then separated because we found it impossible to continue to live together. He had been brought up in Jamaica where the men were lords and the women worked as slaves. For example, he believed in dressing up and going about in other women's company while his wife and children were to go along on the barest necessities and live in seclusion. It became necessary for me to live with my mother as he would not provide for me and my child.

The above document gives some indication of the conflict between the West Indian's attitude towards the subordination of the wife and the American Negro woman's conception of her status in the marriage relation.

Conclusion

In this brief paper an attempt has been made to present certain aspects of conflict in the Negro family which show the influence of cultural factors. First, those conflicts were presented which arose out of rapid changes in social and economic status of the Negro group. As the result of these changes there is a conflict between the ideals, values, and conceptions of life of the older and younger generations, and between members of the same generation occupying different social and economic status. Secondly, it was shown how the absence, to a large extent, of classes based upon a diversity of occupations with established traditions in the Negro group tended to make the behavior of the small upper class subject chiefly to suggestion and imitation, which often involved conflicts between husband and wife. Thirdly, differences of color in the same family were seen to be the basis of conflict when they permitted different degrees of participation in the white world and, in creating conflicting attitudes towards the Negro group, destroyed the community of interest and mutual sympathies and understandings by which the family is held together. Although one is not in the position to determine statistically the extent of these typical conflicts, an analysis of the cultural situations in which they arise will aid in an understanding of certain forms of conflict in the Negro family.

14

PROBLEMS AND NEEDS OF NEGRO CHILDREN AND YOUTH RESULTING FROM FAMILY DISORGANIZATION

1950

Introduction

FAMILY DISORGANIZATION probably has been the most important social problem that has retarded the development of the Negro since his emancipation. For more than half a century, sociologists and social workers as well as other persons interested in the Negro's development have studied and written on the problem of his disorganized family life. Most of the early students of the Negro regarded his failure to measure up to the generally accepted standards of American family life as an indication of moral degeneracy resulting from his racial inheritance or his African social heritage. In fact, many regarded the continued family disorganization as proof that the Negro was unable to acquire American patterns of family life.[1] The early social workers, who were less sophisticated in regard to theories and had a humanitarian interest in the Negro, were bewildered by the phenomenon and

---

Reprinted from the *Journal of Negro Education*, 19 (1950) : 269–77.

[1]   See E. Franklin Frazier, *The Negro Family in Chicago* (Chicago: University of Chicago Press, 1932), chap. 2 for a discussion of theories concerning family disorganization among Negroes.

exhibited a certain pathos toward the Negro's unconventional sex and family life.

As social work increasingly acquired a professional character and sought a theoretical basis for its practices, social workers began to accept the theories of the scholars concerning the cause of family disorganization among Negroes. Other social workers attributed the widespread family disorganization to some single factor as, for example, the low economic status of the Negro. Although DuBois, as early as 1908, had undertaken to relate family disorganization among Negroes to the destruction of the African clan and the demoralization of Negro sex and family life during slavery,[2] few social workers were acquainted with DuBois' study. Nor did sociologists undertake to test DuBois' hypotheses. Not until nearly a quarter of a century after the appearance of DuBois' book was a serious attempt made to study family disorganization among Negroes as a sociological problem.[3]

During the last two decades sociologists have ceased to regard family disorganization among Negroes as a "racial problem," either from the standpoint of the biological heritage or the African social heritage. They have sought to analyze the disorganization of Negro family life in relation to social and economic factors. Only in a general way have they related family disorganization to other problems among Negroes such as crime and delinquency. Moreover, there have been few attempts to study the problems of Negro children and youth resulting from family disorganization. It is the purpose of this paper to deal in a general way, because of the lack of available studies, with the problems resulting from family disorganization. Since this is a field in which few studies have been made, what is offered here is more in the nature of hypotheses to be tested by studies dealing with specific problems of Negro children and youth.

[2]   W. E. B. DuBois, *The Negro Family* (Atlanta: Atlanta University Press, 1908).

[3]   See *The Negro Family in Chicago* where the author undertook the study of the disorganization and reorganization of Negro family life as a phase of the process of the Negro's adjustment to urban life.

Meaning and Forms of Family Disorganization

In discussing the problems of Negro children resulting from family disorganization, it is necessary to make clear at the beginning what is meant by family disorganization. Viewed from the standpoint of its institutional character, the family may be regarded as disorganized when it does not conform to socially accepted norms of family life. But if we also view the family as an organized social group or cooperating unit with which the various members are identified and this identification is recognized by the community, then family disorganization may be defined differently. An illustration will clarify the distinction which we would like to make in regard to family disorganization. In many sections of the rural South, especially in the plantation area, there are Negro families which do not conform to the institutional pattern of the American family. But it would be a mistake to label them as disorganized since they are stable groups and carry on the functions of the family. Therefore, in discussing family disorganization we shall be referring to the disintegration of the family group or its failure to function as a cooperating unit.

The generally accepted indices of family disorganization are illegitimacy, desertion and non-support, and divorce. There is a high incidence of illegitimacy, desertion and non-support among Negroes, while it appears that divorce is rapidly increasing. Among the rural Negroes in the South, a very large percentage of the children are illegitimate; i.e., their parents are not legally married.[4] But, as was suggested above, this fact does not result in family disorganization since the "unwed" parents live as married couples and provide for the economic and social needs of their offspring or, indeed, other children who may be incorporated into the amorphous family group. Even the illegitimate offspring of young unmarried mothers who do not establish families may be incorporated into their mother's family group. However, under different

[4]   These same folkways are found among peasant peoples in various parts of the world. The writer has studied such practices in Brazil and in the West Indies.

circumstances as, for example, in rural communities where the family is on an institutional basis and conventional patterns of sex are supported by the mores, illegitimacy results in family disorganization. Moreover, among the migrants from rural areas to cities, illegitimacy generally results in family disorganization because the rural folkways are opposed to the economic and social demands of urban living.

From all available sources of information, it appears that the incidence of desertion on the part of the male in the family is much greater among Negroes than among other racial or ethnic elements in the population. Although desertion is essentially an urban phenomenon, the increasing mobility of the rural population has some effect upon the organization of the rural Negro family. Desertion is by far the most serious form of family disorganization among Negroes, since it is the chief method of settling marital difficulties and escaping from family responsibilities. Desertion, in the true meaning of the term rather than the legal fiction which goes under this name in divorce cases, takes the place of divorce among lower-class Negroes.

In fact, the different forms of family disorganization are related to the emerging class structure in the Negro community. Just as illegitimacy and desertion are the chief forms of family disorganization among lower-class Negroes, divorce is the most important form of family disorganization among "middle class" and "upper class' Negroes.[5] One of the factors differentiating "middle class" Negroes from lower class Negroes is the fact that marriage has a legal or institutional character. Therefore, when marriages are broken, "middle class" Negroes generally resort to the divorce courts. Although it cannot be definitely established, it appears from many sources that divorces have increased significantly among Negroes during the past thirty years. The increase in the incidence of divorce has followed the increase in the relative size of the Negro "middle class" and the emergence of the "upper

[5]   "Middle class" here refers to the intermediate class in the Negro community. Practically all of the "upper class" Negroes and the top layer of the Negro "middle class" would be identified with the American middle class or middle classes if Negroes did not live in a segregated community.

class" as a socio-economic class rather than a "caste-like" formation at the top of the social pyramid.

The foregoing brief sketch of the meaning of family disorganization and its various forms will serve as a background for the
discussion which follows.

Economic Problems Resulting
from Family Disorganization

The first most important problem of Negro children resulting from family disorganization is economic. A large percentage
of Negro families must depend upon the earnings of the mother
or female head of the family. For example, in 1940 in the South
as a whole 21.7 per cent of the Negro families had a female head.
In the cities of the South 31 per cent of the Negro families had
a female head while in the rural areas the proportion of such families was 11.6 per cent. In some Northern cities the percentage
of Negro families with female heads is as high as in some Southern
cities. The large proportion of Negro families with female heads is
due, as far as we are able to learn, primarily to desertion and
illegitimacy. Therefore, as the result of these two forms of family
disorganization probably nearly a fifth of the Negro children must
depend upon the mother for support. Since the majority of employed Negro women are still in domestic services, the lack of
adequate food, clothing and shelter among nearly a fifth of all
Negro children is attributable to the fact that the Negro woman
must assume responsibility for the support of so large a proportion of Negro families. Of course, the situation has been improved
to some extent by the social services which have been set up to aid
dependent children. But until Negro males assume a larger responsibility for the support of Negro families, Negro children will
continue to suffer because of insufficient family incomes.[6] Moreover, they will continue to leave school at an early age and
assume partial responsibility for the support of their families.

[6]   The extent to which Negro males assume responsibility for the
support of their families is limited partially but not entirely by their limited employment opportunities in industrial occupations.

Social Problems Resulting
from Family Disorganization

Any discussion of the social problems of Negro children resulting from family disorganization should begin with the effects of the absence of family traditions in the vast majority of unstable Negro families. The absence of family traditions is, of course, one of the causes of family disorganization. At the same time the lack of family stability prevents the building of family traditions. The "maternal" families originating from illegitimacy have no continuity with the past and are concerned only with the daily exigencies of making a living. The same is often true of those families where the father has deserted. The deserted mother has less knowledge about her husband's "folks" than she has concerning her own, which is very meagre. What is passed on to her children is generally some trivial scraps of information concerning her mother rather than her father. Thus, as the result of family disorganization, the child fails to acquire the identification which the family normally supplies.

Family traditions play an important role in the socialization of the child. The failure of the disorganized Negro family to pass on traditions to children is only one aspect of its failure in its socializing function. When considering the socializing role of the family one should begin with the emotional needs of the child. Among the motherhood in the rural South, the emotional needs of the children are generally satisfied. This is true even in those "maternal" families where the husband has gone off to work and has left his family to eke out an existence as a sharecropper of some tenant farmer. Among these people the mother's love for her children rather than self-preservation is the first law of nature. Moreover, the community will forgive any transgression rather than condone the mother's lack of love for her offspring. But in the city it is otherwise. Unmarried motherhood brings economic burdens, obstacles to personal gratifications, or shame and a sense of guilt, if not a loss of status. Therefore, illegitimate children are sometimes thrown in garbage cans or disposed of otherwise, or given up to social agencies for adoption. When they are kept by the mother they are often rejected for the reasons indicated. The mother, deserted by the father of her children and bearing the entire burden of their support, may cherish her children despite hardships. But sometimes she reacts as those unmarried mothers in the city who seek personal satisfactions unrelated to family living. Sometimes enforced separation from her children because of the necessity to make a living may make it impossible to give them the love and attention which they need. It is a familiar story to social workers and psychiatrists to hear the child of a broken home recount his or her rejection, imagined or real.

The failure of Negro children to have their emotional needs satisfied because of disorganized family life is not confined to the lower classes. Because of the increasing mobility of Negro life resulting from wider contacts, education, and improvement in economic status, the "middle class" in the Negro community has become relatively larger and the "upper class" has become more sharply differentiated because of its conspicuous consumption. Since Negroes as a whole are a group without deeply rooted traditions, except those stemming from the folk background, the mobility which Negroes are experiencing results in considerable family disorganization. Some of this family disorganization leads to the complete disintegration of family life, which is reflected in divorces. But much of the family disorganization does not reach the divorce courts and is indicated in the individualization of the behavior of those who maintain the forms of family life. As the result of family disorganization among "middle class" and "upper class" Negroes, whether it reaches the divorce court or is concealed, children experience the emotional effects of being neglected or rejected because their parents seek to satisfy the new wishes which a rise in status usually brings.

Even if Negro children who are members of disorganized families have their emotional needs satisfied, love is not enough, to use the title of a recently announced book.[7] Since family disorganization is so widespread, the family environment of a large number of Negro children is precarious and fragmentary. The behavior

[7]   Bruno Bettelheim, *Love is Not Enough: The Treatment of Emotionally Disturbed Children* (Glencoe, Ill.: The Free Press, 1950).

of the adults does not make sense. As Bruno Bettelheim stated in an article, "Above all, they [children] need adults about them whose behavior makes sense, who live a consistent set of values, and after whose image they can form a personality."[8] Since it is generally the father who is absent from the broken Negro family, the boys especially suffer because there is no adult to provide the model or image of the values which should shape their personalities. Perhaps some psychiatrist will undertake to determine the effect upon the personality of Negro boys and youth of female dominance in so many families.

The failure of disorganized Negro families to perform their socializing function is indicated by the lack of discipline and the failure to teach useful habits in such families. In the absence of the father in broken homes the responsibility for any kind of discipline devolves upon the mother. This discipline is often lax and spasmodic. Since the unmarried or deserted mother must spend much of her time away from home as a breadwinner, the children are left without discipline. Because of the lack of discipline, the children in such homes never acquire the most elementary habits in regard to cleanliness or even as to eating. The children are left to act according to their impulses. They do not even acquire the domestic work skills necessary to make a living in the only occupations in which they will find employment. Whatever moral training is provided by these broken homes is generally restricted to a few homely injunctions about sex and honesty which have little meaning in the social environment in which the children grow up.

From the foregoing it is apparent that the disorganized Negro families are characterized by the absence of "family living" which makes of the child a "human being." For example, let us take the simple but important matter of eating. In many of the broken homes the members of the family seldom gather for a meal. Eating is an individual matter, lacking fellowship and communion, and without the ceremony associated with family meals. In fact, there is little ceremony in these families to bind the members together. There is little routine in family living to teach habits and create

[8]   "Love is Not Enough," *The University of Chicago Magazine*, January, 1950, p. 3.

expectations that provide a basis of emotional security. Children in these disorganized families are deprived of the emotional security and sympathy which is one of the main values in family life.

The failure of the disorganized Negro family to perform its socializing function is partly responsible for the large amount of juvenile delinquency and crime among Negroes. There have been numerous studies showing that a large proportion of Negro children, as do white children, come from "broken" homes. But there have been few studies showing specifically how family disorganization results in juvenile delinquency. Juvenile delinquency is primarily a community problem, since its incidence is definitely related to the organization of the community. But since all children living in "delinquent areas" of a city do not become delinquent, the character of the family in these "delinquent areas" plays an important role. Some families in "delinquency areas" manage to maintain their stability and organization and exercise discipline over their children. It appears that the delinquents come not from "broken homes" (for example, "broken" by the absence of a parent) but from *disorganized* families. These disorganized families produce a large number of delinquent Negro youths because they have failed in their socializing function. Many of the Negro juvenile delinquents may be characterized as "wild" (not in the mistaken sense that the term is applied to so-called primitive or non-literate peoples), because they act upon impulse and do not even behave according to the codes of behavior prescribed by gangs. In fact, there is some evidence that Negro juvenile delinquents and criminals act more frequently as individuals than white juvenile delinquents and criminals. At any rate, the life histories of Negro juvenile delinquents and youthful criminals indicate that they are often the products of disorganized families.

The widespread family disorganization among Negroes affects the relations of Negro children and youth to the institutions of the community. The first and most important contact which the child has with the institutions in the community is, of course, with the public school. In providing knowledge and skills, the public school operates upon the assumption that it is possible to establish a certain routine and discipline among the students. The extent to which the students can acquire the knowledge and skills which it offers is determined by the cultural backgrounds of the students. Moreover, the extent to which the students can become adjusted to the routine and discipline of the schools is affected by family training. Negro children from disorganized families often exhibit little interest in the knowledge and the skills provided by the public schools because it has little or no meaning for them in terms of their family backgrounds. The goals and values provided by the public schools have no relation to the values which they have acquired in the family. In addition, children who have never been subjected to the discipline of normal family life find it difficult to conform to the routine and discipline required by the public school. Therefore, they are irregular in their attendance, partly because of the lack of family discipline and partly because of the lack of interest. They are found among the truants who attempt to escape the "dull" subjects and discipline of the public school. Moreover, children from disorganized families are conspicuous among those who "drop out of school" because of "lack of interest" or because of the necessity to "go to work."

We shall not attempt to show how disorganized family life affects the relations of the Negro child and youth to other institutions. For example, children in disorganized families are less likely than children in well organized families to participate in the religious institutions of the community. Moreover, it seems that the lack of family discipline and a failure of the disorganized family to provide models and images of the values of the community are partly responsible at least for the irregular work habits and lack of ambition among many Negro youths.

Conclusion

In this essay we have been concerned with the problems of Negro children and youth resulting from family disorganization. Because of the lack of studies dealing specifically with this problem it has been necessary to draw upon information and insights in numerous studies dealing with Negro children and youth as well as the writer's studies of various aspects of Negro family life. Therefore, what is presented here should be regarded as hypotheses to be tested by studies dealing with the problems which we have treated here. It appears that the first most important problem resulting from the widespread family disorganization among Negroes is economic because about a fifth of the Negro children and youth must depend upon the earnings of the mother or female head of the family. This problem has been alleviated to some extent by the provision of aid to dependent children. However, the lightening of the burden of Negro mothers has not helped much the social problems of children and youth in disorganized Negro families. As the result of family disorganization a large proportion of Negro children and youth have not undergone the socialization which only the family can provide. The disorganized families have failed to provide for their emotional needs and have not provided the discipline and habits which are necessary for personality development. Because the disorganized family has failed in its function as a socializing agency, it has handicapped the children in their relations to the institutions in the community. Moreover, family disorganization has been partially responsible for a large amount of juvenile delinquency and adult crime among Negroes. Since the widespread family disorganization among Negroes has resulted from the failure of the father to play the role in family life required by American society, the mitigation of this problem must await those changes in the Negro and American society which will enable the Negro father to play the role required of him.

V. The Negro Middle Class

15

INFERIORITY COMPLEX AND QUEST FOR STATUS

1957

THE ENTIRE history of the Negro in the United States has been of a nature to create in the Negro a feeling of racial inferiority. During the more than two centuries of enslavement by the white man, every means was employed to stamp a feeling of natural inferiority in the Negro's soul. Christianity and the Bible were utilized both to prove and to give divine sanction to his alleged racial inferiority or, as some contended, his exclusion from the races of mankind. When the system of slavery was uprooted in a Second American Revolution, it appeared for a brief period that the Negro might receive recognition as a man. But as the result of the unresolved class conflict in which the democratic forces in the South were defeated, the demagogues who became the leaders of the disinherited whites but really served the interests of the propertied classes made the Negro the scapegoat. A legalized system of racial segregation was established which stigmatized the Negro as unfit for human association, and every type of propaganda was employed to prove that the Negro was morally degenerate and intellectually incapable of being educated. Living constantly under the domination and contempt of the white man, the Negro came to believe in his own inferiority, whether he ignored or accepted the values of the white man's world. The black bourgeoisie—the element which has striven more than any other element among Negroes to make itself over in the image of the white man—exhibits most strikingly the inferiority complex of those who would escape their racial identification.

I. *A Chattel in an Alien Land*

When the Constitution of the United States was adopted, it provided that the number of representatives from each state in the House of Representatives should be determined by adding to the whole "Number of free Persons, including those bound to service for a Term of Years, and excluding Indians not taxed, three-fifths of all other persons."[1] "Three-fifths of all other Persons" referred, of course, to the Negroes, and the agreement to count the Negro as three-fifths of a person was a compromise between the position that slaves should not be counted at all and the desire on the part of the southern states to have as large representation as possible. Although the Negro was finally counted as three-fifths of a person for the purposes of representation in Congress, his actual status as a person in the southern society was probably more accurately described by the Charleston *Mercury*, which stated that the Negro was as much "an article of commerce" as "the sugar and molasses" which he produced.[2] Despite the "human" relations which developed between Negroes and whites on the plantations where a paternalistic type of control developed, the Negro was, nevertheless, an "article of commerce" or an animate tool, according to Aristotle's definition of a slave. If any recognition were shown him as a person, it was conceded to a person who represented a lower and inferior order of mankind.

During and for a brief period following the American Revolution, some of the leaders who had acquired French ideas concerning human rights expressed their opposition to the enslavement of the Negro. For example, Thomas Jefferson attacked slavery in his original draft of the Declaration of Independence, in which he declared that the king of England had "waged cruel war against

[1]   See William MacDonald, *Documentary Source Book of American History* (New York: Macmillan, 1914), p. 218.
[2]   See Frederick Bancroft, *Slave-Trading in the Old South* (Baltimore: J. H. Furst Co., 1931), p. 365.

human nature itself" in supporting the slave trade.[3] Such sentiments in regard to the enslavement of the Negro were not shared
by the plantation owners in the lower South. Jefferson was Vir-
ginian, and the plantation system of agriculture was becoming
unprofitable in Virginia. When, as the result of technological developments in the textile industries of England, there was a great
demand for cotton, and Eli Whitney perfected his cotton gin, the
"idealism" concerning human rights ceased to have any reference
to the Negro except among a small group of whites in New England. During the period from 1790 to 1808, the year on which
importation of slaves became illegal, over 100,000 slaves were
brought to the United States, and, because of the failure of the
federal government to suppress the slave trade after 1808, between 250,000 and 300,000 were smuggled into the country.[4]

Reduced to a chattel in an alien land, the enslaved Negro
was not only "detribalized" as the African who has had contact
with European civilization, but he was annihilated as a person.
Although the detribalized African may take up permanent residence in a town and sever relations with his chief and his relatives,
there is always the tribal organization to which he can return
or the traditional culture with which he can identify.[5] The enslavement of the Negro in the United States destroyed not only his
family ties and his household gods; it effaced whatever memories
of the African homeland had survived the Middle Passage. The
destruction of a common tradition and religious beliefs and practices reduced the Negro to a mere "atom" without a personality or

3   See Carl Becker, *The Declaration of Independence* (New York:
Knopf, 1942), p. 212.
4   W. E. B. DuBois, *Suppression of the African Slave-Trade* (New
York: Longmans, 1896), pp. 123–24, 178–87.
5   See Ellen Hellman, *Rooiyard: A Sociological Survey of an Urban
Native Slum Yard* (Capetown: Oxford University Press, 1948), p. 110,
where she defines detribalization according to three criteria: "permanent
residence in an area other than that of the chief to whom a man would
normally pay allegiance; complete severance of relationship to the chief;
and independence of rural relatives both for support during periods of unemployment and ill-health or for the performances of ceremonies connected
with the major crises of life."

social identity. The main significance of the proselyting of the Baptist and Methodist missionaries was that Christianity was presented to the slaves in a simple, emotional appeal that provided a release for their frustrated and repressed lives. More than that, it established a bond of union among the slaves and provided them with a meaning of their existence in an alien world.

Although Christianity offered the Negro an interpretation of his existence in an alien world, it did not undertake to change his earthly condition as regards his enslavement. When for economic reasons, during the seventeenth century the Negro indentured servant lost the status which white indentured servants had and became a servant for life, or a slave, the colonial legislatures made it clear that that conversion to Christianity meant freedom not for the body in this world, but for the soul in the afterlife. Nor did the Society for the Propagation of the Gospel in Foreign Parts, which began its missionary efforts among Negroes in the eighteenth century, offer the Negro slave any escape from subordination to the white man in this world.[6] Among the various Christian missionaries who undertook the conversion of the Negroes during the most of the eighteenth century, only the Quakers, who generally met with opposition among the planters, were in favor of the emancipation of the slaves.[7] However, none of the proselyting faiths attracted large numbers of Negroes until the Baptists and Methodists began their missionary efforts during the closing years of the eighteenth century. In the beginning, the Baptist and Methodist missionaries, who brought their message of salvation to the poor and outcast, were in favor of the emancipation of the slaves, but soon they accommodated their message of salvation to the earthly condition of the Negro slave.

Not only did Christianity fail to offer the Negro hope of freedom in this world, but the manner in which Christianity was communicated to him tended to degrade him. The Negro was taught

[6]   See C. F. Pascoe, *Two Hundred Years of the S.P.G.: An Historical Account of the Society for the Propagation of the Gospel in Foreign Parts* (London: 1901), 1:1–13.
[7]   W. E. B. DuBois, *The Negro Church* (Atlanta: Atlanta University Press, 1903), p. 21.

that his enslavement was due to the fact that he had been cursed by God. His very color was a sign of the curse which he had received as a descendant of Ham. Parts of the Bible were carefully selected to prove that God had intended that the Negro should be the servant of the white man and that he would always be a "hewer of wood and drawer of water." While such was being taught the slave, some of the leading ministers of the South were setting forth the same doctrine in books for the American public. One of these books, written by a Presbyterian minister and entitled *The Christian Doctrine of Slavery*, stated that "It may be, that *Christian slavery* is God's solution of the problem [relation of labor and capital] about which the wisest statesmen of Europe confess themselves at fault."[8] Another leading minister published a book entitled *Slavery Ordained of God* in which he defended the doctrine that "slavery is ordained of God, and to continue for the good of the slave, the good of the master, the good of the whole American family, until another and better destiny may be unfolded."[9] These theological justifications of the enslavement of the Negro gave religious support to the philosophical justifications of slavery, the most celebrated of which was that by a Professor of History, Metaphysics and Political Law at William and Mary College, Virginia. In a book published in 1832, he justified the enslavement of the Negro on the grounds that the Negro possessed the strength and form of a man, but had the intellect of a child and was therefore unfit for freedom.[10]

Since the Negro's black skin was a sign of the curse of God and of his inferiority to the white man, therefore a light complexion resulting from racial mixture raised a mulatto above the level of the unmixed Negro. Although mulattoes were not always treated better than the blacks, as a rule they were taken into the household or were apprenticed to a skilled artisan. Partly because of the dif-

[8]   George D. Armstrong, *The Christian Doctrine of Slavery* (New York: C. Scribner, 1851), p. 134.
[9]   Rev. Fred. A. Ross, *Slavery Ordained of God* (Philadelphia: Lippincott, 1857), p. 5.
[10]   See "Professor Thomas R. Dew on Slavery," in *The Pro-slavery Argument* (Philadelphia: 1853), pp. 287–490.

ferential treatment accorded the mulattoes, but more especially because of general degradation of the Negro as a human being, the Negro of mixed ancestry thought of himself as being superior to the unmixed Negro. His light complexion became his most precious possession. Witness, for example, the typical case of the mulatto slave begging Frances Kemble that she "be put to some other than field labor because hoeing in the field was so hard on her *on account of her color.*"[11] Concerning the prestige which white "blood" conferred, Miss Kemble observed that the slaves accepted the contempt of their masters to such an extent that "they profess, and really seem to feel it for themselves, and the faintest admixture of white blood in their veins appears at once, by common consent of their own race, to raise them in the scale of humanity."[12]

The nearly 600,000 mulattoes among the somewhat less than 4.5 million Negroes in the United States in 1860 were the result of the sexual association of white men and Negro women.[13] The character of the sexual association between white men and Negro women ranged from rape based upon physical force or the authority of the master to voluntary surrender on the part of the Negro women.[14] Voluntary surrender on the part of the Negro woman was due at times to mutual attraction, but the prestige of the white race was often sufficient to secure compliance on their part. In giving themselves to their white masters there were certain concrete advantages to be gained, such as freedom from the drudgery of field work, better food and clothing, and the prospect that their half-white children would enjoy certain privileges and perhaps be emancipated. As the mulatto class grew in the South, many slaveholders, if married, set up a separate household for their black, but more often, mulatto concubines. In some cases they lived a monogamous life with their mulatto mistress or concubine, legal marriage being forbidden. But even under the most favorable con-

---

[11]   Frances A. Kemble, *Journal of a Residence on a Georgian Plantation in 1838–1839* (New York: Harper, 1863), pp. 193–94.
[12]   *Ibid.*, p. 194.
[13]   See *Negro Population, 1790–1915*, p. 208.
[14]   See *The Negro Family in the United States*, pp. 65–85.

ditions, the woman and her offspring were stigmatized because of their Negro ancestry.

It was out of such associations that the communities of free mulattoes grew up in the South. In some parts of the South they constituted a sort of lower caste, since no matter how well off they might be economically, they always bore the stigma of Negro ancestry. Even in Louisiana, where the quadroons or *gens de couleur* became wealthy and sent their children to France to be educated, they were still without political rights and could not associate with whites on a basis of equality. But they, like free mulattoes in Charleston, South Carolina, and other localities, would not associate with the blacks. The free Negroes of Charleston, who organized the Brown Fellowship Society in 1790, admitted only *brown* men.[15] This society provided for the education of the free people of color, assisted widows and orphans, and maintained a clubhouse and a cemetery for its members. They identified themselves as far as possible with the interests of the white slaveholding aristocracy and did not even permit a discussion of slavery among their members. Although they were not white, they could thank God that they were not black.

Religion and political philosophy rallied to the support of the planters in the South by confirming the racial inferiority of the Negro. This support became especially urgent as the conflict between the economic interests of the North and South became more acute, and the issue over slavery acquired a moral character. Whether the Negro was only chattel property, and, therefore, had no rights as a human being became an issue in the celebrated Dred Scott Case which was taken to the Supreme Court. In 1857 Chief Justice Taney of the Supreme Court, which was dominated by the South, handed down the famous decision, "A Negro has no rights which a white man need respect."[16] The Court declared that in the meaning of the words "people of the United States," in the

---

[15] E. Horace Fitchett, "The Traditions of the Free Negroes of Charleston, South Carolina," *Journal of Negro History*, 25 (1940):139–52.
[16] MacDonald, *Documentary Source Book of American History, 1608–1898*, pp. 405–20.

Constitution, Negroes were not included in the people of the United States. This represented the final triumph of the southern aristocracy in its struggle to dominate the United States.

II. *Half-a-Man in a White Man's Country*

The primary aim of the North in the Civil War was to save the Union. Lincoln made this clear in a letter to Horace Greeley in August, 1862, in which he stated: "My paramount object in this struggle is to save the Union, and not either to save or destroy slavery."[17] Whatever he did about slavery and Negroes was a part of his official duty and was not intended to modify his "personal wish that all men everywhere could be free."[18] Less than a month after writing this letter, he stated in a speech in Chicago that slavery was "at the root of the rebellion" and that the emancipation of the Negro would help the Union cause in Europe.[19] This growing recognition on the part of Lincoln that the emancipation of the Negro was tied up with the struggle of the North against the South was due partly to the question which had been raised concerning the employment of Negro soldiers in northern armies. In fact, the employment of Negroes as soldiers in the Union Army posed the crucial question of the future status of the Negro in American society.

Lincoln did not have much faith in the ability of Negroes to be trained as soldiers. He had stated that if Negroes were given arms, within a few weeks their arms would be in the hands of the southern rebels. Lincoln shared the prejudices of the masses of northern whites, to whom, as DuBois has well said, "the Negro was a curiosity, a sub-human minstrel, willing and naturally a slave, and treated as well as he deserved to be. He had not sense enough to revolt and help the Northern armies, even if Northern

17   Mervin Roe (ed.), *Speeches and Letters of Abraham Lincoln, 1832–1865* (New York: Dutton, 1907), p. 194.
18   *Ibid.*, p. 195.
19   Charles A. Beard and Mary R. Beard, *The Rise of American Civilization* (New York, 1927), 2:81–84.

armies were trying to emancipate him, which they were not. The North shrank at the very thought of encouraging servile insurrection against the whites."[20] General Hunter, an abolitionist, had recruited Negro soldiers in South Carolina after applying in vain to Washington for reenforcements. His action provoked a long debate in Congress which resulted in the disbanding of his Negro regiment. It was only after the Emancipation Proclamation and a pressing need for manpower that the War Department authorized the employment of Negro soldiers.[21]

The general attitude of the North towards the arming of the Negro was indicated by the fact that when it was planned for the first two regiments authorized by the War Department (the Fifty-fourth and the Fifty-fifth Massachusetts regiments) to pass through New York City, the Chief of Police warned that they would be insulted, and it was necessary for these regiments to go by sea to the theatre of war in South Carolina.[22] Because of the general opposition to the enlistment of Negroes as soldiers, many difficulties beset their recruitment. It was regarded as a stigma for white officers to serve in Negro regiments. Then there was opposition in Congress to giving Negro soldiers the same pay as white soldiers. It was not until 1864 that it was finally agreed that Negro soldiers should receive the same pay as white soldiers. This is not strange in view of the fact that the Negro in the North outside of New England did not live under the same laws as the whites.[23]

Nearly 200,000 Negro soldiers served in the Civil War which became, despite the intention of the majority of northern leaders, a war of emancipation. Since the Negro had contributed to the success of northern arms, they felt that they had earned the right to freedom and citizenship. There has been an attempt to disparage the contribution of the Negro soldiers to the victory of the

[20]   DuBois, *Black Reconstruction*, p. 56.
[21]   I. Wiley Bell, *Southern Negroes, 1861–1865* (New Haven: Yale University Press, 1938), pp. 303–10.
[22]   DuBois, *op. cit.*, p. 97.
[23]   Carl R. Fish, *The Rise of the Common Man* (New York: Macmillan, 1927), pp. 280 ff.

North, but the unprejudiced white officers who led Negro soldiers testified to their courage and efficiency.[24] This was, however, only the beginning of a campaign of disparagement of the Negro soldier which was to continue until World War II. Soon after his emancipation the Negro began to experience disillusionment about the meaning of freedom. The southern States enacted the Black Codes which really re-enslaved the Negro.[25] Restrictions were placed upon the occupations in which the freedmen could enter, provisions were made for them to be "apprenticed" to their former masters, and severe penalties provided for their failure to keep their "Labor contracts" with the planters and for being impudent to whites. It was the enactment of these Black Codes by the Southern States that provided the moral justification for placing the South under military rule and using military power to guarantee the rights of the Negro as a citizen.

For a brief period, less than a decade in most southern States, the Negro enjoyed the rights of a citizen. If the Second American Revolution had not been aborted it would have established a democracy in the South in which the poor whites and black freedmen would have shared power. Leaders like Senator Charles Sumner of Massachusetts and Congressman Thaddeus Stevens of Pennsylvania wanted to divide up the plantations and create a class of black and white small farmers who would have formed the basis of this democracy. But the industrialists in the North were not interested in democracy; they were interested in the exploitation of the resources of the South and in forming an alliance with the emerging middle classes. As a consequence, northern troops were withdrawn from the South when the Negro's vote was no longer needed.[26] The so-called restoration of "white supremacy" really meant the political domination of the "Bourbons" or the

24   See Thomas W. Higginson, *Army Life in a Black Regiment* (Boston: Fields, Osgood, 1870).

25   See *The Negro in the United States*, pp. 126–28.

26   See Louis M. Hacker, *The Triumph of American Capitalism* (New York: Simon and Schuster, 1940), pp. 378–79, and C. Vann Woodward, *Reunion and Reaction: The Compromise of 1877 and the End of Reconstruction* (Boston: Little, Brown, 1951).

alliance of the planters and the new industrial and commercial classes in the South. During the Reconstruction Period, there had never been any Negro domination in the South. Although the Republican Party in the South depended upon Negro voters, it also had southern white supporters who were called "scalawags." The race issue was utilized to defeat not only the Republican Party but the democratic upsurge which was threatened by the alliance of the black freedmen and the poor whites. Under the political dominance of the "Bourbons" the poor whites were in about the same economic condition as the freedmen.

The restoration of "white supremacy" in the South did not resolve the class conflict within the white community. This opened the way for the rise of the southern demagogues who offered a solution to the class conflict that did not threaten the economic interests of the propertied class while offering some relief to the poor whites. Their program provided for the complete disfranchisement of Negroes, the diversion of public school funds from Negro schools to white schools, and the establishment of a system of legalized racial segregation. What has erroneously been called "the rise of the poor whites" in the 1890's inaugurated a period in the history of the Negro in the United States during which a studied campaign was carried on to prove that the Negro was subhuman, morally degenerate and incapable of being educated. Although the "Bourbons" had achieved political power on the racial issue, they often had as little regard for poor whites as for poor Negroes. Once in power, they were willing to leave the voteless and landless Negroes in peace. But the demagogic leaders of the poor whites carried on a ceaseless campaign of terror and vituperation against all persons of Negro descent for over a quarter of a century.

The southern white politicians who carried on this campaign had the support of the propertied classes, the newspapers, and the clergy. They carried their campaign to the halls of the Congress of the United States where they met with scarcely any opposition. The North had become weary and ashamed of its idealism about the Negro and had agreed that the South could best handle the Negro problem. At the same time the Supreme Court of the

United States had been nullifying or curtailing the rights of Negroes which had been written into the Amendments of the Constitution or into laws.[27] During the 1890's two to three Negroes were lynched each week.[28] In 1898 there was a riot in Wilmington, North Carolina, during which Negroes were murdered, their property was destroyed, they were evicted from the petty offices to which they were elected, and driven from the city.[29] In regard to the Negro's fitness to vote, Senator Vardaman of Mississippi declared: "It matters not what his (the Negro's) advertised mental and moral qualifications may be. I am just as much opposed to Booker Washington as a voter, with all his Anglo-Saxon reenforcements, as I am to the cocoanut-headed, chocolate-colored, typical little coon, Andy Dotson, who blacks my shoes every morning. Neither is fit to exercise the supreme function of citizenship."[30] Then there was Senator Tillman of South Carolina who advocated the killing of 30,000 Negroes in his State and declared in a public lecture in Detroit, Michigan, that on one occasion he did not know how many Negroes he had killed.[31] In the Congress of the United States in 1898, David A. DeArmond of Missouri described Negroes as being "almost too ignorant to eat, scarcely wise enough to breathe, mere existing human machines."[32]

While public opinion and the personal attitudes of whites concerning the Negroes were being formed by politicians and newspapers, there appeared in 1900 a book entitled *The Negro a Beast*,

[27]   See Rayford W. Logan, *The Negro in American Life and Thought: The Nadir, 1877–1901* (New York: Dial Press, 1925).

[28]   See Arthur F. Raper, *The Tragedy of Lynching* (Chapel Hill: University of North Carolina Press, 1933), p. 480.

[29]   See *The Negro in the United States*, pp. 160–61.

[30]   Quoted in Paul Lewison, *Race, Class and Party* (New York: Oxford University Press, 1932), pp. 84–85.

[31]   See William A. Sinclair, *The Aftermath of Slavery* (Boston: Small, Maynard, 1905), p. 105. This book contains an excellent account of the methods which were used to reduce the Negro to a subordinate caste in the South.

[32]   Quoted in Logan, *op. cit.*, p. 90. This book provides the only comprehensive study and thorough documentation on the position of the Negro in American society during this period.

published by the American Book and Bible House.[33] The publishers of this book stated in the preface that if this book were "considered in an intelligent and prayerful manner, that it will be to the minds of the American people like unto the voice of God from the clouds appealing to Paul on his way to Damascus." In order that the American people might be convinced of the scientific nature of the "Biblical truths" presented in this book, the author included pictures of God and an idealized picture of a white man in order to prove that white people were made in the image of God, as stated in the Bible, and a caricature of the Negro showing that he could not have been made in the image of God. This book had a wide circulation, especially among the church-going whites, and helped to fix in their minds, as it was argued in the last chapter of this book, that the Negro was not the son of Ham or even the descendant of Adam and Eve, but "simply a beast without a soul."[34]

While this book was giving a religious sanction to current beliefs concerning the inferiority of the Negro, the Negro's inferiority was being engravened in every public edifice—railroad stations, court houses, theatres—with signs showing rear entrances for Negroes or kitchens in which Negroes might be served. Moreover, in every representation of the Negro, he was pictured as a gorilla dressed up like a man. His picture was never carried in the newspapers of the South (the same rule holds today in most parts of the South) unless he had committed a crime. In the newspapers the Negro was described as burly or ape-like and even Negroes who looked like whites were represented in cartoons as black with gorilla features. All of this fitted into the stereotype which represented the Negro as subhuman or a beast, without any human qualities. This vilification of the Negro continued until the second decade of the twentieth century. A so-called authoritative study of the Negro, published as a doctoral dissertation in the Columbia University Studies in History, Economics and Public Law, ac-

[33]   Chas. Carroll, *The Negro a Beast* (St. Louis: American Book and Bible House, 1900).
[34]   *Ibid.*, p. 339.

cepted as scientific evidence the statement that the Negro was "as destitute of morals as any of the lower animals."[35] In the very year in which the first World War started, an advertised authority on the Negro stated in a book that the Negro was an instinctive criminal.[36] Then in 1915, an army surgeon assured the American people that "many animals below man manifest a far greater amount of real affection in their love-making than do negroes" and that it is very rare that "we see two negroes kiss each other."[37] It is not surprising that when this book was written a Negro could not sing a sentimental song on the American stage.

During this campaign to prove that the Negro was subhuman and unfit for human association, the masses of Negroes found a refuge within the isolated world of the Negro folk. Their lives revolved principally about their churches, where they sang their songs of resignation and looked forward to another world in which they might escape the contempt and disdain of the white man. The Negro who migrated to a northern city discovered that he was only half-a-man in the white man's world.[38] The educated middle-class Negroes, who had striven to conform to American ideals and had contacts with a larger social world, could not find a refuge in the world of the Negro folk. In the South they were subject to the same Jim Crow Laws and contempt as the Negro masses, and in the North they were outsiders.[39] The mass migra-

35   Howard W. Odum, *Social and Mental Traits of the Negro* (New York: Columbia University, 1910), p. 171. Dr. Odum who, as head of the Department of Sociology of the University of North Carolina has done much to encourage scientific studies of the Negro, has long ago learned better than to accept any such notions concerning the Negro. Nevertheless, his book was very influential at the time in giving "scientific" support to prejudiced opinion concerning the Negro in the United States.

36   See Charles H. McCord, *The Amercan Negro as a Dependent, Defective, and Delinquent* (Nashville: Benson Printing Co., 1914), p. 42.

37   R. W. Shuffeldt, M. D., *America's Greatest Problem: The Negro* (Philadelphia: F. A. Davis, 1915), p. 47.

38   See Mary White Ovington, *Half a Man* (New York: Longmans, 1911).

39   In 1908, Charles Francis Adams of the famous Adams family, influential in the history of the United States since the American Revolution,

tions of Negroes to northern cities and the impact of two world wars upon the United States changed the relation of the Negro to American society. But Negroes have remained outsiders who still face the problem of being integrated into American society. The black bourgeoisie, who have striven to mold themselves in the image of the white man, have not been able to escape from the mark of racial inferiority.

III. *The Struggle for Status and Recognition*

Although the old black bourgeoisie, or Negro upper class, was not able to find a refuge in the world of the Negro folk, nevertheless, they were sheltered to some extent against the contempt and terror of the white man because they lived within the segregated Negro world. Their privileged position at the top of the social pyramid behind the walls of segregation provided some compensation for their hurt self-esteem. But while the Negro folk were exposed to a greater extent to the violence of the whites, the black bourgeoisie was more exposed in a spiritual sense. Except for the economic relations with whites, the Negro folk could retreat within their own world with its peculiar religious life, recreation, and family and sex life. Moreover, since the thinking of the Negro folk was not affected as that of the black bourgeoisie by the books and papers in which the Negro's inferiority was proclaimed, the black bourgeoisie suffered spiritually not only because they were affected by ideas concerning the Negro's inferiority, but perhaps even more because they had adopted the white man's values and patterns of behavior. Consequently, they developed an intense inferiority complex and because of this inferiority complex sought compensations.

A large section of the old middle class sought compensations

declared that the American theory concerning the assimilation of all races had broken in regard to the Negro since he was "a foreign substance" that could "neither be assimilated nor thrown out." Quoted in Robert E. Park and Ernest W. Burgess, *Introduction to the Science of Sociology* (Chicago: University of Chicago Press, 1924), p. 760.

in their white heritage.⁴⁰ They were not merely proud of their
white complexion, but they boasted of their kinship with the aristocratic whites of the South. In fact, in some cases their white ancestors had helped them to secure an education or had provided
for them economically. They also sought compensations in the
standards of puritanical family and sex mores, which set them
apart from the black masses. But the chief compensation for their
inferior status in American society was found in education. While
their racial heritage and conventional standards of morality only
gave them a privileged position in the Negro community, education gave them access to a world of ideas that provided an intellectual escape from their physical and social segregation in American life. Therefore, they placed an exaggerated importance upon
academic degrees, especially if they were secured from white colleges in the North. If one secured the degree of doctor of philosophy in a northern university, he was regarded as a sort of genius.
Consequently, for the relatively small group of educated Negroes,
education was an indication of their "superior culture" and a mark
of "refinement."

Education was not simply a form of compensation because it
set them apart from the Negro masses; it provided a form of compensation as regards their relations with whites. They constantly
asserted their educational and "cultural" superiority to the majority of the whites whose education was inferior to theirs. Whenever
they had contacts with white men who called them by their first

⁴⁰   See Edward B. Reuter, *The Mulatto in the United States* (Boston:
Richard G. Badger, Gorham Press, 1918) for a study of the extent of race
mixture and the role of the mixed-bloods among Negroes in the United
States. This book is the most important source of information on the mulatto or Negro of mixed ancestry up to the second decade of the present
century, despite the fact that it reflects some of the current prejudices of
whites and contains a number of serious errors. For example, the author
states on p. 317 that "In the United States almost every Negro of prominence from Frederick Douglass to Jack Johnson has married a white
woman or a light-colored mulatto." While it was very likely true that the
majority of prominent Negroes, who were themselves mulattoes, married
mulattoes, only a negligible number of prominent Negroes married white
women.

names or insulted them, they would take consolation in the fact that the white man was ignorant and could not appreciate art and literature or the things of the spirit as they could. Was not DuBois expressing this type of compensation when, while a professor of sociology in Atlanta University during the early years of the century, he wrote. "I sit with Shakespeare and he winces not. Across the color line I move arm in arm with Balzac and Dumas, where smiling men and welcoming women glide in gilded hall"?[41]

Despite their solid achievements and the satisfactions which they derived from their way of life, there was always an atmosphere of unreality surrounding the isolated life of the small black middle class. As we have seen, urbanization and the increasing occupational differentiation of the Negro population undermined the privileged position of the old middle class. But more important still, the compensations which ancestry, puritanical morals, and especially education, provided in a hostile white world were inadequate in the life of the new black bourgeoisie. Having become less isolated and thus more exposed to the contempt and hostility of the white world, but at the same time cherishing the values of the white world, the new black bourgeoisie with more money at their disposal, have sought compensations in the things that money can buy. Moreover, their larger incomes have enabled them to propagate false notions about their place in American life and to create a world of make-believe.

[41]   W. E. Burghardt DuBois, *The Souls of Black Folks* (15th ed.; Chicago, 1926), p. 109.

16

THE NEW NEGRO MIDDLE
CLASS

1955

THIRTY YEARS ago I wrote for inclusion in *The New Negro* a short chapter entitled "Durham: Capital of the Black Middle Class." In that chapter I undertook to show how a small group of Negroes, practicing the philosophy of thrift, had built up businesses which indicated the emergence of the spirit of modern business enterprise. Moreover, I undertook to describe the patterns of behavior and general outlook on life of this new class among Negroes, which I regarded as representative of a new element that was appearing in the evolution of Negro life in the United States. The many changes which have occurred in the economic and social structure of American society since that chapter was written have brought about a transformation of Negro life. One of the most important aspects of this transformation has been the emergence of a sizeable middle class which has acquired a dominant position in the Negro community. It is my purpose in this paper to discuss the development of the new Negro middle class and its present status. But before entering upon the main emphasis of this paper I must say something of the character of the Negro middle class which I described thirty years ago.

The middle class of which I wrote was composed principally of teachers, doctors, dentists, preachers, trusted persons in personal service, government employees, and a few business men. At that time all persons in professional occupations comprised about two

Reprinted from *The New Negro Thirty Years Afterward*, by E. Franklin Frazier (Washington, D.C.: Howard University Press, 1955), pp. 25–32.

and a half per cent of all employed Negroes, while the percentage of all those gaining a living from business enterprises, including clerical workers as well as proprietors, was even smaller. When I speak of this group as a middle class group I am not referring simply to the source of its incomes. This group was distinguished from the remainder of the Negro population not so much by economic factors as by social factors. Family affiliation and education to a less degree were as important as income. Moreover, while it exhibited many middle class features such as its emphasis on respectability and morality, it also possessed characteristics of an upper class or an aristocracy. To this extent the middle class group of which I wrote thirty years ago may be regarded as a caste in the Negro community. This leads me to say something of the sources of the traditions of this class.

From the standpoint of their cultural history, the Negroes in the United States have developed only two really vital traditions. The most important has been the folk tradition which gave the world the Spirituals and the secular folk songs. The second, of less importance but of considerable interest from the standpoint of the stratification of the Negro population, is the tradition of the gentleman. The folk tradition developed out of the experiences of the Negro masses on Southern plantations. The tradition of the gentleman was developed as the result of the close association of Negroes and whites, often in the same household, and led to the amalgamation of the two races. The assimilation of the patterns of behavior and values of upper class whites, mainly Southern aristocrats, established the tradition of the gentleman among a small class of Negroes. Of course, the traditions of the folk have often become mingled with the traditions of the gentleman. This is the reason for my statement in the chapter written thirty years ago that "the Negro has been a strange mixture of the peasant and the gentleman." This fact, as we shall see, has become especially significant in the growing importance of the new middle class today.

But let us return to the middle class of three decades ago. With few exceptions the representatives of the middle class were educated in the missionary schools which had been established by Northern missionaries after the Civil War. These missionaries had inculcated along with their pious teachings the idea of thrift. The influence of the missionaries extended to Tuskegee Institute and other schools under Negro administrations where the idea of thrift and the practice of piety were so conspicuous in the education of Negroes. In the schools of higher education founded by missionaries the teaching of piety and thrift was designed to build character and create a group of leaders with a sense of responsibility for the welfare and elevation of the masses. Moreover, these schools aimed to instill a certain love and appreciation of cultural things—music, literature, and art. The tradition of Yankee piety and thrift was often grafted onto the tradition of the aristocrat and gentleman.

The changes which occurred in the economic and social organization of the United States as the result of two world wars brought into existence a new middle class group among Negroes. The primary cause of this new development was the urbanization of the Negro population on a large scale. Prior to World War I about nine-tenths of the Negro population was in the South, and less than 25 per cent of Southern Negroes lived in cities. As the result of migrations to Southern as well as Northern cities about five-eighths of the Negroes live in cities today. The migration to Northern cities was especially crucial since it created large Negro communities in an area that was relatively free from the legal and customary discriminations under which Negroes live in the South. One of the first effects of the migrations to Northern cities was that it gave Negro children access to a standard American education. Secondly, the entrance of the Negro into industrial employment and into occupations that had been closed to him in the South accelerated the occupational differentiation of the Negro population. The occupational differentiation of the Negro population was accelerated also by the new needs of the Negro communities which were served by Negroes. Finally, the migrations gave the Negro access to political power which helped him to improve his economic as well as his social position.

These changes provided, first, the economic basis of the new middle class. Whereas the middle class of thirty years ago, as we have seen, was composed of a few professionals, mainly teachers and a few persons in other occupations including a few business men, middle class Negroes are found today in a large variety of professional and technical occupations. And what is more important is the significant increase in the proportion of Negroes in clerical and other white collar occupations. This latter development has occurred in the North because whereas in the South Negroes in white collar occupations are restricted to employment in segregated Negro schools and Negro businesses, in the North Negroes have increasingly been employed in white collar occupations in both public services and private enterprises. Then, too, Negro business in the North has become more important than in the South. This has refuted the old belief that Negro business could thrive better in a section where the Negro was segregated and suffered discrimination. However, in discussing the development of Negro business one should remember that some of the most conspicuous successes of Negroes in business have been in the policy racket and other illegal enterprises.

The expansion of the Negro middle class and the change in its character are indicated by the change in its capital, so to speak. Thirty years ago Durham, with its flourishing business enterprises, was rightly regarded as the capital of the black middle class. But today one turns to the North in order to discover what might be regarded as the capital of the black middle class. Although both Chicago and Detroit lay claim to this distinction, the unbiased observer is inclined to regard Detroit as the new capital of the Negro middle class because it is in that city that he finds the most intense expressions of the character and values of the new Negro middle class. The outlook on life and patterns of behavior of the new middle class are not confined to any city, however; they have tended to permeate the new middle class wherever the economic and social conditions have favored the emergence of this new element among Negroes. In the remainder of this paper, I shall undertake to analyze the orientation of this new class and to assess its influence upon the adjustment of the Negro to American civilization.

Let us consider first the economic basis of this class in the light of economic realities. At the present time, about a fourth of the Negroes in the North and West and one-eighth of those in the South may be classed as of middle class status. This estimate is based upon the fact that around three per cent of the employed Negro men in the North and West gain a living in professional and technical occupations and the same percentage as managers, officials, and proprieters, exclusive of farm owners. Slightly more than eight per cent are employed in clerical occupations and as salesmen. To these groups are added the skilled craftsmen and foremen who comprise between ten and eleven per cent of the employed Negroes in the North and West. In the South there are half as many, proportionately, in these occupations.

From the standpoint of incomes, Negroes of middle class status have incomes ranging from between $2,000 and $2,500 upwards. In the South the majority of the Negro middle class do not have incomes amounting to $3,000. In the North and West the Negro middle class is better off since a half of the Negroes of this status have incomes between $3,000 and $4,000. But in any case the less than one per cent of Negroes in the country with incomes between $4,000 and $5,000, who are at the top of the Negro middle class, have incomes about equal to the medium incomes of white collar workers among whites. As we have seen, the group of managers, officials, and proprietors, excluding farm owners, comprise slightly more than two per cent of employed Negroes. It is in this group that belong the Negro business men who are the symbols of the Negro middle class and its aspirations and values. Therefore, it is necessary to say something concerning Negro business.

In our discussion we are interested in Negro business first from the standpoint of its economic significance and secondly from the standpoint of its social significance for the Negro middle class. From the first standpoint, it has little significance in the economic life of the United States and little significance in the economic life of the Negro. It is obvious to anyone that the infinitesimal accumulations of capital represented by all Negro business enterprises have no significance in the American economic system. One small bank in a small town in the state of New York, for example, has more assets than all the Negro banks combined. Then, from the standpoint of providing employment for Negroes, Negro businesses provide employment for less than one-half of one per cent of all the employed Negroes. On the other hand, Negro business has a social significance that can not be ignored or underestimated.

Negro business is not only an economic fact, however insignificant; it is a social myth. The social myth has a long history. It originated in the 1880's when Negro leaders in the South, seeing the Negro supplanted by white workers, began preaching the doctrine that Negroes would achieve economic salvation by building their own businesses. These business enterprises were supposed to give employment to Negro workers. The myth was institutionalized when the National Negro Business League was organized in 1900. Since then the doctrine of salvation through business has been preached in every Negro church and school. Despite the fact that Negro business is no more significant today in the American economy and in the economic life of Negroes than it was fifty years ago, the myth is still perpetuated among Negroes. It is dear to the heart of the Negro middle class and no argument based upon facts can change their faith in Negro business as the means to racial salvation. This is not strange because the Negro middle class lives largely in a world of delusions.

The world of delusions which the Negro middle class has created for itself is due partly to the fact that it has no integral body of traditions. Here, then, it is necessary to consider the social origins of this class and its education. Earlier it was pointed out that two distinct traditions had developed among Negroes: the tradition of the folk and the genteel tradition or the traditions of the gentleman. The small Negro middle class of thirty years ago had its roots on the whole in the latter tradition. Most of the leaders among the Negro middle class were of mixed ancestry and had inherited the traditions of the upper class whites. The missionary education which they received tended to reenforce this tradition. As the result of the rapid social mobility which has brought into existence the new middle class, this tradition has been dissipated. Then, those with the traditions of the Negro folk who have risen to middle class status have shed their social heritage.

This may be seen if one views the changes which have occurred in Negro schools which provide education for the Negro middle class. Formerly, these schools were dedicated to the building of character or the making of men. As a part of this process the students of these schools were expected to become literate in the broadest meaning of the term and to develop some philosophy of life which included a sense of social responsibility. But today these institutions have become a sort of finishing schools for the children of the middle class. The term 'finishing school' is not exactly appropriate, since a finishing school is supposed to give a superficial culture, whereas the graduates of these schools lack even a superficial culture and are generally illiterate. This is not serious from the standpoint of the Negro middle class since these schools are no longer dedicated to the making of men but to the making of money-makers. The students are no longer taught habits of thrift and piety. They take as their models the successful members of the middle class who did not gain their money through such old fashioned virtues as thrift and saving, but through clever manipulations, rackets, and gambling. Moreover, during their college life the students strive to emulate the conspicuous consumption in which their parents and other persons who provide models engage. They have little or no respect for knowledge and learning and often even exhibit a certain contempt for anything involving intellectual achievement. In this respect they tend to perpetuate the anti-intellectualism which sets the new middle class apart from the old middle class that had some respect for education and learning.

The general anti-intellectualism of the new middle classes was shown by the failure of the Negro Renaissance in the twenties, many of the fruits of which are contained in *The New Negro*, edited by the late Professor Alain Locke. The Negro Renaissance of the twenties represented a reevaluation of the Negro's past and of the Negro himself by Negro intellectuals and artists. It failed because at that time the new middle class which was growing in size and importance in the Negro community rejected it. The short stories, novels, and poems which expressed this new evaluation of the Negro and his history in America by his artists and intellectuals were unread and ignored by the new middle class that was eager to gain a few dollars. Instead of being interested in gaining a new conception of themselves, the new middle class was hoping to escape from themselves. Money appeared to them to provide this main avenue of escape. But the escape was to be into a world of make-believe and delusions.

The Negro press has been one of the chief agencies by which the Negro middle class has escaped from the realities of its position in American life. The Negro press has created a world of make-believe into which the middle class attempts to escape from the realities of its position in American life. Some of these realities have been described. But there is still an important fact concerning the middle class which has not been mentioned, namely, the inferiority complex from which the middle class suffers. During its rise to its present position, the middle class has broken with its traditional background and identification with the Negro masses. Rejecting everything that would identify it with the Negro masses and at the same time not being accepted by white American society, the middle class has acquired an inferiority complex that is reflected in every aspect of its life. In creating a world of make-believe for the middle class, the press has provided compensations for their inferiority complex.

Although the vast majority of Negroes of middle class status are in reality white collar workers who derive their incomes from salaries, the Negro press represents them as a wealthy group. The press constantly plays up fantastic stories of rich Negroes. From time to time the Negro millionaires are featured in the Negro press. It carries pictures of their richly furnished homes, their expensive automobiles, their gay and extravagant parties and debutante balls. Since there has been a movement toward integration and white people are increasingly reading about the Negro world behind the walls of segregation, white teachers are asking how Negro teachers can afford debutante balls. But they are only beginning to learn of the gaudy carnival in which the middle class Negroes find an escape from their inferior status in American life.

In fact, much of the news carried in the Negro press is concerned with status. Every bit of news concerning the Negro that indicates that he is given some recognition by whites is recorded as of great consequence. If a Negro has nearly completed his residence work for the doctorate in a Northern university, it is played up as a great intellectual achievement. If a Negro is elected or appointed as a mere police magistrate, he is heralded as a great jurist and is forever afterwards referred to as "Judge." Even if a Negro was supposed to have been intimately associated with some notorious white criminal, he becomes a figure of note. Sometimes a Negro woman gains fame because she was caught in an illicit love affair with a white man. Of course, some of the news showing that the Negro has achieved recognition is mere fiction. Negroes who travel abroad are usually received by royalty, or some count falls madly in love with a Negro woman. Sometimes one reads in the Negro press of some Negro who scarcely knows a word of a foreign language astonishing foreign scholars with his facility in the language as well as his erudition. Thus does any recognition, real or fancied, soothe the inferiority feelings of the Negro middle class.

Much of the world of make-believe created by the Negro press consists of the activities of "Negro society." Nearly everyone who is featured by the Negro press is a socialite. This seems to be the highest compliment conferred upon a person of middle class status, male or female. A very retiring, scholarly friend of mine about whom a notice of his participation in a scientific meeting was carried in the Negro press was surprised to read that he was a leading socialite. Inclusion in "society" implies that a person is wealthy and can engage in all kinds of conspicuous consumption and waste. For example, one hardly ever reads of a socialite getting into her automobile but of her getting into a "chauffeured Cadillac." Minute details are generally provided concerning the cost of a mink coat, the cost of a house, or the cost of a party. But extravagant expenditure is not the only feature of being a socialite. It involves exclusiveness, and exclusiveness is always a means of overcoming one's feeling of inferiority.

The attempt of the middle class Negro to escape from the realities of his position in American life is really an attempt to escape from himself. This is shown partly in the case of the religious life of the middle class. At one time the Negro middle class was identified with the Congregational, Episcopal, Presbyterian, and, in a few cases, the Catholic churches. When one acquired middle class status it often meant a change from membership in the Baptist or Methodist denomination to affiliation with one of the above churches. But today, the new middle class has lost much of its religion and is constantly seeking some new religious or quasi-religious affiliation. But since the middle class has no philosophy of life and can only draw upon scraps of a religious tradition which it has rejected, it seeks solutions of life's problems in spiritualism and other forms of superstition. In fact, the world has become a world of chance for the middle class. After all, don't most of the most successful prominent members of the middle class owe their achievement to chance? This accounts for its almost religious devotion to poker, horse racing, and other forms of gambling.

The middle class owes its growth and form of existence to the fact that the Negro has been isolated mentally, socially, and morally in American society. Therefore, in some respects, the Negro community may be regarded as a pathological phenomenon. It is not surprising, then, that the Negro middle class shows the mark of oppression, to use the title of a recent study of the Negro, in its mental and psychic make-up. The middle class Negro shows the mark of oppression more than the lower class Negro who finds a shelter from the contempt of the white world in his traditional religion, in his songs, and in his freedom from a gnawing desire to be recognized and accepted. Although the middle class Negro has tried to reject his traditional background and racial identification, he cannot escape from it. Therefore, many middle class Negroes have developed self-hatred. They hate themselves because they cannot escape from being identified as Negroes. This self-hatred is really the hatred of the Negro turned against themselves. The inefficiency of the middle class Negro in the running of businesses and the management of educational institutions is notorious, but he excuses his deficiencies by exaggerating the defects of the Negro masses. Yet the middle class Negro pretends that he is proud of being a Negro while rejecting everything that identifies him with Negroes. He pretends that he is a leader of Negroes when he has no sense of responsibility to the Negro masses and exploits them whenever an opportunity offers itself. As a result, the middle class Negro is often plagued by feelings of guilt. Much of the neurotic behavior of the middle class Negro is doubtless due to his self-hatred and guilt feelings.

The middle class Negroes are haunted by feelings of insecurity. None of the compensations of the world of make-believe can completely efface their deep feelings of insecurity. The reality of the world about them breaks through the pretenses about wealth and recognition and social status. These feelings of insecurity become more urgent as the walls of segregation cease to protect them from the competition and requirements of American society. While middle class Negroes are often vociferous in their fight against segregation, many of them are afraid of the competition and the demands of the larger community. Some hope to come to terms with the white world by shedding as far as possible the last vestige of their racial identification. But this will provide no solution of their problems which arise from their rejection of their racial identification and their refusal to accept their real role in the economic organization of American life. As they become integrated into American society, they can achieve personal dignity and peace within themselves only through acceptance of their racial identification and their real position in American economic life.

17

THE FAILURE OF THE
NEGRO INTELLECTUAL

1962

DURING THE past forty years the relations of Negroes to American society have undergone fundamental changes. The tempo of these changes has been accelerated during the past two decades. The changes in the relationships of Negroes to American society have been the result of changes in the economic and social organization of American life which have in turn had their repercussions upon the Negro community and its institutions.

As a result of the changes in the character of the Negro community all the platitudes and clichés about Negroes and race relations have lost their meaning and relevance. The changes in the Negro community and American society have reached a stage where we are beginning to see in rather clear outlines the real problem of Negroes in American society.

There can be no question at the present time that the Negro must be integrated into the American community. But the integration of the Negro into the economic and social organization of American life is only an initial stage in the solution of some of the problems of the Negro.

There still remains the problem of the assimilation of the Negro, which is a more important and more fundamental problem. It is with this second problem that I am primarily concerned. But in order to clarify the issue it will be necessary to make clear the distinction between integration and assimilation. . . .

It is relevant at this point to say something concerning integra-

---

Reprinted from *Negro Digest*, February, 1962, pp. 26–36.

tion and the Negro community. . . . In the generally accepted meaning of the term, integration involves the acceptance of Negroes as individuals into the economic and social organization of American life. This would imply the gradual dissolution of the Negro community, that is, the decline and eventual disappearance of the associations, institutions and other forms of associated life in what constitutes the Negro community.

We do not expect anything approaching this to occur in our lifetime. Moreover, any discerning person will be aware of the fact that certain aspects of the organized aspects of Negro community life will be affected sooner and more fundamentally than other aspects.

For example, Negroes have always been forced to depend upon the economic institutions in the American community for employment and a living. Despite the vain hopes that Negroes have had concerning Negro business as a means to economic salvation and independence, the integration of Negroes into the industry and as white collar workers into the manufacturing and commercial institutions of the country has increased the economic welfare of Negroes and provided them with more business experience than all the so-called Negro business enterprise in the country.

On the other hand, there are certain cultural institutions such as the church and the fraternal organizations that will not dissolve or disappear. However, it has already appeared that in those sections of the country where newspapers carry news about Negroes as normal human beings and Negro reporters are employed, the circulation of Negro newspapers is declining.

I mention these facts concerning the Negro community because it is necessary to emphasize the fact that integration involves more than individuals, but the organized life of the Negro community vis-a-vis the organized white community. . . .

How does integration differ from assimilation? Assimilation involves, of course, integration for it is difficult to see how any people or group can become assimilated without being integrated into the economic and social organization of a country.

But assimilation involves integration into the most intimate phases of the organized social life of a country. As a consequence, assimilation leads to complete identification with the people and culture of the community in which the social heritages of different people become merged or fused.

In 1908, Charles Francis Adams stated in a lecture in Richmond that the theory of the complete assimilation and absorption of all peoples because of the absence of fundamental racial differences had broken down in the case of the Negro.

The Negro, according to Adams, could only be partially assimilated or, in our language, integrated but not assimilated. When he spoke of absorption he was evidently referring to amalgamation.

In recent years there has been much talk about the integration of the Negro but hardly any attention has been given to his assimilation. There have been some wild guesses about the amalgamation or absorption of the Negro and his disappearance in 300 to 500 years. It is to the question of the assimilation of the Negro that I want to devote the remainder of this talk.

It may seem strange if I tell you that the question of integration and assimilation of the American Negro has not been considered or raised by American Negroes but by African intellectuals. Only recently at a luncheon in Washington an African intellectual spoke on the subject and afterwards asked me to write an article on the subject. But the contrast between the attitude and orientation of American Negro intellectuals and African intellectuals was revealed most sharply at the congresses of Negro writers held in Paris in 1956 and in Rome in 1959.

At these congresses the African, and I might add the West Indian intellectuals, were deeply concerned with the question of human culture and personality and the impact of western civilization on the traditional culture of Negro peoples. It was to be expected that African intellectuals would be concerned with such questions.

But the amazing thing was that American Negro intellectuals who were imbued with an integrationist point of view were not only unconcerned with this question but seemingly were unconscious of the implications of the important question of the relation of culture and personality and human destiny.

I insist that these are the fundamental questions with which all thinkers should be concerned and that it is unfortunate that Americans have not concerned themselves with these questions. The lack of interest in this important question or lack of understanding of it is responsible for much of the confusion in regard to integration which is changing the entire relationship of the Negro to American society.

As far as I have been able to discover, what Negro intellectuals have had to say concerning integration has been concerned with the superficial aspects of the increasing participation of Negroes in the economic and social and political organization of American society.

Practically no attention has been directed to the rather obvious fact that integration involves the interaction of the organized social life of the Negro community with the wider American community.

Moreover, there has been an implied or unconscious assimilationist philosophy, holding that Negroes should enter the mainstream of American life as rapidly as possible leaving behind their social heritage and becoming invisible as soon as possible. This has been due, I think, to the emergence of a sizeable new middle class whose social background and interests have determined the entire intellectual orientation of educated Negroes.

In my *Black Bourgeoisie* I have considered this phenomenon and it is unnecessary to go into the question here. There are certain phases of this phenomenon which are relevant to this discussion.

The first aspect is that the new Negro middle class is the stratum of the Negro population that is becoming integrated most rapidly because of its education and its ability to maintain certain standards of living. In its hope to achieve acceptance in American life, it would slough off everything that is reminiscent of its Negro origin and its Negro folk background.

At the same time integration is resulting in inner conflicts and frustrations because Negroes are still outsiders in American life. Despite integration, the middle class, in escaping from its sheltered and privileged position in the Negro community, has become more exposed to the contempt and discriminations of the white world. Thus, the new Negro middle class is confronted with the problems of assimilation and their intellectuals have not provided them with an understanding of the problems.

This lack of understanding on the part of the so-called intellectual fringe of the new middle class is due partly to the general anti-intellectualism of this class and partly to the desire to achieve acceptance in American life by conformity to the ideals, values, and patterns of behavior of white Americans.

This is no speculation on my part. Every study that has been made reveals that they think very much the same as white Americans, even concerning Negroes.

Moreover, so-called Negro intellectuals continue to repeat such nonsense as "No race has made as much progress as the American Negro in the same period and that his remarkable progress has been due to oppression."

Yet, anyone knows that after 250 years American Negro intellectuals cannot measure up to African intellectuals.

If was the white scholar, Buell Gallagher, in his book, *Color And Conscience*, who showed clearly that Negroes in every part of the world where they enjoyed freedom had achieved more intellectually and artistically than the American Negro. All of this drive towards conformity to dominant beliefs and values is implicit or unconscious striving of the middle class to become assimilated.

The great difference between the orientation of the African intellectual and the American Negro intellectual is striking when one considers their starting point in their analysis of the position of the people for whom they are supposed to provide intellectual leadership.

All African intellectuals begin with the fact of the colonial experience of the African. They possess a profound understanding of the colonial experience and its obvious effects upon not only their traditional social organization, but of the less obvious and more profound effects upon the culture and the African personality.

The American Negro intellectual goes his merry way discussing such matters as the superficial aspects of the material standard of living among Negroes and the extent to which they enjoy civil rights. He never begins with the fundamental fact of what slavery has done to the Negro or the group which is called Negroes in the United States.

Yet it is as necessary for the American Negro intellectual to deal with these questions as it is for the African intellectual to begin with the colonial experience.

The American Negro intellectual is even more remiss in his grasp of the condition and fate of American Negroes. He has steadily refused to recognize what has been called the "mark of oppression." It was the work of two white scholars that first called attention to this fundamental aspect of the personality of the American Negro. Moreover, it was the work of another white scholar, Stanley M. Elkins, in his recent book on *Slavery*, who has shown the psychic trauma that Negroes suffered when they were enslaved, the pulverization of their social life through the destruction of their clan organization, and annihilation of their personality through the destruction of their cultural heritage.

Sometimes I think that the failure of the American Negro intellectual to grasp the nature and the significance of these experiences is due to the fact that he continues to be an unconscious victim of these experiences. After an African intellectual met a group of Negro intellectuals, he told me that they were really men who were asleep.

All of this only tends to underline the fact that educated Negroes or Negro intellectuals have failed to achieve any intellectual freedom. In fact, with the few exceptions of literary men, it appears that the Negro intellectual is unconscious of the extent to which his thinking is restricted to sterile repetition of the safe and conventional ideas current in American society.

This is attributable in part, of course, to the conditions under which an educated and intellectual class emerged in the American society. This class emerged as the result of white American philanthropy. Although the situation has changed and the Negro intellectuals are supported through other means, they are still largely dependent upon the white community. There is no basis of economic support for them within the Negro community. And where there is economic support within the Negro community it demands conformity to conservative and conventional ideas.

Witness, for example, the vote of the National Medical Association in New York City against placing medical care for the aged under social security. The action of this group might be attributable partly to ignorance and what they conceived to be their economic interests; nevertheless, it was done under the domination of the American Medical Association which ignored the whining complaints of Negro doctors against racial discrimination.

I could cite other examples which more clearly represent the absence of intellectual freedom in regard to national and international issues. Most Negro intellectuals simply repeat the propaganda which is put out by people who have large economic and political interests to protect.

Of course, Negro intellectuals are in a different position from the standpoint of employment. If they show any independence in their thinking they may be hounded by the F.B.I. and find it difficult to make a living. At the present time many of them find themselves in the humiliating position of running around the world telling Africans and others how well-off Negroes are in the United States and how well they are treated.

One is reminded of the words of Langston Hughes in his recent book, *Ask Your Mama*, where he says that the African visitor finds that in the American social supermarket blacks for sale range from intellectuals to entertainers. Thus, it appears that the price of the slow integration which the Negroes are experiencing must be bought at the price of abject conformity in thinking.

One of the most important results of the lack of freedom on the part of Negro intellectuals has been their failure to produce men of high intellectual stature who are respected by the world at large.

We have no philosophers or thinkers who command the respect of the intellectual community at large. I am not talking about the few teachers of philosophy who have read Hegel or Kant or James and memorized their thoughts. I am talking about men who have reflected upon the fundamental problems which have always concerned philosophers such as the nature of human knowledge and the meaning or lack of meaning of human existence.

We have no philosophers who have dealt with these and other problems from the standpoint of the Negro's unique experience in this world. I am not talking about the puerile opportunistic rationalizations of the Negro's effort to survive in a hostile world. The philosophy implicit in the Negro's folklore is infinitely superior to the opportunistic philosophy of Negro intellectuals who want to save their jobs and enjoy material comforts.

The philosophy implicit in the folklore of the Negro folk is infinitely superior in wisdom and intellectual candor to the empty repetition of platitudes concerning brotherly love and human dignity of Negro intellectuals who are tyrants within the Negro world and never had a thought in their lives.

This brings me to say something of what Negro intellectuals or scholars have failed to accomplish as the intellectual leaders of Negroes.

They have failed to study the problems of Negro life in America in a manner which would place the fate of the Negro in the broad framework of man's experience in this world. They have engaged in petty defenses of the Negro's social failures. But more often they have been so imbued with the prospect of integration and eventual assimilation that they have thought that they could prove themselves true Americans by not studying the Negro.

Since integration has become the official policy of the country they have shunned more than ever the study of the Negro. They have remained intellectually sterile while propounding such meaningless questions as: Should Negro scholars study the Negro? Should Negro painters paint Negro subjects? Should Negro writers and playwrights write Negro novels and plays above Negroes?

This is indicative of the confusion among Negro intellectuals. But more important still, it has meant that Negro intellectuals have cut themselves off from a vastly rich source of human experience to which they had access.

It is scarcely believable that the only significant studies of Negroes in politics have been the work of white scholars. I have already mentioned other fields of interest in which scholars have made significant contributions. Of course, some of this failure has been the result of ignorant administration of Negro schools which have refused the intelligent proposals of Negro scholars.

Let us take the case of Conant's book, *Slums And Suburbs*,

which deals with the tragic position of Negroes in America. As long as 25 years ago I pointed out that urbanization had changed the entire relationship of Negroes to American society and that comprehensive and fundamental research should be done on Negroes in cities. But those Negroes who have controlled the destiny of Negro intellectuals ignored this and even today no Negro college or university is concerned with this fundamental problem.

Conant's book, which reveals the poverty, ignorance and social disorganization of Negroes, emphasizes a phase of the integration and assimilation of Negroes to which I have only vaguely referred. It deserves special attention in what I am undertaking to discuss.

Not only has Conant devoted attention to the position of Negroes in slums, but I have noted that Ashmore has published a book dealing with this problem and the frustrations of the Negro middle class.

The significance of the large proportion of unemployed, impoverished and socially and personally disorganized Negroes in cities for our discussion can not be overemphasized. It shows clearly that whereas a relatively large middle class is emerging in our cities, at the same time a large degraded proletariat is also appearing.

It reveals the wide economic and social cleavage which is becoming more manifest between the middle class and the masses of Negroes.

These Negroes have little education, practically no skills, and what is more, they have never known a normal family life. Because of their lack of socialization, they can hardly take advantage of the educational institutions, they are unprepared for employment in an industrial society, and they are unfit for normal social life.

Conant is afraid that they will become susceptible to Communist propaganda, but he does not know Negroes. If they were to become Communist their lives would be organized about objectives and goals which would have some stabilizing influence.

But most of these Negroes will become the victims of liquor, dope, and disease and they will engage in all forms of crime and anti-social behavior. Those who seek an escape from their frustration and bewilderment will not join communist movements; they will join all types of religious sects and cults, some of which will have nationalistic or racial aims.

In fact, the growth of the Black Muslim movement represents disillusionment on the part of Negroes concerning integration and a repudiation of the belief in assimilation which is so dear to the middle classes.

Recently we have been hearing about the revolt against the leaders of the Negro. The most significant symptom of this revolt has been the revolt of Negro youth against the old respectable and conventional leadership which acted as mediators between the Negro community and the white community.

The most dramatic aspect of the revolt has been the "sit-in" movements which are a direct attack upon segregation. The aim is integration and ultimately assimilation, if I gauge correctly the aims of the leaders. This seems to emphasize the failure of Negro intellectuals. They can only see assimilation beyond integration. But there are problems of American life that Negroes will have to meet in becoming integrated and assimilated and they concern the economic and social organization of American life.

I pointed out at the beginning that whatever change had occurred in the status of Negroes was due to changes in the economic and social organization of American life. American Negro intellectuals seem to be unconscious of this fact and seemingly believe that integration and ultimate assimilation will solve the problems of the Negro.

It is very important for our discussion on integration and assimilation that the leaders of the non-violence technique have gone to India for philosophical and ideological justification of their revolt against segregation and discrimination in American society.

That the technique should be non-violent is natural since Negroes, who are outnumbered by whites and threatened by the armed might of whites, could not resort to violence or revolutionary tactics.

I do not think that it represents any moral superiority on their part. Moreover, I do not think that Gandhism is really applicable to the Negro's situation in the United States.

Nevertheless, I recognize that it achieves a certain moral respectability because of its religious basis. This is especially important where Negroes confront the guilt-ridden respectable white middle classes. In analyzing the movement and in seeking its religious and moral inspiration, we should recognize that it has its roots in the religious experiences and culture of the Negro folk.

The leaders may speak in philosophical and ideological terms that are drawn from an alien culture but the dynamics of the movement are to be found in the religious experiences of the Negroes. When Negroes are forced to face hostile white mobs, they do not sing Indian hymns, they sing Negro Spirituals and the hymns of their fathers which embodied the faith of their fathers in a hostile world.

That the Negro leaders should turn to an alien culture for the philosophical and ideological justification of their revolt shows the extent to which Negro intellectuals are alienated from the masses. It is also an indication of the failure of the intellectual leaders to perform their role in relation to the Negro. They have failed to dig down into the experiences of the Negro and provide the soul of a people.

With exceptions, and I will name Langston Hughes as a conspicuous example, they have tried to escape from the Negro heritage. It was their duty to put this heritage in history books, in novels and in plays, in painting and in sculpture.

Because of their eagerness to be accepted as Americans or perhaps sometimes because of their fear, they have written no novels and plays about Denmark Vesey, Harriet Tubman or Schields Green who went with John Brown. They have accepted supinely as heroes the Negroes whom white people have given us and told us to revere. Even today they run from DuBois and Paul Robeson.

In view of the Negro's history, the Negro intellectual and artist had a special opportunity and special responsibility. The process by which the Negroes were captured and enslaved in the United States stripped them of their African culture and destroyed their personality. Under the slavery regime and for nearly a century since emancipation everything in American society has stamped the Negro as subhuman, as a member of an inferior race that had not achieved even the first steps in civilization.

There is no parallel in human history where a people have been subjected to similar mutilation of body and soul. Even the Christian religion was given them in a form only to degrade them. The African intellectual recognizes what colonialism has done to the African and he sets as his first task the mental, moral, and spiritual rehabilitation of the African.

But the American Negro intellectual, seduced by dreams of final assimilation, has never regarded this as his primary task.

I am aware that he has carried on all sorts of arguments in defense of the Negro but they were mainly designed to protect his own status and soothe his hurt self-esteem.

I am talking about something entirely different. I am referring to his failure to dig down into the experience of the Negro and bring about a transvaluation of that experience so that the Negro could have a new self-image or new conception of himself.

It was the responsibility of the Negro intellectual to provide a positive identification through history, literature, art, music and the drama.

The truth of the matter is that for most Negro intellectuals, the integration of the Negro means just the opposite, the emptying of his life of meaningful content and ridding him of all Negro identification. For them, integration and eventual assimilation means the annihilation of the Negro—physically, culturally, and spiritually.

Guy Johnson has written recently that in the next 25 years there will be more integration but far less than the Negro hopes for, and as a consequence there will be much frustration. Moreover, as Park once wrote, the Negro will be treated as a racial minority rather than a racial caste.

I am inclined to agree on the whole with this prediction, especially for the South. But even in the North where Negroes will achieve greater integration, I can not envision any assimilation in the foreseeable future. The best evidence of this is the manner in which the centennial of the Civil War is being celebrated. The important fact about the Civil War is the emancipation of the Negro and Lincoln's achievement of worldwide immortality as the Emancipator—not as the savior of the Union, which was a local political event.

Yet, the nation has ignored and repudiated the central fact which is the most important element in the boosted moral idealism of the United States. The Negro is left out of the celebration both physically and as a part of the heritage of America.

The Civil War is supposed to have been the result of a misunderstanding of two brothers, white brothers, of course, and the Emancipation of the Negro is forgotten.

Confronted with this fact, the Negro intellectual should not be consumed by his frustrations. He must rid himself of his obsession with assimilation. He must come to realize that integration should not mean annihilation—self-effacement, the escaping from his identification.

In a chapter entitled, "What can the American Negro Contribute to the Social and Economic Life of Africa" in the book, *Africa Seen By American Negroes*, I pointed out that the American Negro had little to contribute to Africa but that Africa, in achieving freedom, would probably save the soul of the American Negro in providing him with a new identification, a new self-image, and a new sense of personal dignity.

I want to emphasize this by pointing out that if the Negro is ever assimilated into American society his heritage should become a part of the American heritage, and it should be recognized as the contribution of the Negro as one recognizes the contributions of the English, Irish, Germans and other people.

But this can be achieved only if the Negro intellectual and artist frees himself from his desire to conform and only if he overcomes his inferiority complex.

It may turn out that in the distant future Negroes will disappear physically from American society. If this is our fate, let us disappear with dignity and let us leave a worthwhile memorial—in science, in art, in literature, in sculpture, in music—of our having been here.

VI. The Negro and Desegregation

18

HUMAN, ALL TOO HUMAN: THE NEGRO'S VESTED INTEREST IN SEGREGATION

1947

BEHIND THE walls of segregation that prevent the Negro from participating fully in American life, an organized life has grown up similar to that in the larger white community. There are institutions, such as the church and fraternal societies, which are deeply rooted in the culture and traditions of the Negro. There are the more consciously planned business enterprises and professional associations.

Then there are institutions and organizations, notably the schools, which embody both cultural and material interests. Some of these agencies have grown out of the long history of the race, while others represent changing adjustments to the pattern of segregation. The various institutions and organizations reflect the economic and social stratification of the Negro community which owes its character largely to economic discrimination and to the isolation of its members from their fellow Americans.

All these various bodies—even the class structure itself—have become vested interests, of a sort, for some elements in the Negro group. They have become vested interests in the sense that Negroes feel that they have a right to the exclusive enjoyment of the social and material rewards they derive from the system of segregation.

Reprinted from *Survey Graphic*, 1947, pp. 74–75, 99–100.

As the system is under attack today, it is necessary to take into account these special interests behind its walls.

Separate Churches

The various independent Negro churches represent the vested interests associated with institutions and organizations rooted in Negro traditions and history. These religious bodies came into existence because the Negro was denied an opportunity for self-expression and equal status with whites within the church.

When Richard Allen and his colored associates withdrew from St. George's Church in Philadelphia in 1787, he expressed the opinion that Methodism was better suited to the needs of Negroes than the Episcopal form of worship. Although Allen did not attribute the peculiar religious needs of Negroes to racial factors, both racial and cultural influences have been used since as justification for separate Negro churches.

For example, in a recent article in *The Quarterly Review*, published by the Sunday School Board of the Southern Baptist Convention, E. P. Alldredge states that because of the Negro's religious endowment he should have separate church organizations. While Mr. Alldredge is obviously attempting to justify his racial prejudices, Mr. Allen had referred to something that had nothing to do with race. Sixty years ago, George W. Cable pointed out in his book "The Silent South" that the failure of the white Methodists to incorporate Negroes in their churches after the Civil War was not due to racial differences but to the fact that the Protestant churches had never been able "to get high and low life to worship together."

It is generally recognized today that the form of worship preferred by Negroes is due to their level of culture rather than to some peculiar racial endowment or African background. Both illiterate poor whites and Negroes of like condition always have enjoyed the same type of emotional religious expression. So, separate churches turn out to be factors in the attempt to keep the Negro in the position of a lower caste.

Because of the exclusion of Negroes from full participation in

American life, the segregated church has provided a field in which leaders could obtain social and economic security. Moreover, the separation of the races has placed the Negro minister in a very special relationship to the members of his church.

To many Negroes there is something incongruous in having a representative of the dominant white race preach brotherly love and Christian humility and offer them the solace of religion in sickness or bereavement. A white doctor may enjoy prestige among Negroes because he may possess special professional skill; but for the things of the spirit, they feel that only a black minister who has the same peculiar relation to God as have they themselves can give help and comfort.

The Shepherd and His Flock

Many Negro pastors, for their part, feel they have a vested interest in ministering to the spiritual needs of Negroes. Of course this involves certain social and material advantages. Moreover, in the Methodist church organizations, there is the coveted office of bishop, which not only provides a good living but confers considerable authority over large numbers of people. This concentration of power within a segregated Negro institution also places the Negro minister in a strategic position in relation to the white community.

Thus, recently it was suggested in a midwestern city that as a means of breaking down segregation in churches, a white church might take on an assistant Negro minister. The suggestion was immediately opposed by the Negro ministers in the city. Seemingly, they feared that if the plan were carried out members of the segregated Negro churches would be drawn away, into the white church.

In view of the shortage of trained Negro ministers and the difficulty of attracting young Negroes to the theological seminaries, it might be assumed that the vested interest of Negro pastors in the separate churches would be easy to overcome. Because of the historic background of the Negro church and its place in the life of the Negro, this is not the case. The elimination of segregated Negro churches, in all probability, will follow rather than precede the breakdown of the secular color line.

This is also true of fraternal and similar organizations that have provided the chief means by which Negroes have accumulated capital. Consequently, their leaders wield power and enjoy financial rewards.

Job Rights and Segregation

Vested interests in separate Negro schools, libraries, hospitals, and welfare organizations (some, but by no means all of them, rooted in historic tradition) offer resistance to the removal of the color line. In the separate schools, as in the separate churches, many Negroes have found a field for leadership. Some of the separate schools in the South have enabled their heads to accumulate means; more often they have been the source of authority in interracial relations. In border states and even in northern cities, some Negroes have regarded separate school as an opportunity to acquire an exclusive right to employment.

Some Negro social workers have favored separate agencies to handle the problems of colored people. The Negro's professional interest in segregated schools, hospitals, and welfare agencies is generally accompanied by rationalizations about the peculiar needs of the race; or the exclusion, real or potential, of trained Negroes from employment in non-segregated institutions.

Thus, Negro physicians may advocate separate hospitals on the grounds that in them they would have more opportunities to develop their skill and to serve their "own people." But this, too, is only a rationalization because there is abundant evidence that the standard of medical care in segregated hospitals, where Negro physicians are supposed to have every professional opportunity, is lower than in unsegregated institutions. It is scarcely necessary to point out that to abolish segregation would create technological unemployment for Negroes who secure a living from the existence of segregation.

Clearly, only certain elements in the Negro community have a vested interest in segregation. Since this fact is often overlooked, its implications should be made clear. It is the Negro professional, the business man, and to a less extent, the white collar worker who profit from segregation. These groups in the Negro population enjoy certain advantages because they do not have to compete with whites.

For example, the writer heard a Negro college president excuse the inefficiency of his administration on the grounds that the Negro was a "child race" and only seventy years out of slavery. In thus flattering his white listeners, he was fortifying his own position in the segregated Negro world. Imagine, on the other hand, a Negro steel worker or shipyard riveter excusing his inefficiency thus.

The Negro doctor who favors separate hospitals is in a position similar to that of the Negro college president. In fact, in one northern city, Negro doctors, instead of fighting the exclusion of Negro patients from municipal hospitals, have opened their own hospitals to which only Negroes are admitted, with the city paying a daily stipend for each patient. Very seldom, however, is the vested interest of the Negro professional man in segregation so patently opposed to the interests of his racial group.

Negro Enterprises

The institutions and organizations embodying the more material interests of the Negro have never acquired great importance because they have had to compete with similar institutions in the larger white community. This is shown especially in regard to business establishments. Negro enterprises are no more signficant today as a source of income for Negroes than they were fifty years ago when the Negro began to place so much faith in them as a means of economic salvation. Nevertheless, these organizations represent vested interests, and since every such interest by its very nature is opposed to competition, it is in this field that the Negro's vested interest in segregation finds its clearest expression.

But as a rule, Negro businesses are not willing to compete with businesses generally; they expect the Negro public to support them because of "race pride." Colored people are told that Negro enterprises are rendering a service to the "race." In fact, however, the majority of Negro businesses are operated by the owners themselves, and therefore provide few, if any, jobs for Negro workers. Moreover, patrons of these enterprises usually have to pay high prices for inferior goods and services.

Negro restaurants in the black ghettos of our cities are a striking example of this fact. Not only are Negro patrons forced to pay higher prices than are charged in comparable white restaurants, but they must often tolerate poor service and outright incivility on the part of the employes. The chief benefits of Negro enterprises are enjoyed by the operators who have a monopoly on services which Negroes cannot get elsewhere.

If segregation were eliminated, the social justification for the existence of Negro business would vanish and Negro businessmen would have to compete with other businessmen. Undoubtedly, many Negro enterprises would disappear, along with the sentimental justification which helps support them.

Negro insurance companies and newspapers are the largest and most successful business undertakings among Negroes. Both provide employment for Negro white collar workers, both have enabled a few Negroes to acquire enough wealth to maintain the standards of the moderately well-to-do.

If segregation were abolished, the efficient white collar workers would probably be absorbed in the business enterprises of the community—but the Negro entrepreneurs would no longer enjoy the vested interest which segregation provides. Despite all the talk about discrimination on the part of white insurance companies, their rates are lower than those of insurance companies which are compelled to use actuarial tables based solely upon the life expectancy of Negroes.

Segregation and discrimination provide prime reasons for the existence of Negro newspapers. In fact, they thrive upon the injustice under which Negroes suffer. The integration of the Negro into American life offers a threat to their very existence.

During the war, there was a growing disposition on the part of white papers to handle news about Negroes just as they handled similar items concerning white people. On one occasion when white papers were about to carry a story of a distinguished achievement of Negroes in the military forces, they were requested to withhold the story until Negro newspapers had carried it.

The Question of Status

The class structure which has grown up in segregated Negro communities is due partly to discrimination in employment and partly to the social isolation of the Negro. Consequently, occupations and incomes in the Negro community do not have the same relation to social status as they do in the white community. Persons whose jobs and resources would place them in the middle class, or perhaps lower middle class, in the white community are at the top of the social pyramid in the Negro community. Further, a fair complexion often plays an important role in social distinctions and preeminence among Negroes.

The extent to which certain occupations, a fairly secure income, or a light complexion cause some colored people to attempt a leisured, upper class style of living depends upon the degree of isolation of the Negro community. In northern cities where the Negro professional and white collar workers often associate freely with whites of similar occupations, they are more likely to conform to middle class standards. But where the Negro community is completely segregated, as in border and southern cities, the professional and white collar workers are more likely to assume an upper class style of life.

As members of the "aristocracy" of the Negro community, professional and business men and women acquire certain vested interests in segregation. For example, a Negro doctor who has acquired a certain skill has been known to keep it within an upper class clique of doctors.

Usually, however, the status of a Negro doctor or college professor in the Negro community bears little or no relation to his professional achievements. In fact, he is relieved of competing with white men in the same profession.

He enjoys certain rewards and advantages solely because of his social position in the Negro world. Like other members of the upper class, he is treated with a certain deference by the general Negro public and the attention of the Negro world is focused upon him through reports of his activities in the Negro press. If the walls of segregation were broken down, the Negro doctor or college professor would be thrown into competition with whites in his profession and, in most instances, he would suffer a deflation of his social status. In addition to the organized phases of their life, many Negroes as individuals have vested interests in the pattern of segregation. Although these include certain pecuniary rewards, material interests are not always as important as other elements in such vested interests—the psychological and social.

Because of segregation, the dominant white group has been forced to select certain Negroes to act as mediators between the two races. These Negro go-betweens have acquired an eminence unrelated to intellectual ability or moral character. Oftentimes Negroes have been chosen for this role because they lacked these very qualities. But as long as they played the role assigned them by white individuals and organizations, they have been "built up" as great "interracial statesmen" or great "intellectual leaders" or great "spiritual leaders." Simply because of their strategic position in the pattern of segregation, they have enjoyed prestige and power among Negroes and whites as well. If there had not been a pattern of racial segregation, many of these mediators would have become faithful servants, successful traveling salesmen, or small town revivalists.

Double Standards of Achievement

The pattern of segregation has created generally an attitude of tender condescension on the part of many whites toward the Negro. This is shown especially in the exaggerated evaluation of the Negro's intellectual and artistic achievements. In fact, it is difficult to obtain an objective appraisal of the work of Negro students and artists. A foreign visitor once said to the writer that he was tired of being told that a certain Negro was a great scholar when it was obvious that he had a mediocre mind and had not produced any outstanding work. Such designations as "Negro psychologist" or "Negro artist" reveal the double standard implicit in the criticism of the work of Negroes by whites.

The achievements of Negroes in scholarship and the arts are most likely to be overvalued when they conform to what whites think Negroes should study, write, or paint. These warped estimates of the work of Negroes form a part of the folklore of race relations which has grown out of segregation. The road to distinction and to more concrete rewards in the segregated Negro world is not as rough as whites who invest the Negro with pathos think it is.

The segregated Negro community, which is essentially a pathological phenomenon in American life, has given certain Negroes a vested interest in segregation—involving more than dollars-and-cents considerations. As the walls of segregation "come tumbling down," the Negro will lose all these petty advantages. If this results in the social and psychological deflation of some, it will nevertheless cause Negroes generally to acquire a saner conception of themselves and of their role in American society. Through the same process, white people will come to regard Negroes as human beings like themselves and to make a more realistic appraisal of their personalities and of their work.

19

THE NEGRO MIDDLE CLASS
AND DESEGREGATION

1957

THE STUDY of the black bourgeoisie is in a sense the logical outgrowth of the study of the Negro family which I began thirty years ago. At that time it was my conviction that the study of the Negro in the United States had a wider significance than what was regarded then as a social problem and generally referred to as the "Negro problem." Consequently, it occurred to me that the study of the Negro would gain in significance if it were placed in a wider frame of reference and defined in terms of a fundamental sociological problem. It is from this standpoint that I shall undertake to discuss the Negro middle class desegregation.

The problem of desegregation involves much more than racial attitudes or interpersonal relations. Economic and political factors must be taken into account as well as institutions and other aspects of organized social life. It is especially significant then that on this occasion we are celebrating the seventy-fifth birthday anniversary of Professor MacIver, who while claiming for sociology a special field of interest has insisted upon the relevance of psychological, economic, political and cultural factors in the analysis of social relationships. Although I am restricting myself to the limited role which a new social stratum in the Negro community is playing in desegregation, my discussion will nevertheless be within the context of larger economic and social forces in American life.

Reprinted from *Social Problems*, 4 (April, 1957): 291–301, by permission of The Society for the Study of Social Problems.

From whatever standpoint one may undertake an analysis of the process of desegregation, it is necessary to recognize the existence of a Negro community in the United States with a set of institutions which closely duplicate those in the American community. It is necessary to emphasize this fact because in most discussions of desegregation there is an implicit assumption that Negroes are merely atomized individuals who have been excluded from full participation in the life of the white society. The recent decision of the Supreme Court of the United States concerning the admission of Negroes to white schools has tended to focus attention upon the institutional life of the Negro community. Nevertheless, it is necessary to emphasize the organized aspects of Negro life in order to gain a clear insight into the sociological aspects of the problem of desegregation. Since there is a Negro community or, perhaps better, there are Negro communities in the United States, they have a locus in space. Some attention has been given to the location and character of these communities with reference to the plantation system of agriculture. More detailed studies have been carried on in cities, especially northern cities, where large Negro communities have grown up in response to the demands of northern industry. The ecological studies of Negro communities are important because of the light which they throw on the whole subject of desegregation. If those who are concerned with desegregation in public education in the North had some knowledge of the ecological organization of our cities, they would not be puzzled or confused about segregated schools in northern cities which are generally the result of an ecological process rather than a policy of racial segregation. And if those in southern cities who are honestly concerned with bringing about a transition from segregated to non-segregated schools had some knowledge of the ecological organization of cities, they could meet more effectively the arguments of opponents who claim that desegregation will result in social anarchy and at worst sexual promiscuity.

We are more especially interested in the institutions and association in the Negro community since their relation to the process of desegregation is even less understood. For the purpose of this discussion, an attempt will be made to classify these institutions according to their significance for a sociological analysis of the desegregation process. The first type includes those institutions and associations which serve the cultural needs of the Negro community. The most important of these institutions are the religious institutions. The religious institutions, especially the Baptist and Methodist, have a history spanning nearly two centuries. They embody more than any other institution the unique experiences, aspirations, and outlook on life of the Negroes in the United States. Whatever African survivals might have influenced the early history of these institutions, they are the result of the experience of the Negro in the New World and embody the beliefs, patterns of thought, and behavior which the Negro acquired from Europeans. In this same category should be placed mutual aid associations, Negro schools and colleges under the control of Negro church organizations, fraternal organizations, Greek letter societies, and professional societies, although the latter two reveal more definitely the influence of the white community.

In the second category of institutions and associations I would place those organized form of social life which have their roots both in the Negro community and in the larger American community. This category is represented by the public schools which reveal to varying degrees the extent to which these institutions are rooted partly in the Negro community and partly in the white community. In the South the Negro public schools are controlled by the white community but may embody to some extent the traditions and patterns of behavior of the Negro community. On the other hand, in the North the public schools which are attended mainly by Negro students are part of the wider American community. I would place in this same category those Negro schools and colleges which were established by white philanthropists and missionaries and where the support and ultimate control remain in the white community. One would place in this same category various public recreational institutions which serve primarily the Negro community.

The third category includes those institutions and associations which have their roots entirely in the white community. These forms of organized social life are concerned principally with the economic activities of Negroes. The segregated Negro labor unions are an outstanding example of this type of association. Although the Brotherhood of Sleeping Car Porters is a Negro association, it owes its existence to the Negro's relation to the economic institutions of the American community. The relatively few Negro political organizations would also come within this category. But how shall we classify the Negro economic institutions which are owned by Negroes and cater specifically to the needs of the Negro community? I would answer this question by saying that such institutions present an anomaly and that their anomalous position explains their insignificance in the economic life of Negroes as well as in the American economy.

In the institutions of the first category, middle class Negroes have generally played an important role as leaders. They have provided the ministers in many of the leading churches and the leadership in the fraternal societies. These organizations have been the source of the incomes which enabled many Negroes to maintain middle class standards. However, the middle class leadership has always been under the scrutiny of leaders who rose from the Negro masses. Middle class Negroes have been more at home in the professional associations and in the Greek letter fraternities. Moreover, their leadership in the schools and colleges was generally undisputed. It was in those institutions where the control and support remained in the white community that they have played the difficult role of mediators between the white and Negro communities.

In some of the institutions of the third category such as, for example, segregated public welfare agencies, middle class Negroes have played a similar role. But only recently have they begun to play a significant role in the labor organizations. Although middle class Negroes have had a longer history in politics, their role has always been one of serving two masters. They have generally attempted to reconcile the interests and demands of the Negro masses with their desire for power which was subject in the final analysis to the white community.

During the past fifty years the Negro community, despite the system of racial segregation, has been slowly breaking up or dissolving, so to speak. The process has been accelerated during the past twenty-five years. This may be seen first in the decline in the size and population of the Black Belt or those counties in the South where Negroes form 50 per cent or more of the total population. During this same period the proportion of Negroes in the population of the South declined from about one in three to close to one in five and the proportion of Negroes living in the South declined from nine-tenths to two-thirds. These changes are significant not only from the standpoint of the distribution of Negroes in the United States but from the standpoint of the change in the nature of the contacts between Negroes and whites. In the South it has meant that about one-half of the Negroes have contacts with whites in cities and in the North it has had even greater significance. As the result of the greater freedom of the North, Negroes are escaping to some extent from the Negro community. They are entering a variety of occupations and associations which are not based in the Negro community and their contacts with whites are more secular and on the basis of individual competence. In recent years the legal attacks upon the residential segregation of Negroes and the integration of Negroes into housing projects, both public and private, have tended to break up the Negro community in cities.

The emergence of a sizeable Negro middle class during the past two decades has tended to emphasize in some respects the dissolution of the Negro community. This has been characteristic of the Negro middle class in the North rather than in the South, since in the South the Negro middle class still has its economic roots in the Negro community. This explains the fact that the black middle class is still relatively small in the South and its income is less than that of the middle class in the North. The significance of the difference between the middle class in the two regions will be revealed as we view briefly the origin, economic basis, and social heritage of the middle class way of life among Negroes.

The economic roots of the Negro middle class go back to the efforts of the Negroes who were free before the Civil War to acquire wealth. These efforts consisted mainly of their success in acquiring land or real estate and of the small businesses established by independent artisans. For example, at the opening of the Civil War, the real estate holdings of the free Negroes in the District of Columbia amounted to $630,000 and in Baltimore to about half a million dollars. Among the free Negroes in Charleston, S.C., in 1860, there were listed 371 free persons of color, including 13 Indians, who paid taxes on real estate valued at about a million dollars and 389 slaves. It has been estimated that the free Negroes accumulated $50,000,000 in real and personal property before the Civil War. The savings and business undertakings of the Negroes who were free before the Civil War reflected the "old-style" bourgeois spirit which was current among white American artisans.

The spirit of modern business enterprise did not take root among Negroes until after Emancipation. The development of the spirit of modern business was due primarily to the establishment of the Freedmen's Savings Bank. This institution was set up by an Act of Congress in order to encourage thrift on the part of the newly emancipated Negroes. The headquarters of the Bank was in the national capital and there were thirty-four branches in various cities—thirty-two being in the South. Although the Freedmen's Savings Bank failed for reasons which we cannot go into here, the spirit of modern business enterprise caught fire among Negro leaders. As evidence of this one might cite the fact that between 1888 and 1934, Negroes organized 134 banks. These banks were short-lived, since by 1905 only seven of all the banks organized by Negroes were still in existence.

It was during this period that the social myth grew up among Negroes that business enterprise would provide the solution of the Negro's economic and social problems. The Negro had experienced a brief period of high hopes during the Reconstruction Period that he would have the rights of other American citizens. But this was succeeded by a period when not only "white supremacy" was restored in the South but as the result of the unresolved class conflict within the white community, the Negro was disfranchised and lost his right to the same education as the whites, and was subjected to a legalized system of racial segregation. He then accepted the myth of economic and social salvation through Negro business which was preached by Negro leaders all over the South. The myth became institutionalized when Booker T. Washington organized the National Negro Business League in 1900. From then on the myth was propagated through the Negro press, from the pulpits of Negro churches, and through pilgrimages throughout the South and to a lesser extent in the North.

There is another phase of the social heritage of middle class Negroes that was of equal importance in shaping their early outlook. This was the education which they received in the schools established by northern white missionaries. These missionaries followed in the wake of the advancing Union armies and founded schools all over the South. Living in close association with their Negro charges and guiding their behavior twenty-four hours a day, the missionaries were able to mold the mind of the Negro in the image of the Puritan heritage. The Negro students were reared in an atmosphere of piety, thrift, and respectability. These three virtues were to distinguish them from the great masses of Negroes who practiced a highly emotional religion, who were reputed to be thriftless, and whose general behavior was anything but respectable. To these schools came the children of the Negroes who were free before the Civil War, among whom there was a large percentage of mulattoes. The teachings of the missionaries only tended to reinforce the tradition of respectability and gentlemanly behavior which existed among the descendants of these free Negroes. Those who had a background of unconventional sex behavior, especially the mulattoes, could overcome the fact that they had been conceived in sin by living a pious life. Booker T. Washington, who was the product of missionary education, carried the tradition of piety, thrift, and respectability to Tuskegee Institute. The National Negro Business League represented in a way an attempt to bring the gospel of piety, thrift, and respectability to the entire Negro race.

At one time the city of Durham, North Carolina, with its successful banks and insurance companies and respectable middle class, was regarded as a sort of capital of the old Negro middle class. As the result of the changes in the economic organization of American life as well as of the changes in the Negro community, the capital of the black middle class has shifted to Chicago or Detroit. This shift has been indicative of the emergence of the new Negro middle class which no longer cherishes the values and social distinctions of the old middle class. The old middle class which placed considerable value upon family stability, mulatto ancestry, and thrift constituted a sort of caste in the Negro community. As a privileged caste the old middle class enjoyed a rather secure position behind the walls of segregation.

The emergence of the new Negro middle class has been due to the migration of Negroes to northern cities where, as the result of the expansion of the American economy, the occupational differentiation of the Negro population has been accelerated. A glance at the federal census of occupations will reveal that in the North Negroes are found in practically all of the occupations whereas in the South they are still excluded from most of the white collar occupations—managerial, salaried professional, sales people, and office workers. Even where Negroes appear in these middle class occupations in the South, they are working within the segregated Negro community. Consequently, according to the best estimates, in the South middle class Negroes constitute an eighth of the employed Negro population whereas in the North they constitute about a fourth.

Significant differences between the Negro middle class in the North and the same class in the South appear in regard to their incomes. Contrary to the social myth concerning the great significance of Negro business in the South, Negro business enterprises in the North represent a larger investment of capital, larger business operations, and larger incomes for Negroes. Of more importance are the differences in incomes derived from salaries and wages. In the South the incomes of middle class Negroes begin at about $2,000 a year and the majority of them do not have annual incomes amounting to $3,000. On the other hand, in the North the annual incomes of middle class Negroes begin at about $2,500 and about a half of them have incomes between $3,000 and $4,000. Moreover, whereas in the South less than one per cent of the Negroes have incomes of $4,000 or more, in the North and West slightly more than two per cent have annual incomes of $4,000 or more and one employed Negro in every hundred has an income of $5,000 or more. Thus the Negro middle class is comprised almost entirely of white collar workers. The so-called wealthy Negroes and black millionaires about whom one reads in the Negro press derive their incomes from the entertainment world, undertaking, and from the "numbers" rackets and other forms of illegal activities. There are no Negro captains of industry or managers of large corporations.

Nevertheless, the values of the new Negro middle class and the style of life which it attempts to maintain give the impression that it has an economic base different from what it has in reality. This can be explained partly by some of the social traditions of this class and partly by the social origins of Negroes who have suddenly acquired incomes in recent years which allow them to lead a style of life different from that of the masses. The descendants of the old middle class continue to think of themselves as aristocrats whose status is determined by certain standards of behavior as well as of consumption. Those members of the new middle class who have been able as the result of education and larger employment opportunities to rise to middle class status have intermarried into the old middle class. Since the new middle class are not the true heirs of the old middle class with its solid virtues which had some real meaning among a privileged caste behind the walls of segregation, they seek to confirm their new status by conspicuous consumption. They may scoff at the virtues and values of the old middle class because of their own feeling of inferiority. They may dismiss family traditions and general refinement as of little value or they may pretend that they place no value on a light complexion. Nevertheless, they pretend to have a certain "culture" which they do not possess and they still place a high value on a light complexion, especially in women.

The change in the character of the schools and colleges in which the middle class has been educated explains the confused outlook of the new middle class. The Negro schools, which had once placed great value upon the making of men or the development of a cultivated civilized person, have turned their attention to the making of money makers. The social myth of "Negro business" as the means of economic and social salvation is cultivated as a crude philosophy of life. The white missionaries who were the representatives of piety, thrift, and respectability have been long dead and their places were filled by middle class Negroes who have given a new content to piety, thrift, and respectability. The new content is partly of a negative type and it involves the rejection of everything represented by the Negro folk. The Negro literary and artistic renaissance which turned to the Negro folk for inspiration was rejected by the emerging new middle class and it is completely forgotten today. Nevertheless, the new middle class cannot escape from its folk background and this background mixed with some elements of genteel tradition explains the fact that the middle class Negro is often a strange mixture of a gentleman and a peasant.

With this background of the new Negro middle class and its place in the Negro community, we are prepared to discuss in some detail its role in desgregation.

We shall begin by considering the role of the Negro middle class in desegregation from the standpoint of the organization of the Negro community. First, there is no likelihood that the institutions and associations which are rooted in the Negro community and serve its cultural needs will disappear in the foreseeable future as the result of desegregation. The Methodist and Baptist church organization with nearly two centuries of continuous history and the fraternal organizations and some social clubs which embody the historical traditions of the Negro community will not be liquidated because of desegregation. Consequently, middle class Negroes who are identified with these organizations and derive their incomes from them will not work for their dissolution.

In this connection, it should be noted that many middle class Negroes have acquired vested interests in segregation. These vested interests are of both a material and a non-material nature. The material nature of these vested interests is most clearly revealed in the Negro business enterprises. The owners of these business enterprises have always tried to convince the Negro masses that it is in the latter's interest to pay higher prices even for inferior goods and services when they are provided by Negroes. The material advantages which middle class Negroes have derived from segregation include also salaries and incomes which are received from segregated institutions. Then there are certain vested interests of a non-material nature which are provided by segregated institutions. Middle class Negroes have been able to enjoy a certain prestige and status behind the wall of segregation which would be threatened by desegregation. Moreover, middle class Negroes enjoy a certain emotional security by not being forced into competition with whites in the American community. Often this means that they may occupy positions for which they are unqualified and that they can excuse their inefficiency on the grounds that the Negro is, to use their words, "a young race" or "is only a few decades out of slavery."

Middle class Negroes do not have the same vested interests in the second category of institutions which I have mentioned, namely those which have their roots in the white community as well as in the Negro community. The system of racial segregation may provide them with good incomes from public schools and recreational facilities but middle class Negroes are willing nevertheless to compete with whites in unsegregated public institutions. This is especially true in the North. It is not as true of middle class Negroes in border States and it is less true of the same class in the South. As the Negro carries on the struggle for equality, middle class Negroes who derive their support from publicly supported institutions are showing a greater disposition even in the South and border States to accept the consequences of desegregation. This was demonstrated when the presidents of Negro land grant colleges took a stand against the continuance of segregated colleges even if it threatened their own economic security.

Middle class Negroes have been most inclined to wipe out segregation in those institutions which are based in the white community and in those associations which owe their existence to the economic activities of the Negroes in the general American community. An outstanding exception is to be found in the case of the National Negro Business League which represents, as I have said, an unrealistic attempt to foster a separate economy. But even in the case of this organization there has been an attempt to remove the designation, Negro, from its name because the younger and more prosperous members of the League are employed as salesmen by large white corporations. Some of the older Negro business men who cling to the myth of Negro business and have a vested interest in the myth are sounding warnings against the disastrous effects of too rapid desegregation.

As the walls of segregation are broken down, middle class Negroes bring to the new world certain attitudes, values, and patterns of behavior which they have acquired in the segregated Negro world. Some of these attitudes, values, and patterns of behavior are liabilities but others can be regarded as assets. Let us begin with the assets. There can be no gainsaying that middle class Negroes conform more nearly to the American standards of behavior than any other element in the Negro population. Because of their incomes they are able to maintain a physical appearance similar to that of the general American population. Moreover, I think it can be said that they accept the dominant values of white America. In fact, in the experiments to establish racially mixed housing projects an attempt is made to secure Negroes of the middle income group who have a stable family life and conform to generally accepted standards of behavior.

Although middle class Negroes have always taken a lead in the struggle of Negroes for equality in American life, they have always respected and supported the basic American values. The old middle class that drew upon the heritage of the Negroes who were free before the Civil War cherished many of the conservative values of the white southern aristocracy and sought to gain their ends through respectable means. When the urbanization of the Negro population stirred new currents of thought among Negroes, they shunned the communists and showed only contempt for the masses who followed Marcus Garvey. Although the militant leadership of the N.A.A.C.P. should be distinguished from the compromising leadership of the National Urban League, both have supported American values and have insisted upon the use of legal and respectable means to secure civil rights or job opportunities. The N.A.A.C.P. has constantly resisted the pressure to make the organization a mass organization. Needless to say, since the National Urban League is a welfare organization which receives its support from white philanthropy, there has been no such pressure.

However the N.A.A.C.P. is faced today with the rise of the masses of Negroes under leaders like Reverend Martin Luther King, who has introduced unconventional tactics in the struggle for Negro rights. Although the N.A.A.C.P. is willing to join King and his followers who are carrying their protests to Washington, the Association insists that it be a respectable pilgrimage and not a march on Washington.

This indicates a cleavage in the Negro community that cannot be ignored. Although middle class Negroes have been the leaders in the Negro's struggle for equality, they have always had an ambivalent attitude towards the Negro masses. Even in the days when the Negro "Talented Tenth" went forth from the colleges under missionary control to lead the masses, the middle class could not identify itself completely with the great masses of poor illiterate black peasants. They were too self-conscious of their achievements and of the burden of proving to whites that they were as intelligent, thrifty, and respectable as whites. The new Negro middle class that has none of the spirit of service and little of the social heritage of the old middle class attempts to dissociate itself as much as possible from identification with the Negro masses. The respectability which its members seek is generally the kind which enables them to maintain standards of consumption out of the reach of the masses. The lip service which they give to solidarity with the masses very often disguises their exploitation of the masses.

Nevertheless, middle class Negroes cannot escape altogether the discrimination and contempt to which Negroes are generally subjected. At the present time they have often become the targets of violence in the South. In the past they were able to escape some of the harsher forms of prejudice in the South because they enjoyed some degree of economic independence and were not in direct competition with whites. But they have suffered in a more intimate way a hurt to their self-esteem. This is because it is this class in the Negro community which has striven most to conform to the standards of behavior of the white community and yet they are rejected by whites. The masses of Negroes, though exposed more to physical violence, can find a refuge in their churches and in associations that represent a way of life from which whites are excluded. The new Negro middle class is more exposed than the old to appear prejudiced. The lack of responsibility and seriousness middle class. Their rejection of the masses and their conspicuous consumption cannot insulate them against their inferior status in American society. As a consequence middle class Negroes have a feeling of inferiority despite their demands for equality and as they participate in American society they cannot escape feelings of insecurity and frustration. Many teachers and other professional people have admitted that despite their competence they feel insecure when faced with competition in the white world.

It is not surprising then that when middle class Negroes face desegregation they retain handicaps of their sheltered and privileged life behind the walls of segregation. Because of their ambivalent attitude in regard to identification with the Negro masses, they are confused about maintaining the racial identification of a number of organizations. The National Council of Negro Women decided to drop the term Negro but reversed its decision. The Colored Methodist Episcopal Church with eighty-six years of history decided to change the "Colored" to "Christian." But, when it was suggested that the African Methodist Episcopal Church with 170 years of continuous history change "African" to "American," there was such an uproar that the suggestion was dropped. While objection to the identification of Negroes where their behavior might reflect upon the "race," middle class Negroes still insist upon the identification where the slightest recognition might be gained.

The segregation of the Negro in American society has tended to engender a spirit of irresponsibility among middle class Negroes. Middle class Negroes have played, so to speak, at the running of their schools, their hospitals, their businesses, their churches and other organizations. This was natural since they were not held responsible for their inefficiency and failures and liberal whites were especially indulgent because they did not want to appear prejudiced. The lack of responsibility and seriousness has coincided with the refusal of the white man to take the Negro seriously except where his behavior affected the white community. As middle class Negroes are being integrated into the institutions of the white community, they are forced to assume a more serious and a more responsible attitude towards life. For, while white people may not take seriously the inefficiency of an ignorant head of a segregated institution, and may even pretend that he is a great man, they would not tolerate such behavior on the part of a Negro federal judge.

Shut up within a world where serious matters are not taken seriously, middle class Negroes carry on a serious struggle for status and recognition. This seems to provide some compensations for the lack of status and recognition in the white world. This struggle for status is constantly reflected in Negro newspapers which provide exaggerated reports on the achievements of Negroes and the least recognition which they receive in the white world. The Negro press also reveals the great emphasis which is placed upon "social" life among the middle classes. In its reports upon the activities of Negro "society," one may get a glimpse of the struggle for status in the world of make-believe in which middle class Negroes live. In the world of make-believe middle class Negroes engage in all sorts of conspicuous consumption which set them apart from the Negro masses. It is not unusual to read of Negro Greek letter societies spending more than two million dollars during the Christmas holidays or of parties where fountains flow with champagne and women dripping in diamonds and wearing mink coats arrive in "chauffeured" Cadillacs. The world of make-believe which the Negro press helps to create seems to cushion the effects of the world of reality. In the world of reality Negro business men have no real wealth and Negro professional men and women are only white collar workers. When they assert their superiority over so-called poor white people who are often better paid professional workers, they are merely attempting to compensate for their rejection by the white world.

There is another phase of the role which the middle class plays behind the walls of segregation that deserves attention when one considers desegregation. Because of the middle class Negro's position in the social structure, he has acquired an authoritarian attitude which is not so readily revealed to whites. As a matter of fact, he must generally conceal this aspect of his personality because of his subordinate role in relations with whites. But as heads of schools and churches and lodges, the middle class Negro is generally an autocrat. In the Negro schools and colleges his autocratic power is backed up by the white community. White professors in Negro institutions have been startled by the autocratic attitude of Negro college presidents. As desegregation has taken place in some public school systems, Negro teachers have been shocked to learn that their opinions would be respected and they would have to act in a responsible manner to which they were not accustomed. Moreover they have been surprised that they could not act in the same authoritarian manner in regard to the students as in the segregated schools. The differences in style of life and in values, rather than race, are often the main barriers between middle class Negroes and whites. For example, because of their position in the Negro community, the Negro teachers are likely to be members of "society", which means that they engage in a form of conspicuous consumption that is unknown to white teachers. It also means that they do not read, or attend the theatre, or travel. Some white teachers and other white professionals and white collar workers have been puzzled that their colored colleagues lived in $50,000 homes, wore mink coats, drove Cadillac cars, gambled for high stakes, and gave debutante balls for their daughters in expensive desegregated hotels.

It should be noted, however, that the differences in the style of life and in values are greatest in those areas where the walls of segregation are highest or, shall I say, thickest. In the large cities of the North where Negroes of middle class status have increasingly been integrated into the institutions of the community, they are more likely to think of themselves as middle class and white collar workers rather than as an upper class in the segregated Negro community. Consequently, their pattern of living and their values are likely to be the same as those of middle class whites. This may seem to contradict what I have said about the capital of the Negro middle class being in Chicago or Detroit. But it only indicates that middle class Negroes are not assimilated into the wider community even in the North and that in their more intimate association they are still identified with the institutions of the Negro community.

Nevertheless, middle class Negroes are becoming detached from the Negro community. They are increasingly finding acceptance on the basis of their competence and skills and they are becoming a part of the associations which are coming into existence as the result of the changes in the economic organization of American life. They may not feel completely accepted and may think of themselves as one Negro professional told me: he was only an ambassador to the white middle class from the Negro community. This causes, of course, inner conflicts and arouses feelings of hostility towards whites. When inner conflicts, frustrations, and hostilities of the middle class Negro are viewed from the standpoint of what has occurred generally in the so-called American melting pot that has created and is creating an American nation, they do not appear as a unique experience. The Negro's physical visibility may prolong the painful experience of assimilation since, despite the emergence of African nations, it does not appear that Negro ancestry will cease to be a taint in the near future.

In concluding this discussion of the role of the Negro middle class in desegregation, it is possible to note certain important facts of sociological significance. The first is that the emergence of the Negro middle class has been inseparable from changes in the economic and social organization of American society. The second fact is that the economic role of the Negro middle class in the American economy has been restricted by the social heritage of the Negro and his racial identification. Third, the Negro middle class has been restricted to the role of an upper class within the segregated Negro community. Fourth, as the barriers to general participation in American life have been breaking down, middle class Negroes are gaining an opportunity to sell their professional knowledge and skills on the same basis as whites. Fifth, this is resulting in an escape from the segregated Negro community where they have lived in a world of unreality into the world of reality where they can play a more responsible role as salaried professional and white collar workers. Sixth, the Negro community will only "wither away" slowly and will not only form a refuge for the Negro masses but for those middle class Negroes who continue to be identified with Negro institutions within the Negro community.

20

DESEGREGATION AS AN OBJECT OF SOCIOLOGICAL STUDY

1961

A REVIEW of the relevant literature indicates that much more attention has been given to the study of the historical, political, and especially social psychological aspects of racial desegregation than to the sociological aspects of the problem. Outstanding among the sociological contributions to the subject is an article by Blumer in which he has presented a theoretical analysis of desegregation as a social process with special emphasis on the ecological aspects of the problem and on the role of functionaries and organized activities in the desegregation process (1). Recently greater attention has been directed to the role of the Negro community, especially the role of Negro leaders in the movement for racial desegregation.[1] But scarcely any studies have been concerned primarily with the manner in which the organization and social life of the Negro community and its interaction with the wider American community influence the nature and extent of desegregation. It is the purpose of this essay to explore and analyze this phase of the process of desegregation.[2]

Reprinted from *Human Behavior and Sociological Processes: An Interactionist Approach,* ed. Arnold Rose (Boston: Houghton Mifflin Co., 1961), pp. 608–24, by permission of the publisher. Copyright 1961 by Houghton Mifflin Company.

[1]   See, for example, Lewis M. Killian and Charles U. Smith (14).
[2]   Desegregation and integration are often used interchangeably. There is some justification for this usage since desegregation and integra-

In the article referred to above, Blumer has made a clear analysis of the difference between racial segregation as a natural ecological process and racial segregation resulting from conscious social policies (1). It is with the effect upon desegregation of racial segregation as an ecological process that the sociological study of desegregation should begin. Racial segregation resulting from social policies should be considered as a phase of the conflicts arising over the status of the Negro in the social organization. Racial segregation as an ecological process has been in operation almost from the time when Negroes were introduced into the American colonies. One phase of the ecological process was the concentration of Negroes who were free before the Civil War in cities and in areas outside the plantation.[3] But more important was the fact that as the cotton plantations developed, the concentration of Negroes in the "Black Belt" of the South provided the basis of a pattern of race relations which has persisted until the present. Although there has been a decrease in the area of the "Black Belt" and a corresponding decline in the number of Negroes in the "Black Belt," the area which comprised the old plantation South constitutes the hard core which shows the greatest resistance to desegregation.[4] In October 1960, according to the *Southern School News*, 27 per cent, or 768 of the 2,834 biracial school districts in 17 Southern and Border states, including the District of Columbia, had begun or had

---

tion are correlated aspects of the same social process. Generally speaking "desegregation" refers to the process by which Negroes are being integrated into the institutional and other phases of the social life of the wider American community or American society. Unfortunately, however, the term "integration" is often used to refer to assimilation, which has a more restricted or specified denotation.

3   See chap. 4, "The Free Negro," in the writer's *The Negro in the United States.*

4   The "Black Belt" in the South consists of those counties in which Negroes constitute 50 per cent or more of the total population. From 1900 to 1950 the number of such counties declined from 286 to 158 and the total Negro population of the "Black Belt" counties decreased from 4,057,619 to 2,078,168.

accomplished desegregation.[5] There were no desegregated school districts in Alabama, Georgia, Louisiana, Mississippi, and South Carolina and very few desegregated school districts in other states outside the Border states. A similar pattern in the distribution of registered Negro voters will be considered later.

The relevance of racial segregation as an ecological process for sociological analysis is not based upon the assumption that there is a mechanical relationship between the proportion of Negroes in a white community and the emergence of a system of racial segregation.[6] The sociologist is interested in human ecology because it provides the basis of divergent social orders—economic, political, and moral—which form a hierarchy. (See 21, p. 157.) In the "Black Belt" of the South, one can recognize these different systems of human interaction. The southern plantation represented, in a sense, a racial division of labor (23, p. 52). However, it should be noted that this racial division of labor was in harmony with the distribution of power. Therefore, the plantation was not only an industrial or economic institution, but it was also a political institution. In the areas dominated by the plantation system of agriculture, there was a paternalistic regime in which Negroes had no rights as citizens. Since the decision of the Supreme Court of the United States outlawing the white primary (13, p. 54), the only significant increases in the number of Negro voters has been outside the "Black Belt." In Mississippi, where there are 31 "Black Belt" counties, between 1947 and 1952 the number of registered Negro voters increased from 5,000 to less than 20,000.

[5]   Vol. 7 (October, 1960). In 1957, of the 3,700 biracial school districts, 684, or 18 per cent, were desegregated or had begun desegregation (Vol. 3, June, 1957).

[6]   This was the position of Alfred H. Stone when he stated that segregation by law was inevitable where the proportion of Negroes exceeded 10 per cent because the white man experienced an instinctive feeling of "pressure" in the presence of a mass of people of a different race (25). In St. Louis, for example, where racial desegregation of the public schools was carried out smoothly after the Supreme Court decision of May 17, 1954, 36 per cent of the school enrollment and 20 per cent of the population is Negro (*Look*, April 3, 1956).

On the other hand, in Texas, where there were only two "Black Belt" counties, the number of registered Negro voters increased from 100,000 to 214,000 (24). During this same period, the number of registered Negro voters in Louisiana, where the number of "Black Belt" counties declined during this period from 31 to 13, shot up from 10,000 to 160,000; but subsequent political action on the part of whites removed 40,000 Negroes from the registration rolls.

We have noted above that as a result of the ecological process the Negroes who were free before the Civil War were concentrated in cities and in other areas outside the plantation region. It has been in the cities and other areas not dominated by the plantation regime that Negroes have been able to escape from the social control which grew up under the plantation system. It has been in Border states where the Negro population is largely urbanized that school desegregation has progressed farthest. Even in the cities of the lower South there are movements toward integration (3). However, it is in the cities that are least dominated by the plantation system that Negroes are beginning to register to vote. For it is in the matter of voting that the influence of the political system which grew up on the plantation system makes itself most evident. For example, it is easier for Negroes to register and vote not only in the cities but even in the rural areas of North Carolina and in Savannah and Atlanta, Georgia, than in Birmingham, Alabama. According to the report of the Southern Regional Council, "Birmingham and surrounding Jefferson County present one of the gloomiest pictures for Negroes in the South. In no other major city of the region has it been so difficult for them to vote. Only about 7,000 of 121,500 Negroes over 21 are registered; at least that many more have been turned down." (24)

Within the cities themselves, both in the South and in the North, racial segregation has occurred as the result of an ecological process. In the larger cities of the South, there have been two types of Negro concentration (5, 82). In the older cities of the South the Negro population was widely scattered. This was due to historic factors, the most important of which was the fact that Negro settlements grew up in places close to the homes of whites in which Negroes worked. These settlements represented in a way the symbiotic relationship which exists between people on the ecological level of human relations. But this type of racial settlement should be differentiated from the racial segregation which results from the impersonal economic forces which are responsible for the ecological organization of modern industrial and commercial cities. This new type of racial segregation has appeared in the new cities of the South, or in cities where industry and commerce have determined their spatial pattern. In these newer cities there are several large concentrations of Negroes and the remainder of the Negro population is scattered lightly over a large area. These light scatterings of Negroes over a large area are generally the remnants of the historic conditions which we have indicated.

The location of the Negro communities in the Border cities tends to conform to the pattern of Southern cities, though there are large concentrations of Negroes similar to those in Northern cities (11, pp. 242 ff.). It appears that neither historic nor economic factors have been solely responsible for the location of the Negro communities in the Border cities. It is perhaps because neither factor exercised a decisive influence in determining the location of the Negro population that the battles over the residential segregation of Negroes were first fought in the Border states.[7] On the other hand, it is in the large cities of the North that the most important studies of racial segregation as an ecological process have been carried out. The concentration of Negroes in certain areas of Northern cities was the result of the same eco-

---

[7]   In St. Louis the first popular vote on the residential segregation of the Negro in the United States was held in 1916. It was in the Louisville segregation case that the Supreme Court of the United States handed down the unanimous decision that it was unconstitutional to prohibit Negroes by law from buying and occupying property. The United States Supreme Court decisions of May 3, 1948, outlawing the enforcement by state or federal courts of covenants restricting the sale or rental of property to Negroes, were based upon two covenant cases from the District of Columbia, one case from St. Louis, and a fourth case from Detroit.

nomic and social processes as were responsible for the segregation of other minority groups.[8]

Racial segregation as an ecological process is important for sociological analysis because the spatial pattern of the community is the basis of a moral order.[9] It is an indication of the place of the racial group within the organization of the community and the interactions of people within the community. At the same time, racial segregation as an ecological process provides an index to the absence of communication between Negroes and other peoples and their moral isolation. The attempts to integrate Negroes into public housing projects represent an effort to break down the moral isolation of Negroes in the urban environment. (See 7, 18, 28.)

Despite the success of some of these efforts to develop integrated housing and break down residential segregation, the moral isolation of the Negro has continued. It has continued not so much because of segregation resulting from an ecological process as because of the social organization of the Negro community. The ecological process which creates segregation on the basis of language, culture, and race brings about segregation "based upon vocational interests, upon intelligence and personal ambition" within the racial group (21, p. 170; 9). Because of their isolation within American life, Negroes have developed a community life with a set of institutions which duplicate the institutions of the wider American community. These institutions embody the social traditions and values which are current within the social world of the Negro. Moreover, there is an economic and social stratification of the Negro population with its different norms of behavior,

---

[8]   In a pioneer article (4, p. 105), Ernest W. Burgess stated: "The residential separation of white and Negro has almost invariably been treated by itself as if it were a unique phenomenon of urban life. In fact, however, as recent studies already prove, this is only one case among many of the workings of the process of segregation in the sorting and sifting of the different elements of the population of the city. There are immigrant colonies, the so-called Ghettoes, Little Sicilies, Chinatowns, as well as Black Belts."

[9]   See chap. 9, "The Urban Community as a Spatial Pattern and a Moral Order," in Park, *Human Communities* (21).

different expectations, and certain vested interests. When the sociologist studies desegregation, he must take this fact into account in studying the attitudes and behavior of Negroes in regard to desegregation.

Although the Negro community is more or less isolated spatially from the wider American community and the social life of Negroes revolves around the institutions and associations of the Negro community, Negroes are, nevertheless, dependent economically upon the economic institutions of the American community. In the rural South, farm ownership among Negroes has never exceeded the 25 per cent level which was attained in 1910; and as Negroes have moved into cities their dependence upon the economic institutions of the American communities has increased. At the opening of the present century, because of the competition of white workers and discrimination in employment, some Negro leaders advocated the development of Negro businesses which would give employment to Negroes. But this proved an empty dream, for one finds that in 1960 Negro businesses, from the standpoint of Negro employment and income from capital investment, were no more important than they were in 1900. The integration of Negroes into the economic institutions of the American community has become the only hope for survival.

In the South the integration of Negroes into the economic institutions of the American community is complicated by both social and economic factors. These factors include traditional notions and attitudes concerning the status of Negroes and their fitness for certain types of work; their relationship of employers and the labor unions; the relations of Negroes and whites, especially white women, in the plants; the competition of whites and Negroes for employment in the new industries; and changing conditions of a market economy (19, pp. 179 ff.). In most of the industries in Southern cities there is a color bar which restricts Negro workers to unskilled occupations. The greatest barrier, however, to the upward mobility of Negro workers is the relative inaccessibility to them of white collar and professional occupations. Negroes in white collar and professional occupations are confined almost entirely to the Negro community.

In the North, on the other hand, Negroes have been able to break through many of the barriers to their entering white collar and professional occupations. This can be attributed partly to the absence of a deeply rooted tradition of caste. But it is also due to those changes in the organization of American life which have enabled the large industrial unions to play an increasingly important role. These industrial unions have from the beginning had a much more liberal racial policy than the older craft unions. In the South, on the other hand, the older craft unions have continued to exclude Negro workers and the political forces in Southern communities have tended to reduce the effectiveness of the industrial unions. There are other factors which should be studied by the sociologist and the most important of these is the fact that Negroes in Northern cities have political power. A large number of Negro white collar and professional workers in Northern cities are in municipal employment. This is not ture in the South because the Negro does not have the right to vote. Thus, although theoretically one might assume that desegregation in economic relations would be easy, social status and political power are always involved in the economic relations of men.

Those who have been faced with the problem of the desegregation of public schools in the North as well as in the South have come up against the fact of the residential segregation of Negroes. Residential segregation, as we have seen, is partly due to an impersonal ecological process. But it is also the result of deliberate activities on the part of whites (27). Where the whites have resorted to laws and covenants in order to restrict the free movement of Negroes into areas, the sociologist will be concerned not with the ecological process but with changes in the economic organization of race relations and with the conflicts which arise in the struggle of the Negro for status (29). The conflict over status will involve the poitical power of Negroes most especially in Northern cities. It appears that at the present time the efforts to desegregate are directed mainly against segregation resulting from ecological factors and to a less extent against resistance on the part of whites. In the South, on the other hand, it appears that the resistance of whites to desegregation is directed mainly against the ecological process which accounts for racially mixed school districts.

When the organization of the Negro community is considered in relation to desegregation, the first fact which should be considered is the stratification of the Negro community. The stratification of the Negro community has been accelerated by the urbanization of Negroes and the resulting occupational differentiation. Increasingly, the older stratification, which consisted of a simple class system based upon social distinctions, has been effaced by a stratification based upon socio-economic classes. The process has progressed much farther in the North than in the South because of the restrictions upon the occupational mobility of Negroes in the South. In the South, the majority of the Negro population is still found in the lower class, which is composed of laborers and unskilled workers who are drawn from the rural areas. The behavior and outlook of the lower-class Negroes are largely influenced by the folk tradition of the Negro. Their family life, which lacks an institutional character, is often unstable and their children lack discipline and are poorly socialized. Above this lower class is an intermediate class which is struggling to maintain middle-class standards of life. At the top of the social pyramid is an upper class which is really a middle class according to American standards. The members of this class have broken away from the folk traditions or they are the descendants of the Negroes who were free before the Civil War or the slaves who were house servants and skilled mechanics. This new middle class, which constitutes about 13 per cent of the Negro population, is only relatively half as large as the Negro middle class in Northern cities (10, Chapter 2).

In the North, the stratification of the Negro community is based mainly upon occupation and income (8, Chapters 19, 20, 21, 22). This is the result of the fact, as we have seen, that Negroes have been able to enter most of the occupations. In the North there is a small upper class, which is becoming differentiated from an intermediate class on the basis of incomes which permit it to maintain a standard and style of life above the majority of those who derive their incomes from professional and white collar occupations. Within this upper class, which from the standpoint of income would be included in the middle class in the white American community, and the intermediate class are found about a fourth of the Negroes in the North. This new middle, class in the Negro community is especially influential in determining the values and outlook of Negroes.

In studying the processes of desegregation, it is important to study the interaction of the various strata in the class structure of the Negro community to the new relation of Negroes to American society. It should be pointed out that these strata represent important differences in the extent and nature of the exposure of Negroes to American culture and differences in the extent and nature of contacts with white people. The new Negro middle class, which has become increasingly important in the Negro community, has a social heritage which differentiates it from the white middle classes. In fact, the social heritage of this class is a mixture of the so-called "aristocratic" heritage of mulattoes or Negroes who were free before the Civil War and the heritage of the Negro folk who have risen to middle-class status (10, Chapter 5). Therefore, they have a style of life and set of values which do not permit them to participate easily in the social world of white middle classes. The differences in style of life and values have become evident when whites and Negroes have been brought together. If these differences are conspicuous in the case of middle-class Negroes, the class which is closest in culture and outlook to white Americans, it is hardly necessary to emphasize the difficulties involved in contacts between whites and lower-class Negroes, with their free and uninhibited behavior.

A study of the changing class structure of the Negro community is important in order to understand the social heritage and attitudes of the new strata which are rising to middle-class status and are assuming leadership in the process of desegregation. This may be seen in the movement which is being led by Reverend Martin Luther King and in the sit-ins by the Negro college students in the South. Reverend King is representative of a new leadership which is supplanting the old "accommodating" leadership. This new leadership has appeared in response to the rise of new strata to middle-class status as the result of the increasing numbers of Negroes who are attending colleges. The rise of these new strata is dramatized in the spontaneous movement on the part of Negro students who are in revolt against the former leaders (16, 17). The new strata have a different social heritage from the older leadership, who represented the "genteel tradition" of the small Negro upper class. They had become the leaders in the Negro community because they enjoyed economic and social advantages which differentiated them from the masses of Negroes. The new strata are rooted in the Negro masses, and as they have become articulate they have given a "new definition" to the problem of desegregation. In fact, it might even be said that the old "accommodating" leadership had a vested interest in segregation which the new strata do not have.

Among the institutions which have grown up among Negroes, the Negro church is the most important. The Negro church is important because it provided the earliest basis of social cohesion and cooperation among Negroes. The Negro church as an institution has a continuous history that goes back to the last quarter of the eighteenth century. This institutional form is rooted in the social traditions and the mores of Negroes and embodies their highest aspirations and peculiar outlook on life. It has been in the Negro church that the Negro has been able to give rein to his emotions and find satisfaction for his longings. Moreover, the Negro church has provided a refuge in which Negroes could find protection against a hostile white world. For a people who were isolated from the political life of the American community, the Negro church has been a political arena and provided an area of social existence in which Negroes could aspire to leadership and gain recognition. As a consequence, the Negro church continues to enlist the Negro's deepest loyalties.

These facts concerning the Negro church must be taken into account when he sociologist studies desegregation generally and especially the desegregation of the churches. From the standpoint both of the organization of the Negro community and the white community, the church offers one of the most important barriers to desegregation.[10] The Negro church organizations, like the churches in the white community, reflect the class structure of the Negro community. For the great mass of the Negro population the Baptist and Methodist churches provide emotional satisfactions and participation in a meaningful social existence, or a way of life. Upper-class and middle-class Negroes who have broken away from the traditions and way of life of the Negro masses find a more congenial religious experience in the Presbyterian, Congregational, Episcopal, and Catholic churches. Desegregation for them is not so much the desegregation of Negro churches as the desegregation of white churches. But no amount of acceptance in the white churches will bring about the dissolution of Negro churches, which are the most important cultural institutions among Negroes.[11]

In the Negro community there are, besides the Negro church, other institutions and associations which represent the peculiar traditions and special interests of Negroes. These include fraternal organizations, the Greek-letter societies, and social clubs. Then there are professional organizations among Negroes which have a long history. At the present time there are some indications that Negroes will increasingly be admitted to the local chapters of the

10   This will sound strange to those who assert that the Christian Church should be the last place where a policy of racial exclusiveness is practiced. The Negro church is admonished that it should abandon its racial character and thus aid in the process of racial desegregation. But this shows a complete lack of an understanding of the nature of social organization. Some middle-class Negroes, in their present confusion about their racial identity and the meaning of integration, have undertaken to change the names of Negro churches. The Colored Methodist Church was changed to *Christian* Methodist Church. When a similar attempt was made to change the name of the African Methodist Church to the *American* Methodist Episcopal Church, the mass of the Negro membership revolted against the proposal.

11   Recently the President of the National Baptist Convention, Inc. (Negro), condemned the "kneel-ins," or the attempt of Negroes to enter white churches in the following words: "If you have religion in your church, use it. Don't go kneeling in somebody else's church." (*The Pittsburgh Courier*, November 5, 1960.)

American Medical Association. But this trend does not seem to forecast the early dissolution of the National Medical Association, the Negro professional association. The Negro professional associations, like the white, are not simply concerned with their professional interests but provide social contacts of a more or less intimate character. It is because of the intimate social contacts within professional organizations that barriers to the acceptance of Negroes in associations representing the secular interests of the community continue to exist. This is often given as the reason for not admitting Negro workers to labor unions in the South. Labor unions are important, as we have been before, because they provide the means by which Negroes gain access to the economic institutions of the American community. Thus they are important in desegregation, since they form a bridge between the Negro social world and the wider American society.

The sociologist should give attention to the integration of Negroes into sports and into the world of entertainment because it reveals certain important facts concerning both the changes in status of the Negro and the relation of desegregation to the changes in the organization of American life. Forty or fifty years ago, a Negro could neither sing a sentimental song on the American stage nor appear on the stage with whites. Within the past 25 or 30 years this has changed; however, the change has been much more radical in the North than in the South. It appears that the change is the result of two factors: first, the fact that the Negro has always been able to secure an acceptance more easily in those areas of American life which were outside of conventional society; and, secondly, the change in the organization of American life—urbanization, the growth of gigantic corporations, and the growth in power of labor unions. As a result of the change in the organization of American life, the assimilation of Negroes has become a process of assimilation in secondary groups (15; 20, pp. 204–20). The Negro is being incorporated into the institutions and associations of the metropolitan communities and he is acquiring the superficial uniformity and homogeneity of manners and fashions characteristic of cosmopolitan groups. But his loyalties and deepest attachments are still rooted in the Negro community or the social world of the Negro. Negroes may be integrated into baseball, the respectable national sport, but there is not intimate association between Negro and white players (2). The intimate social life of the Negro players is in the Negro community. It is only in Hollywood, a world removed from conventional American society, that there are signs that intimate association between whites and Negroes is becoming acceptable.

There are other aspects of desegregation which are important in the sociological study of the problem. Because of the change in the organization of American life and the change in the relation of the United States to the rest of the world, there has been a change in public policy (31). At the opposite pole of race relations is intermarriage, involving the most intimate relations of mankind. Hardly any fundamental sociological studies of the marriage of Negroes and whites have been undertaken. Most of the studies of sociologists have been no more than a priori judgments on intermarriage without empirical data to support them. The fact of primary sociological importance is that intermarrying couples should be studied in relation to their position in the organization or structure of the white and Negro communities and the interactions between those two social worlds.

By way of summary and conclusion, I shall undertake to state the important points which have been brought out in this attempt to define desegregation as an object of sociological study. First, it was shown that it was necessary to study the effect of segregation as an ecological phenomenon upon the desegregation process. Although, as Wirth has pointed out, human ecology is outside of the field of sociology, it nevertheless "provides us with one of the hitherto neglected aspects of the matrix within which social events take place" (30, p. 142). Or, as we have noted, the ecological organization of the community is the basis of the social organization. It is the relation of the desegregation process to social organization that is of primary interest to the sociologist. It has been shown that the sociologist should concern himself with the social organization of the Negro community and the social organization of the wider American community because desegregation is the result of the interaction between both the Negro and white communities, both of which are undergoing changes. Therefore, of particular interest to the sociologist are those areas of interracial contacts which are on the fringe or outside of the traditional or conventional social organization of both the white and Negro communities. It is in these "vulnerable" areas of social life that desegregation progresses most rapidly. In the final analysis, complete racial desegregation would mean the dissolution of the social organizations of the Negro community as Negroes are integrated as individuals into the institutional life of American society.

References

1. Blumer, Herbert. "Social Science and the Desegregation Process," *Annals of the American Academy of Political and Social Science*, 304 (March, 1956) :137–43.
2. Boyle, Robert. "The Private World of the Negro Ballplayer," *Sports Illustrated*, March 21, 1960.
3. Bullock, Henry A. "Urbanism and Race Relations," in Rupert R. Vance and Nicholas J. Demerath (eds.), *The Urban South*. Chapel Hill, N. C.: University of North Carolina Press, 1959, pp. 207–29.
4. Burgess, Ernest W. "Residential Segregation in American Cities," *Annals of the American Academy of Political and Social Science*, 140 (November, 1928) :105–15.
5. Demerath, Nicholas J., and Harlan W. Gilmore. "The Ecology of Southern Cities," in Vance and Demerath (eds.), *The Urban South*, pp. 242 ff.
6. *Desegregation: Some Propositions and Research Suggestions.* New York: Anti-Defamation League of B'nai B'rith, 1958.
7. Deutsch, Morton, and Mary E. Collins. *Interracial Housing: A Psychological Evaluation of a Social Experiment*. Minneapolis: University of Minnesota Press, 1951.
8. Drake, St. Clair, and Horace R. Cayton. *Black Metropolis.* New York: Harcourt, Brace and Co., 1945.
9. Frazier, E. Franklin. *The Negro Family in the United States.* Chicago: University of Chicago Press, 1931.
10. Frazier, E. Franklin. *Black Bourgeoisie.* Glencoe, Ill.: The Free Press, 1957.
11. Frazier, E. Franklin. *The Negro in the United States*, rev. ed. New York: The Macmillan Company, 1957.
12. Frazier, E. Franklin. "The Negro Middle Class and Desegregation," *Social Problems*, 4 (April, 1957) :291–301.
13. Hill, Herbert, and Jack Greenberg. *Citizen's Guide to Desegregation.* Boston: Beacon Press, 1955.

14. Killian, Lewis M., and Charles U. Smith. "Negro Protest Leaders in a Southern Community," *Social Forces*, 38 (March, 1960):253–257.

15. Lohman, Joseph D., and Dietrich C. Reitzes. "Note on Race Relations in Mass Society," *American Journal of Sociology*, 58 (November, 1952):240–46.

16. Lomax, Louis E. "The Negro Revolt Against 'The Negro Leaders'," *Harper's Magazine*, June, 1960, pp. 41–48.

17. Lomax, Louis E. "The Negroes Act," *Dissent*, Summer, 1960.

18. Merton, Robert K. "The Social Psychology of Housing," in W. Denis (ed.), *Current Trends in Social Psychology*. Pittsburgh: University of Pittsburgh Press, 1948, pp. 163–217.

19. National Planning Association. *Selected Studies of Negro Employment in the South*. Washington, D.C.: National Planning Association.

20. Park, Robert E. *Race and Culture*. Glencoe, Ill.: The Free Press, 1950.

21. Park, Robert E. *Human Communities*. Glencoe, Ill.: The Free Press, 1952.

22. Reid, Ira DeA. (ed.). "Racial Desegregation and Integration," *Annals of the American Academy of Political and Social Science*, vol. 304 (March, 1956).

23. Reuter, Edward B. "Competition and the Racial Division of Labor," in Edgar T. Thompson (ed.), *Race Relations and the Race Problem*. Durham, N. C.: Duke University Press, 1939, pp. 46–60.

24. Southern Regional Council. "The Negro Voter in the South," *Special Report*. Atlanta, Ga., July 18, 1957.

25. Stone, Alfred H. "Is Race Friction Between Black and Whites in the United States Growing and Inevitable?" *American Journal of Sociology*, 13 (1907–08):677–96.

26. Tumin, Melvin M. *Desegregation: Resistance and Readiness*. Princeton, N.J.: Princeton University Press, 1958.

27. Weaver, Robert C. *The Negro Ghetto*. New York: Harcourt, Brace and Co., 1944.

28. Weaver, Robert C. "Integration in Public and Private Housing," *Annals of the American Academy of Political and Social Science*, 304 (March, 1956):86–97.

29. Weaver, Robert C. "Class, Race and Urban Renewal," *Land Economics*, 36 (August, 1960):235–51.

30. Wirth, Louis. "Human Ecology," in Elizabeth Wirth Marvick and Albert J. Reiss, Jr. (eds.), *Community Life and Social Policy: Selected Papers by Louis Wirth*. Chicago: University of Chicago Press, 1956, pp. 133–42.

31. Wirth, Louis. "Race and Public Policy," in Marvick and Reiss (eds.), *Community Life and Social Policy*, pp. 334–53.

32. Woofter, Thomas J., Jr. *Negro Problems in Cities*. New York: Doubleday, Doran & Company, 1928.

The Bibliography of E. Franklin Frazier

"The Folk High School at Roskilde." *Southern Workman* 51 (July, 1922) : 325–28.

"Danish People's High Schools and America." *Southern Workman* 9 (September, 1922) :425–30.

"Cooperation and the Negro." *Crisis* 5 (March, 1923) :228–29.

"Training Colored Social Workers in the South." *Journal of Social Forces* 1 (May, 1923) :440–46.

"Neighborhood Union in Atlanta." *Southern Workman* 52 (September, 1923) :437–42.

"The Cooperative Movement in Denmark." *Southern Workman* 52 (October, 1923) :479–84.

"The Negro and Non-resistance." *Crisis* 27 (March, 1924) :213–14.

"A Note on Negro Education." *Opportunity* 2 (March, 1924) :75–77.

"Social Work in Race Relations." *Crisis* 27 (April, 1924) :252–54.

"A Negro Industrial Group." *Howard Review* 1 (June, 1924) : 196–211.

"Discussion" (Health Conditions in the South). *Opportunity* 2 (August, 1924) :239.

"Some Aspects of Negro Business." *Opportunity* 2 (October, 1924) : 293–97.

"Cooperatives: The Next Step in the Negro's Development." *Southern Workman* 53 (November, 1924) :505–9.

"Psychological Factors in Negro Health." *Social Forces* 3 (March, 1925) : 488–90.

"All God's Chillun Got Eyes." *Crisis* 29 (April, 1925) :254.

"Social Equality and the Negro." *Opportunity* (Journal of Negro Life) 3 (June, 1925) :165–68.

"A Community School." *Southern Workman* 54 (October, 1925) :495–64.

"Durham: Capital of the Black Middle Class." in *The New Negro*, by Alain Locke. New York: A. and C. Boni Company, 1925, pp. 333–40.

"Family Life of the Negro in the Small Town." *Proceedings of the National Conference of Social Work* (1926), pp. 384–88.

"How Present Day Problems of Social Life Affect the Negro." *Hospital Social Service* 13 (1926) :384–93.

"King Cotton." *Opportunity* 4 (February, 1926) :50–55.

"What is Social Equality?" (with John Haynes). *The World Tomorrow* 9 (April, 1926) :113–14.

"Three Scourges of the Negro Family." *Opportunity* 4 (July, 1926) :210–13, 234.

"Garvey: A Mass Leader." (New York), 128 (August, 1926) :147–48.

"The Garvey Movement." *Opportunity* 4 (November, 1926) :346–48.

"The Pathology of Race Prejudice." *Forum* 70 (June, 1927) :856–62.

"Is the Negro Family a Unique Sociological Unit?" *Opportunity* 5 (June, 1927) :165–8.

"Negro in the Industrial South." *Nation* 75 (July, 1927) :83–84.

"Professional Education for Negro Social Workers." *Hospital Social Service* 18 (1928) :167–76.

"The American Negro's New Leaders." *Current History* 28 (April, 1928) : 56–59.

"Folk Culture in the Making." *Southern Workman* 57 (1928) :195–99.

"The Mind of the American Negro." *Opportunity* 6 (September, 1928) : 263–66, 284.

"The Negro Family." *The Annals of the American Academy of Political and Social Science* 130 (November, 1928) :21–25.

"La Bourgeoisie Noire." in *Anthology of American Negro Literature*, V. F. Calverton. New York: The Modern Library, 1929, pp. 379–88.

"The Negro Community, a Cultural Phenomenon." *Social Forces* 7 (March, 1929) :415–20.

"Chicago A Cross Section of Negro Life." *Opportunity* 7 (March, 1929) : 70–73.

"Occupational Classes Among Negroes in Cities." *The American Journal of Sociology* 35 (March, 1930) :718–38.

"The Negro Slave Family." *The Journal of Negro History* 15 (April, 1930) :198–206.

"The Occupational Differentiation of the Negro in Cities," *Southern Workman* 57 (May, 1930) :196–200.

"The Changing Status of the Negro Family." *Social Forces* 9 (March, 1931) :386–93.

"Some Aspects of Family Disorganization Among Negroes." *Opportunity* 9 (July, 1931) :204–7.

"Certain Aspects of Conflict in the Negro Family." *Social Forces* 10 (October, 1931) :76–84.

"An Analysis of Statistics on Negro Illegitimacy in the United States." *Social Forces* 9 (December, 1932) :249–57.

The Negro Family in Chicago. Chicago: University of Chicago Press, 1932.

The Free Negro Family. Nashville: Fisk University Press, 1932.

"The Negro and Birth Control." *Birth Control Review*, March, 1933, pp. 68–70.

"Children in Black and Mulatto Families." *The American Journal of Sociology* 39 (July, 1933) :12–29.

"Graduate Education in Negro Colleges and Universities." *The Journal of Negro Education*, 2 (July, 1933) :329–41.

"Traditions and Patterns of Negro Family Life." in *Race and Culture Contacts*, Edward B. Reuter (ed.). New York: McGraw-Hill Company, 1934, pp. 191–207.

"The Status of the Negro in the American Social Order." *The Journal of Negro Education*, 4 (July, 1935) :293–307.

"The DuBois Program in the Present Crisis." *Race* 1, no. 1 (Winter, 1935–36) :11–13.

"A Critical Summary of Articles Contributed to Symposium on Negro Education." *Journal of Negro Education* 5 (July, 1936) :531–33.

"Negro Harlem: An Ecological Study." *American Journal of Sociology* 43 (July, 1937) : 72–88.

"The Impact of Urban Civilization Upon Negro Family Life." *American Sociological Review* 2 (August, 1937) :609–18.

"Some Effects of the Depression on the Negro in Northern Cities." *Science and Society* 2 (Fall, 1938) :489–99.

"The Present Status of the Negro Family in the American Social Order." *The Journal of Negro Education* 8 (July, 1939) :376–82.

The Negro Family in the United States. Chicago: University of Chicago Press, 1939.

Negro Youth at the Crossways. Washington, D.C.: American Council on Education, 1940.

"The Negro Family and Negro Youth." *The Journal of Negro Education*, 9 (July, 1940) :290–99.

"The Role of the Negro in Race Relations in the South." *Social Forces* 19 (December, 1940) :252–58.

"The Negro Family in Bahia, Brazil." *American Sociological Review* 7 (August, 1942) :465–78.

"Brazil Has No Race Problem." *Common Sense* 11 (November, 1942):
363–65.

"Ethnic and Minority Groups in Wartime With Special Reference to the
Negro." *The American Journal of Sociology* 48 (November, 1942):
369–77.

"Some Aspects of Race Relations in Brazil." *Phylon*, Third Quarter
(1942), pp. 284–95.

"Rejoinder" to Melville J. Herskovits' "The Negro in Bahia, Brazil: A
Problem in Method." *American Sociological Review* 8 (August, 1943):
402–4.

"A Negro Looks at the Soviet Union." *Proceedings of the Nationalities
Panel, The Soviet Union, A Family of Nations in the War*. National
Council of American-Soviet Friendship, New York, N.Y., November,
1943.

"A Comparison of Negro-White Relations in Brazil and in the United
States." *Transactions of the New York Academy of Sciences*, Series 2,
6, 7, (May, 1944):251–69.

"The Role of Negro Schools in the Post-War World," *The Journal of
Negro Education*, 13 (Fall, 1944):464–73.

"Race Relations in the Caribbean," in *The Economic Future of The Caribbean, Seventh Annual Conference of the Division of the Social Sciences*, Eric Williams and E. Franklin Frazier (eds.). Washington:
Howard University Press, 1944, pp. 27–31.

"The Booker T. Washington Papers." *The Library of Congress Quarterly
Journal of Current Acquisitions* 2 (February, 1945):23–31.

"The Negro and Racial Conflicts." in *One America*, Francis J. Brown
and Joseph S. Roucek (eds.). New York: Prentice Hall, 1952, pp.
492–504.

"The Negro Now." *Contact*, Book 2: *Britain Between West and East*
(1946), pp. 61–63.

"Children and Income in Negro Families" (with Eleanor Bernert). *Social
Forces* 25 (December, 1946):178–82.

"Human, All Too Human, The Negro's Vested Interest in Segregation," in
Race Prejudice and Discrimination, Arnold Rose (ed.). New York:
Knopf, 1951.

"Sociological Theory and Race Relations." *American Sociological Review*
12 (June, 1947):265–71.

"The Racial Issue," in *Unity and Difference in American Life*, R. M. Mac-
Iver (ed.). New York: Harper and Bros., 1947, pp. 43–59.

"A World Community and a Universal Moral Order," in *Approaches to Group Understanding*, for Conference on Science, Philosophy and Religion in their Relations to the Democratic Way of Life, Inc., Lyman Bryson, Louis Finkelstein, and R. M. MacIver (eds.). New York: Harper and Bros., 1947, pp. 443–52.

"The Negro Family," in *The Family: Its Function and Destiny*, Ruth Nanda Anshen (ed.). New York: Harper and Bros., 1948, pp. 142–58.

"Post-High-School Education of Negroes in New York State," chap. 8 in Inequality of Opportunity in Higher Education, a study of Minority Group and Related Barriers to College Admission, published in *A Report to the Temporary Commission on the Need for a State University*, by David S. Kerkowitz. Albany: William Press, 1948, pp. 159–74.

The Negro Family in the United States (Rev. and Abr. Ed.). New York: The Dyden Press, 1948.

"The Social Status of the Negro." *Les Etudes Americaines*, 1948.

"Ethnic Family Patterns: The Negro in the United States." *The American Journal of Sociology* 53 (May, 1948):435–38.

"Race Contacts and the Social Structure." *American Sociological Review* 14 (February, 1949):1–11.

"Sociologic Factors in the Formation of Sex Attitudes," in *Psychosexual Development in Health and Disease*. New York: Grune and Stratton, 1949, pp. 244–55.

"Problems and Needs of Negro Children and Youth Resulting from Family Disorganization." *The Journal of Negro Education* 19 (1950): 269–77.

"Sociological Aspects of Race Relations." *Courier*, Publication of UNESCO, August-September, 1953, p. 1.

"Theoretical Structure of Sociology and Sociological Research." *The British Journal of Sociology* 4 (December, 1953):293–311.

"Problèmes de L'Etudiant Noir aux Etats-Unis," in *Les Etudiants Noirs Parlent*. Paris: Presence Africaine, 1952, pp. 275–83.

Commentary on "The Impact of Western Education on the African's Way of Life," in *Africa Today*, C. Grove Haine (ed.). Baltimore: Johns-Hopkins Press, 1955, pp. 166–71.

"The New Negro Middle Class," in *The New Negro Thirty Years Afterward*, Papers contributed to the Sixteenth Annual Spring Conference of the Division of Social Sciences. Washington, D.C.: Howard University Press, 1955, pp. 25–32.

"Impact of Colonialism on African Social Forms and Personality," in

Publication of Norman Wait Harris Memorial Foundation Lectures on Africa in the Modern World, Calvin W. Stillman (ed.). Chicago: University of Chicago Press, 1955, pp. 70–96.

"The Negro in the United States," in *Race Relations in World Perspective*, Andrew W. Lind (ed.). Honolulu: University of Hawaii Press, 1955, pp. 339–70.

Bourgeoisie Noire. Paris: Plon, 1955. American edition published as *Black Bourgeoisie*. Glencoe, Ill.: The Free Press, 1957.

The Negro in the United States. New York: The Macmillan Company, 1949; rev. ed., 1957.

Race and Culture Contacts in the Modern World. New York: A. A. Knopf, 1957.

"Introduction" to *Caribbean Studies: A Symposium*, Vera Rubin (ed.). Jamaica, B.W.I.: University College of the West Indies, 1957.

"Race Relations in World Perspective." *Sociology and Social Research* 41 (May-June, 1957) :331–35.

"The Negro Middle Class and Desegregation. *Social Problems* 4 (April, 1957) :291–301.

"The Cultural Background of Southern Negroes," in *Selected papers of the Institute on Cultural Patterns of Newcomers*. Welfare Council of Chicago, Chicago, Illinois, October, 1957, pp. 1–14.

"Areas of Research in Race Relations." *Sociology and Social Research* 42 (July-August, 1958) :424–29.

"Urbanization and Social Change in Africa." *Sais Review* 3 (Winter, 1959) :3–9.

"Education and the African Elite." *Transactions of the Third World Congress of Sociology*, vol. 5. *Changes in Education*. Amsterdam, 1956, pp. 90–96.

"The Present State of Sociological Knowledge Concerning Race Relations." *Transactions of the Fourth World Congress of Sociology*. Milan and Stressa, 1959, pp. 73–80.

"The Negro Family in America," in *The Family: Its Function and Destiny*, Ruth Nanda Anshen (ed.), rev. ed. New York: Harper and Bros., 1959, pp. 65–84.

"What Can the American Negro Contribute to the Social Development of Africa?" in *Africa: Seen by American Negroes*. Paris: *Presence Africaine*, 1959, pp. 263–78.

"Racial Problems in World Society," in *Race Relations Problems and Theory: Essays in Honor of Robert E. Park*, Jitsuichi Masuoka and

Preston Valien (eds.). Chapel Hill: The University of North Carolina Press, 1961, pp. 38–50.

"Negro Harlem: An Ecological Study," in *Studies in Human Ecology*, George A. Theodorson (ed.). Evanston, Ill.: Row, Peterson and Company, 1961, pp. 165–74.

"The Socialization of the Negro Child in the Border and Southern States" (based upon *Negro Youth at the Crossways: The Personality Development in the Middle States.*) A Casebook edited by Yehudi A. Cohan. New York: Holt, Rinehart and Winston, 1961, pp. 45–53.

"Desegregation as an Object of Sociological Research," in *Human Behavior and Social Processes: An Interactionist Approach.* Arnold Rose (ed.). Boston: Houghton Mifflin Company, 1961:608–24.

The Negro Church in America. Liverpool: Liverpool University Press, 1961.

"Negro, Sex Life of the African and American," in *The Encyclopedia of Sexual Behavior.* New York: Hawthorn Books, 1961, pp. 769–75.

"Urbanization and Its Effects Upon the Task of Nation-Building in Africa South of Sahara." *The Journal of Negro Education* 30 (Summer, 1961):214–22.

"The Failure of the Negro Intellectual." *Negro Digest*, February, 1962, pp. 26–36.

DATE DUE